# *Infusing* Technology
## *in the* K-5 Classroom

A Guide to Meeting Today's Academic Standards

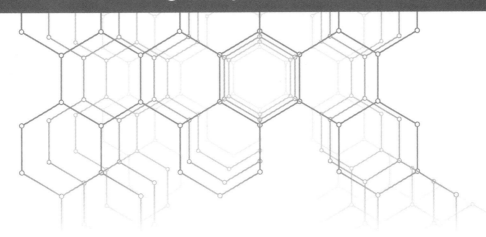

**VALERIE MORRISON, STEPHANIE NOVAK, TIM VANDERWERFF**

International Society for Technology in Education

PORTLAND, OREGON • ARLINGTON, VIRGINIA

Infusing Technology in the K-5 Classroom
A Guide to Meeting Today's Academic Standards
Valerie Morrison, Stephanie Novak, and Tim Vanderwerff

Editor: *Emily Reed*
Copy Editor: *Karstin Painter*
Proofreader: *Corinne Gould*
Indexer: *Wendy Allex*
Book Design and Production: *Jeff Puda*
Cover Design: *Edwin Ouellette*

Library of Congress Cataloging-in-Publication Data available.
First Edition
ISBN: 978-1-56484-745-4
Ebook version available.

Printed in the United States of America
ISTE® is a registered trademark of the International Society for Technology in Education.

# About ISTE

The International Society for Technology in Education (ISTE) is the premier non-profit organization serving educators and education leaders committed to empowering connected learners in a connected world. ISTE serves more than 100,000 education stakeholders throughout the world.

ISTE's innovative offerings include the ISTE Conference & Expo, one of the biggest, most comprehensive edtech events in the world—as well as the widely adopted ISTE Standards for learning, teaching, and leading in the digital age and a robust suite of professional learning resources, including webinars, online courses, consulting services for schools and districts, books, and peer-reviewed journals and publications. Visit iste.org to learn more.

## Related ISTE Titles

*Integrating Technology in the Classroom, Second Edition: Tools to Meet the Needs of Every Student* (2019), by Boni Hamilton

To see all books available from ISTE, please visit iste.org/books.

# About the Authors

 **Valerie Morrison** graduated with an elementary education degree from Northern Illinois University (NIU) and began her career as a classroom teacher. She became interested in teaching with technology early on and was a computer teacher for two years at a K–8 private school. Morrison then switched to the public school system, where she obtained a master's degree in instructional technology with an emphasis in media literacy from NIU, and is currently pursuing a doctoral degree from National Louis University in Advocacy, Policy, and Curriculum. She gained fourteen years of experience as a technology director/technology integration specialist and technology coach. Morrison worked closely with teachers and students to plan and differentiate lessons and projects that integrate technology. She taught technology workshops and classes for teachers and oversaw the technology program at her school. (She loves working with kids, teachers, and technology!) Like her coauthor Tim Vanderwerff, Morrison regularly served on her district's technology committee and was involved with integrating current state and district standards with the latest educational technologies. She presented at various conferences, including a presentation in Springfield, Illinois, to state legislators, where she and coauthor Stephanie Novak briefed legislators on how schools use technology. Morrison has switched career paths and is now teaching education classes at the college level; she enjoys using technology to teach the next generation of teachers. She also uses her time to write, which allows her to further educate the current generation of teachers.

 **Stephanie Novak** knew from a very young age that teaching and working with kids was the right career path for her. She graduated from Northern Illinois University with a master's degree in education and earned a reading specialist certificate from National Louis University. Novak started teaching at the middle school level but eventually settled in the elementary school system. As a classroom teacher for twenty-seven years, and an extended-learning teacher and coach for the last seven years of her career, she has always felt learning should be fun and meaningful. Novak was on her school district's technology committee for many years and regularly tried new technology in her classroom. As an instructional coach, she

encouraged teachers to help students grow in their learning at a pace that allowed for the most intellectual and personal growth. For the last two years of her career, Novak guided Grades 1–5 teachers through the Common Core State Standards, teaching them how to blend these standards with rigorous curriculum and prepare students for the digital age. After many years in education, Novak retired in 2014. She now applies her years of experience in lesson development by writing and publishing a blog depicting current instructional practices in the field of education and technology.

**Tim Vanderwerff** has an extensive background in teaching and technology that began in the 1970s. Although writing was a new experience, trying out new experiences in education are second nature to him. After graduating from Illinois State University and then earning a master's in educational administration from Northern Illinois University, Vanderwerff saw many federal and state initiatives come and go in his thirty-three years of teaching. Starting as a classroom teacher in Grades 2–5, he was on his school district's technology committee for many years and regularly tried new technology in his class during that time. Vanderwerff eventually moved to the library and media center at his elementary school. He was the librarian and the technology teacher, and he provided tech support for the building for many years. In 2010, he was asked to be a teaching coach in his school district where he worked extensively with Valerie Morrison and Stephanie Novak; advising grade-level team meetings, finding resources for the standards, supporting individual teachers and teams in the classroom (with both technology and the newest educational strategies), and coaching new teachers. Vanderwerff is now retired, allowing him to devote more time to writing and advocating for the field about which he is so passionate.

## Acknowledgments

We are grateful for the contributions of our friends, teammates, colleagues, and assistants with whom we worked throughout the years and who helped us come up with ideas for the books in this series. Working with so many talented people, we appreciate the collaboration and teamwork that allowed us to learn a great deal about coaching and technology.

We would also like to thank our families for all of their amazing support during the writing of these books. During the time we spent meeting, editing, and struggling to write, their unwavering support was truly appreciated.

Also, we would like to thank the editors and staff at ISTE for their insight, guidance, and patience. Their ongoing support has been much appreciated.

## Dedications

*To my husband, Glenn, and for my three daughters—Allana, LeeAnn, and Annaleese—who motivate me to inspire educators for the sake of children.*
—Valerie Morrison

*To my husband Bill—thank you for your advice and patience while working on this book; to Helene, Estin, Jacob, Wyatt, and Abby—I wish great things for you in school and your future.*
—Stephanie Novak

*To my ever-patient wife, Kim; my children Eric, Michael, and Kristina; and my grandson, Tyler, who motivate me every day to make our future the best that it can be.*
—Tim Vanderwerff

# Contents

About ISTE.............................................................................................iii

About the Authors..............................................................................iv

## Introduction........................................................................................1

What are My State Standards?.........................................................2

What Is In This Book? ........................................................................3

Who Is This Book For? .......................................................................4

How Can We Keep This Book Up-to-Date? ..................................5

### CHAPTER 1

## Today's Students...............................................................................6

Who Are Your Students?....................................................................6

What Does This Generation Know and Do? ................................7

How Has Technology Affected
   Students' Minds?............................................................................8

How Has Technology Affected Behavior? ....................................9

How Do We Move Beyond the ABCs?............................................9

How Can Educators Succeed
   in the Digital Age? .....................................................................10

### CHAPTER 2

## Parent Education.............................................................................12

Why Do Parents Need to Know about Technology Standards? ...............13

What Issues Do Parents Have with Technology in CCR Standards? .........14

How Can Parents Help with Assessment Technology?............15

How Can Parents Help Students Meet Technology Standards? ..............16

What Are the Roadblocks to  Accessibility? ...............................18

CHAPTER 3

## Roadblocks to Technology ................................................... 18

How Do We Overcome Software and Hardware Roadblocks? ................. 20

What Other Roadblocks Must We Solve? ........................................ 24

How Do You Get the Help You Need? ........................................... 25

CHAPTER 4

## Staff Development .............................................................. 28

How Do You Create a Technology Plan? ....................................... 29

What Are Some Staff-Development Ideas? ..................................... 32

Where Can You Learn about Staff Development? ............................. 33

How Are the ELA Standards Organized? ....................................... 36

CHAPTER 5

## Organization of the Standards .............................................. 36

How Do You Find ELA Standards by Subject and Grade? ................... 40

How Does the Organization of Math Standards Differ? ..................... 41

Where Is Technology in the ELA Standards? .................................. 45

CHAPTER 6

## Technology in the Common Core ............................................ 45

Where Is Technology in the Math Standards? ................................. 46

What About Using Technology in All Subjects? ............................... 47

How Do You Put ELA Technology Standards into Context? ................. 47

What about Assessment? ......................................................... 49

What Are the ELA Standards with Technology? ............................... 50

What Are the ELA Grade-Level Standards with Technology? ............... 52

What Is the Math Standard with Technology? ................................ 56

How and Where Do I Begin? ..................................................... 58

CHAPTER 7

## Implementing Practical Ideas ........................................................ 58

What Strategies Can I Use? ............................................................. 59

How Do I Determine What Works Best? ........................................... 61

CHAPTER 8

## Practical Ideas for Kindergarten ................................................. 63

Writing Resources .......................................................................... 64

Speaking and Listening Resources .................................................. 66

Math Resources ............................................................................. 69

Literacy Lessons ............................................................................ 75

Social Studies/Science Lessons ...................................................... 78

Math Lessons ................................................................................ 80

A Final Note .................................................................................. 85

Reading Resources ......................................................................... 87

Writing Resources .......................................................................... 88

Speaking and Listening Resources .................................................. 90

Math Resources ............................................................................. 94

Literacy Lessons ............................................................................ 99

Social Studies and Science Lessons ................................................ 102

Math Lessons ................................................................................ 104

A Final Note .................................................................................. 108

CHAPTER 9

## Practical Ideas for First Grade .................................................... 90

Reading Resources ......................................................................... 91

Writing Resources .......................................................................... 92

Speaking and Listening Resources .................................................. 94

Math Resources ............................................................................. 98

Literacy Lessons ............................................................................ 103

Social Studies and Science Lessons ................................................ 106

Math Lessons ....................................................... 108

A Final Note ........................................................ 112

CHAPTER 10
## Practical Ideas for Second Grade ...................... 109
Reading Resources .................................................110

Reading Ideas .....................................................111

Writing Resources ...............................................113

Speaking and Listening Resources.....................117

Language Resources ............................................121

Math Resources ..................................................122

Literacy Lessons ..................................................129

Science and Social Studies Lessons ...................132

Math Lessons ......................................................134

A Final Note ........................................................139

CHAPTER 11
## Practical Ideas for Third Grade ....................... 140
Research Ideas ....................................................141

Writing Resources ...............................................145

Speaking and Listening .......................................149

Resources.............................................................152

Math Resources ..................................................153

Literacy Lessons ..................................................158

Science/Social Studies Lessons ..........................163

Math Lessons ......................................................166

A Final Note ........................................................174

CHAPTER 12
## Practical Ideas for Fourth Grade ..................... 175
Reading Resources ..............................................176

Reading Literature ............................................................... 176

Reading Information ............................................................ 180

Writing Resources ............................................................... 182

Writing Research ................................................................. 186

Speaking and Listening ....................................................... 190

Language.............................................................................. 193

Math Resources .................................................................. 194

Literacy Lessons .................................................................. 200

Social Studies and Science Lessons .....................................207

Math Lessons ...................................................................... 210

A Final Note ........................................................................ 216

## CHAPTER 13
# Practical Ideas for Fifth Grade

Practical Ideas for Fifth Grade................................................ 217

Reading Resources ..............................................................218

Reading Information ............................................................218

Writing Resources ...............................................................222

Writing................................................................................222

Writing Research .................................................................226

Speaking and Listening .......................................................231

Language Resources ............................................................233

Language..............................................................................234

Math Resources ..................................................................234

Literacy Lessons ..................................................................239

Social Studies and Science Lessons .....................................246

Math Lessons ......................................................................248

A Final Note ........................................................................255

## References ............................................................................ 256

## ISTE Standards for Students .............................................. 259

## Index ................................................................................... 263

# Introduction

Have you ever found yourself sitting in a meeting wondering, "How am I ever going to cover all these standards and get to everything I'm supposed to be teaching this year?" At that moment, you also realize your district wants you to integrate the latest digital technology, and that may have you asking yourself, "Where will I get the technology I need? Who will help me learn and implement the technology?"

All of this might seem overwhelming—what is a teacher to do? First, you might turn to your teammates and colleagues for help and support. Perhaps your district provides current technology development for staff on a regular basis and has instructional coaches to help teachers chart this new territory, planning new lessons, bringing in resources, and infusing technology. In reality, most districts don't have all of this support. Yet teachers are especially in need of technology when considering their clientele: students.

We have an important role in helping you and your students implement technology into the standards. Our hope is that you are in a place that regularly provides high-quality professional learning experiences to help teachers understand the state standards and supports you with the latest in equipment and software. Professional development, along with this book and its resources, will help guide your instruction using the standards with technology, and it will support you in transferring new knowledge and skills to the classroom. It is a large task, but focusing on specific goals for student learning utilizing the state standards with technology will have a positive effect on student achievement. This will improve your teaching.

# What Are My State Standards?

Until 2010, every state was doing its own thing when it came to state standards. The Common Core State Standards (CCSS) initiative was a state-created drive that sought to bring diverse state curricula into alignment by following the principles of standards-based education reform. Despite the public perception that it was a federal program, CCSS was sponsored by the National Governors Association Center for Best Practices (NGA Center) and the Council of Chief State School Officers (CCSSO), and a vast majority of the fifty U.S. states are members of the initiative. So, even if you're in a state that did not adopt Common Core, there is a high likelihood your curriculum looks very similar to CCSS.

As of the writing of this book, there are forty-six states that use CCSS in some form. Please see the map (Figure 0.1) to check if your state is one of them. But even the four states that never adopted Common Core have standards that are similar to them. Thirteen states adopted and subsequently, over the next several years,

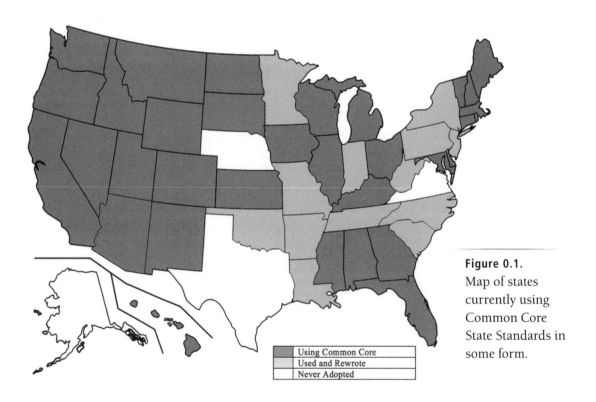

| Using Common Core |
| Used and Rewrote |
| Never Adopted |

**Figure 0.1.** Map of states currently using Common Core State Standards in some form.

rewrote the Common Core standards as their own. States have also renamed them, with the most popular alternate title being College and Career Readiness Standards (CCRS), and there are many others names used. According to an *Education Week* article about states' rewrites,

> [N]early 70 percent of the changes that were made in either math or language arts across all grades were simply wording or format clarifications . . . Another 25 percent of the changes added a standard or a concept to an existing math or reading standard. In only 6 percent of the math or reading changes did states delete a standard, and none lessened their rigor. (Sparks, 2017)

Many articles have been written about the demise of CCSS, but a vast majority of states still have CCSS in place. In fact, most states would have problems getting textbooks and resources for their own standards if they did not adhere to, or closely resemble, CCSS.

Why? Because most publishers, lesson creators, and online purveyors write for, and align to, CCSS. Recently, the assessments have come under fire; several states have changed, opted out, or created their own assessments for students, but the Common Core (or its close approximation) remains.

If you would like to explore the history behind CCSS, review the Common Core State Standards Initiative's "About the Standards" page **(tinyurl.com/26f7amp)**.

## What Is in This Book?

This is the first book in a two-book series designed to help teachers connect technology to CCSS in their K–12 classrooms. Although we refer to "standards," "College and Career Readiness Standards," and "CCSS" often in this book, we mean Common Core State Standards. We have reviewed the CCSS and selected those specific standards that implicitly or explicitly refer to technology. In other words, we do not cover every standard, only those that direct teachers to use technology as part of their instruction and assessment. Here is what you will find in this book.

- We address some of the issues that your students face and discuss how important it is to tailor their learning experiences.

- We give you ways of engaging and educating parents about the standards and assessments.

- We discuss the equipment you need to teach the standards.

- We show you how to address the roadblocks that stand between you and this technology.

- We explain how the CCSS are organized and list the specific standards with the technology aspect in bold for the grade level you teach.

- We show you how to offer several classroom-tested lesson ideas by grade level from Chapter 8 through the end of the book. This ensures that your students are satisfying the tech-related benchmarks outlined in the CCSS.

## Who Is This Book For?

Our intentions for this book, and the second book in this series, is that it be used as a resource for K–12 teachers, administrators, school librarians, and home-school providers in the United States. Additionally, we believe the books will greatly benefit college instructors of elementary, middle school, and high school teachers. Really, any educator who is responsible for developing and delivering instruction to students in the United States and its territories will love this book!

We intend you to use this book as your technology coach when you need support for your lessons, especially when you are working with the standards. We experienced firsthand how to do this when teaching together and working as technology coaches. We have more than eighty-five years of combined teaching experience. As a team, we worked with teachers, students, administrators, and parents to integrate technology in our district. We hope that you will view this book as your own individual technology support, because we can't be with you personally. Please consult this book often, especially if you're in a school, district, or state that does not provide enough professional development in this area. We hope to show you how to integrate the embedded tech-related language found within the CCSS into your everyday curriculum.

# How Can We Keep This Book up to Date?

We realize that technology is constantly changing and that digital tools come and go. To make certain that you continue to have the most current resources at your fingertips, visit our website, Infusing Technology in the Classroom **(tinyurl.com/y9dfltpr)**. The website password for the K–5 book is: k5ITITC. There, you will find an updated list of the apps, software, and websites mentioned in this book.

Book Website

We should also mention that, although we are sharing many tools and resources with you, we are not affiliated with any company. The programs, apps, and websites listed in this book are simply those that we feel support the CCSS. There are many wonderful digital tools available that are not included due to space and time constraints. If you come across a particularly good or new resource that fits a specific standard, we hope you will visit our website and share that resource.

Let's begin by taking a closer look at today's generation of tech-savvy students and the skills they bring to the classroom.

# CHAPTER 1
# Today's Students

A two-year-old taking a selfie? Seven-year-olds tweeting? No doubt about it, today's students come to school knowing more technology than ever before. New educational research suggests that offering a variety of learning opportunities, including lots of technology options, may be the best way to engage today's generation of learners. Educators must respond to this generation and address its unique learning needs. We believe this so passionately that we think a chapter about this subject is a must in any book about teaching children in the digital age. Technology must be made available to students. Technology must become ubiquitous.

The CCSS are designed to upgrade our school system's standards to meet the needs of prospective high school graduates who want to get into a good college or land a great job. They are designed with the tech-savvy child in mind. More specifically, the standards are designed with students' future workplaces in mind. That is the driving force behind the technology we see in the standards, and it is why teaching to your students' future needs is extremely important. Please keep this mind as you read this chapter.

## Who Are Your Students?

Today's students grew up using digital technology and mass media. According to Debra Szybinski, executive director at New York University's Faculty Resource Network (tinyurl.com/y22s3kzo), this generation is:

> [A] generation characterized by some as self-absorbed, short attention spanned digital addicts who disrespect authority and assume that they can control what, when, and how they learn, and by others as smart, self-assured technology

wizards who follow the rules and who are on their way to becoming the pow-
erhouse generation. Clearly, this is a generation like no other, and that has
posed an entirely new set of challenges both in and out of the classroom for
faculty members and administrators alike. (2016)

This current generation is ever-changing. New technologies and new media are constantly invented and refined, creating pressure on schools to evolve. Most students
entering school now are completely immersed in technology outside of school.

Ironically, at many schools, there is a disconnect from students' real lives and their
way of learning. Schools are often islands of twentieth-century thinking in what is
now a digital age. Schools must do a better job of reaching the current generation
of students; making technology available to students at school helps educators
respond to and address students' unique learning needs.

# What Does This Generation Know and Do?

Most students entering kindergarten now have access to desktop computers, smartphones, tablets, and laptops at home. These children begin using most of these
devices by the time they are three years old. Whether you go to playgroups, parks,
or other places frequented by young children, you're likely to see them working
on their parents' tablets or smartphones (or begging to use them!). These students
come to us with skills that include (but are not limited to) swiping to work an
app; navigating a mouse to play computer games; operating their own electronic
devices, such as children's learning tablets, handheld learning devices, and interactive video games; and hunting and pecking on the keyboard to send emails. Also,
our tech-savvy students can take videos and photos using a tablet or smartphone,
as well as converse with someone by texting, blogging, and messaging. Most have
been exposed to the internet and understand that they can find almost any information there.

Because they have so much information at the touch of a button, and constant
stimulation around them, this generation often attempts to multitask. It makes
sense to them to watch TV, send a text, and find out what the weather will be all at
the same time!

Some say that the current generation has hovering parents and a sense of entitlement. While this may be taken as a negative, having parents who are involved with their children and their children's school is a good thing, as it strengthens the home–school connection. Students with parents who are involved in their academic lives can be better students, and they are less afraid to try new things. We, as educators, need to recognize these traits and use them to help students reach their maximum potential.

Being social is very important to the students in this tech-savvy generation. They are certainly the "in-touch" generation, with immediate access to texts, emails, social networking sites, and even the sound of a human voice at the other end of the line. This generation is lost when their smartphones or tablets break; they feel "cut off from the world" when they don't have instant access to the internet.

## How Has Technology Affected Students' Minds?

By the time they're in their twenties, today's students will have spent thousands of hours surfing the internet and playing video games. This vast amount of screen time seems to be shortening their attention spans. At a time when their brains are particularly sensitive to outside influences, excessive screen time affects the way they learn and absorb information.

Furthermore, this generation rarely reads books to find information. Online search engines are prevalent in providing all of the information they need quickly, without having to go through a book from cover to cover. With access to an overabundance of information, they need to be skilled hunters who know how to sift through data quickly and efficiently. This new type of learner doesn't necessarily read from left to right or from beginning to end. Visuals help today's students absorb more information than they do from straight text. Thus, students become better scanners, a useful skill when confronted with masses of online information in a world that's full of noise and multiple stimulations. So, most modern students have learned to block out distractions while they focus on the task at hand.

# How Has Technology Affected Behavior?

There is less and less face-to-face communication taking place because of constant technology use. We have seen instances of parents and children sitting next to one another without speaking at a restaurant. Instead, they simply sit and quietly engage with their individual tablets or smartphones.

There are many debates about how technology helps or harms the development of a student's thinking. Of course, this depends on the specific technology used, as well as how and with what frequency it is used in school. Our duty as educators is to decide what technology to use in the classroom and when, because technology influences students' thought processes. We must be aware of this effect to guide our students as digital age learners.

# How Do We Move beyond the ABCs?

Education has gone through a monumental transformation in the last twenty years. Some changes have greatly improved the way teachers educate, while others are still under evaluation. Great educational debates, such as teacher-directed versus self-directed learning, are cases in point. What we have found during our years of experience is that to progress in the classroom, teachers must adapt to the times, adopting new techniques while using time-tested methods. Success in teaching a new generation of students isn't based solely on what educators are teaching students but *how* educators are teaching them.

We have seen our share of success stories and our share of students who struggled for reasons that are completely preventable. For these highly activity-scheduled and gadget-oriented students, traditional one-size-fits-all teaching is no longer effective. Sitting behind a desk, listening to the teacher talk, and reading from a textbook are completely ineffective. This generation of students needs to be engaged in active and interactive learning to enhance their knowledge. They do not want technology just because it is "cool." They need technology because it drives their world (now and in the future). They are looking for something dynamic to make learning come alive—to make it different and interesting every day. Being connected accomplishes that goal.

# How Can Educators Succeed in the Digital Age?

Thinking of technology as a new toy that will go away or doesn't have a place in education is no longer an option. Educators need to embrace technology and tap into what our students are already coming to us with, using it to advance their learning. But this technology cannot just be digital worksheets!

This is not always easy, especially when students know more about how to use the technology than many teachers. Therefore, it is our duty to catch up and make sure we know what our students know. This can be done in many different ways; however, the easiest way is to do what they do: pick up tablets or smartphones and start using apps that they use! Once we have the background skills to know what our students know, we can move forward. We simply need to remember that technology is a tool. And we can use these tools like anything else we use in education—manipulatives in math, novels in reading, and microscopes in science, to name a few.

Of course, this new reality being imposed on and by the current generation has implications for you as a teacher. It used to be that students conducted research by using books that were from credible publishers, and those books had been rigorously edited and fact-checked. This generation uses the internet almost exclusively. If your students get all of their information from the internet, then you must teach them media literacy skills. This skill set has become extremely important in an information age where children need to discern fiction from fact on the internet when, sometimes, adults have trouble differentiating it for ourselves.

You need to tap into what your students are experiencing every day and use it to your advantage. Many of your current students will work in very social settings but in a different way than previous generations. Let them work often as partners or in groups to create multimedia presentations or digital videos. Because they love to send texts and video chat, let them text, instant message, or video chat with students around the world! This generation is good at multitasking. Allow them to do more things at once, such as collaborate with others while taking notes on a research paper. Students all know how to use a smartphone, so when on a field trip, let them record a video of what they are seeing. They are used to constant noise and stimulation. Do not make them work quietly at their desks; rather, they should work with hands-on activities like live apps, green-screen technology, or maker labs. Students know at a very young age how to navigate the internet. Let them use a computer when they have a question instead of asking you for the answer.

We know this new generation of children, teenagers, and young adults can be challenging because of how digital technology has changed their way of learning and behaviors. The following chapters will further address some of these issues and how their learning must be specialized, giving more examples of how to integrate technology with the CCSS and how to use the ISTE standards as a guide. These standards keep this new generation of students in mind, and so will we.

# 2 Parent Education

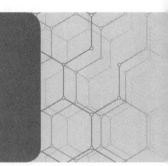

The past decade has been financially difficult for schools. States across the country have had to slash education budgets due to economic downturns. If your district's budget was unaffected by financial cuts, it is among the few. As for the rest of us, we have had to achieve more with less. To make matters more challenging, we had to implement new standards that ask schools to immerse students in technology—a very expensive task. Having parents on your side in this budget struggle can be very helpful.

In the years since the CCSS were written and adopted by most states, some attitudes toward the standards have changed. More recently, parents and community members have questioned them. So it is important, as a teacher, to be proactive in getting the word out about what is going on in your classroom. Work with parents and the community to educate them about CCR standards in your state, district, and school. Parents only want what is best for their children, and a little reassurance from you can go a long way.

This reassurance begins with listening to parents. Ask them about their concerns. Answering their questions with facts will help them to better understand why your state adopted the standards. The following topics cover a few of the technology concerns that have been raised about CCSS recently. Knowing about these and other controversial issues allows you to defuse concerns before they become major issues.

# Why Do Parents Need to Know about Technology Standards?

You don't need technology to read or do math—civilizations have been doing both for centuries. Nevertheless, technology does help in both areas. If we were still at the turn of the last millennium (1000 CE), we would be hand copying books. The printing press brought books to the commoner and education to those who wanted to learn. The abacus is fine but cannot compete with a calculator or computer. Technology marches on so that we can advance, learn more, and pass that knowledge along to the next generation.

The computer revolution of the last century hit the classroom with the encouragement of the CCR standards. Before these standards, computers were for schools with money or those who won grants. Even so, many schools that were considered advanced had not integrated technology into everyday learning. These were the first set of widely recognized standards to do that. There are several reasons for parents to know about CCSS.

First, keeping students versed in the fundamentals of technology will enhance your teaching tremendously, and students' parents can help with this at home. Survey parents to see how many students have internet access at home. What kind of equipment do they use—do they have cameras or video capabilities? What do they allow their children to use? Knowing what your students have at home improves equitable access in the classroom. Encourage parents to teach their children how to properly use tablets, computers, smartphones, and other mobile devices so students come to school more prepared.

Second, learning doesn't happen only at school. You need to educate parents because they are the main support system for learning outside of school. Consistent, clear standards put forward by CCR standards enable more effective learning. Knowing what technology and what software will be used to master these standards greatly assists parents and, in turn, their children. Look at the Global Family Research Project **(tinyurl.com/hguh777)** for the latest research and insights on how to get students' parents involved.

Third, technology can instantly link parents to what their children are learning. Communicating with teachers, seeing assignments, and understanding what is expected are all improved with today's technology. There is even a principal out there who tried "flipping" parent communication, which you might try too (DeWitt, 2013). Whatever you implement is a win-win for you and your students. Take advantage of technology in communication; don't shun it. It will make your life easier.

Finally, we are becoming a smaller, more codependent world. To have a world-class education that keeps our nation and civilization moving forward, all students need to be well versed in the newest technologies. That is what the CCR standards are all about! The CCSS Initiative's mission statement affirms, "The standards are designed to be robust and relevant to the real world, reflecting the knowledge and skills that our young people need for success in college and careers" (National Governors Association Center for Best Practices & Council of Chief State School Officers, 2010). In other words, the CCSS are designed for your students' success as adults in the workplace, of which technology is an integral part.

Even so, parents must be a part of this endeavor or their children will struggle to succeed. Involving them is as important to you, as a teacher, as is any other aspect of your students' learning. Do not think of parent education in the standards as an add-on, a tool to be used if you have time. Investing in your students' parents and having them on your team benefits you and lessens your load. In a synthesis of studies done on families, communities, and schools, Henderson and Mapp stated, "Efforts to improve children's performance in school are much more effective if they encompass their families. Regardless of income level or education background, all families can—and often do—support their children's success" (2002, p. 208).

## What Issues Do Parents Have with Technology in CCR Standards?

Parents may ask you about some of the controversial things they hear related to the standards. One controversy involves a misunderstanding about standards and curriculum. Standards describe what students should know; curriculum is how they get there. For example, even though there is no standard for cursive writing or keyboarding, that doesn't mean it won't be in your school's curriculum. Curriculum is still developed locally. Educate parents who are concerned that they have no control over their child's curriculum—they still have the ability to contribute to how it is taught in their local school.

Another controversy centers on decreased test scores from 2015 and 2017 National Assessment of Educational Progress. Although it may or may not be true in your district, scores quite often decrease when the format of the test changes. One example is when students go from paper-and-pencil tests to digital assessments. According to Swanson (2013), if your school changed tests, then a result might be decreased scores until students become familiar with the new format. The best way to combat this is to have other digital tests in the classroom throughout the year, to familiarize students with the new format. Also, the NAEP tests are still in trial stages, even four years after implementing the standards. Some states have changed their tests to new assessments. Cumulative results from standards-based teaching and assessment will tell more as parents, teachers, administrators, and policy makers look at the data and adjust the test accordingly.

A common concern we have heard is that the federal government will be able to collect the data of individual students because of these digital tests. This has been a particularly heightened apprehension recently. The U.S. Congress (2010) passed laws that prohibit the creation of a federal database with students' personally identifiable information. Although the law is in place, you should still be vigilant about keeping this sensitive data secure. You are the first line of defense and need to have procedures in place. Please go over your district's privacy policy. If there is none, push hard to make one.

## How Can Parents Help with Assessment Technology?

Teachers should help parents and community members understand the types of questions and problems that students are asked to solve on the new digital assessments. During parent nights, open houses, and/or in newsletters, introduce parents to the kind of testing their son or daughter will be experiencing. The Partnership for Assessment of Readiness for College and Careers (PARCC), **(parcconline.org)** and Smarter Balanced Assessment Consortium **(smarterbalanced.org)** websites are still the most commonly used assessments. If your state is using a different format, choose questions from these tests. You can download sample questions to show to parents; it can also be helpful to put new assessment questions next to old assessment questions so everyone can directly observe the shift.

If your state is going to use the Smarter Balanced test, have parents use the sample questions on the PARCC site to test their children at home. The sample Smarter Balanced test can also be used to prepare for the PARCC test. Both tests' questions are similar, based on the CCR standards, and can be used prepare students for state written tests.

Don't forget the basics. Make sure parents know what kind of equipment the students will be using for the test, and have them use similar equipment at home if possible. This will make the device a secondary concern so your students can focus on the test's content. Send home a sample question weekly so parents can become familiar with the changing assessments. Make sure some of the sample test questions you send home require students to use technology to answer the question, as this will be included on the assessments.

## How Can Parents Help Students Meet Technology Standards?

Parents need to see the value of having technologies at home that can help their children achieve more. At the same time, home technology helps you accomplish these new curriculum tasks that, as we teachers know, are daunting, to say the least.

A poll by the Leading Education by Advancing Digital (LEAD) Commission found that parents and teachers believe students who lack home access to the internet are at a significant disadvantage (2012, p. 23). Home access to broadband is viewed as important to learning and succeeding in school for the following reasons:

- It greatly exceeds anything that your students could ever bring home in their backpacks.

- It allows parents to be more involved in their child's schoolwork and allows more effective communication between parent and school, thus promoting greater student success.

- It vastly expands the time your students can learn and explore.

- It leads to greater collaborative work, engaging students in online group home-work. (This last point dovetails perfectly with many of the CCR technology initiatives.)

Home access requires your active support. At the beginning of the year, run a work-shop for parents about the kinds of technology you will be using and why. Teach them how to monitor their children for internet safety. You may want to call on your library media specialist or tech specialist to help, if they are available in your school.

Of course, you may teach in an area where parents do not have the funds for broad-band access or technology at home. Following are a few ways to address the issue.

- For homes that have broadband but no computers/tablets, start a program that allows students to check out resources from the school.

- Have after-school clubs or homework help where technology is available.

- Open the school in the evenings for parents and students, providing them access to teachers and technology.

- Apply for one of many grants available from different levels of government, foundations, and companies to help with your school community's access to technology.

- Ask parents to allow their children to use their smartphones that have cellular access.

Wherever you teach, parent education is the key to student success with the state standards. Lack of information is one of the main reasons parents have been opposed to the CCR standards. Being a proactive partner will defuse most objec-tions that arise—from parents and others in the community—and actually create proponents of what is going on in your classroom. Having parents as partners can only help when you are faced with technology needs, such as lack of hardware and software, lack of assistance, and gaps in your students' tech knowledge.

However, parent education is only part of the puzzle; you must first educate yourself about the standards and technology before you can effectively educate others. To address this, we have included a chapter on staff development (Chapter 4). But before we explore your professional development options, let's take a closer look at the road-blocks you may encounter on your journey to get technology into your classroom.

# 3 Roadblocks to Technology

Unless your school or district has unlimited funding and gives you completely free reign on your purchases, you have hit roadblocks in your quest for classroom technology. Chances are that you do not have the student technology to become a fully stocked digital age learning environment, but you are not alone. In this chapter, we provide ideas to use and manage the equipment and software/apps you already have, and we explore ways to add more. It is our hope that when we come to the later chapters on practical ways to integrate your technology with the CCR standards and your curriculum, you will be better prepared to maximize your resources.

## What Are the Roadblocks to Accessibility?

If it is not possible to provide all of your students with tablets or laptops, providing them to half the class is the next best thing. This allows you to work with small groups or pairs of students. Another option is to share technology with the classroom next door to gain at least some time with a full class set of laptops or tablets.

### Lack of Funding for 10–12 Laptops/Tablets per Classroom

One option is to have each grade level share a cart of fifteen laptops or tablets in addition to a mobile lab that any classroom can access. We suggest grade-level sharing of technology with no more than three sections, as more sections are likely to be too limiting. If there are four or more sections in a grade, add more carts. This will allow the grade level to have access to at least half of a class set. When you need a full class set, use the mobile cart to fill in the gaps. Another way to share additional mobile devices is to divide the fifteen laptops or tablets into sets of five for each of three classrooms and then have teachers share devices when necessary. You could also place all fifteen laptops or tablets on a cart and provide a signup sheet for as-needed use.

## Only 4–6 Laptops/Tablets per Classroom

You can use four to six laptops or tablets as a learning center or have half the class double up. You can also share with other classrooms. Pick a time every day when two or three classrooms share their laptops or tablets for an allotted amount of time; arrange certain days when each class has all of the devices or teachers can request them informally. The key is easy accessibility.

## Computer Lab Limitations

A computer lab with enough computers for all of your students is another great resource, especially if it includes a tech or media center teacher or assistant. This is great because everything is in a set location and there is another knowledgeable teacher available. The down side is that teachers have to schedule certain times and everyone must work on the computers at the same time. If you have access to tables in the lab or a nearby learning space, you have the opportunity to do other things with students who finish their work  early, forming smaller work groups as in a traditional classroom.

## Additional Equipment

How do you choose additional technology to better equip your classroom when your computer budget is already tight or inadequate? Aside from laptops and tablets, it is imperative to have a multimedia projector so that all students can see lesson materials, projects, resources, and so on. Other valuable equipment includes:

**Document cameras:** You will use these every day to display written books, worksheets, student work, and the like. Once you have one, you won't know how you got along without it!

**Interactive whiteboards:** These are great for engaging students, especially during whole-group instruction.

**Color printer:** Access to a color printer makes student work come to life. (Young children especially love color!)

**Scanner:** Access to a scanner will help when you wish to scan documents or student work.

With so many new websites that can turn laptops, tablets, or smartphones into interactive technology, buying interactive response systems is no longer necessary.

Free interactive websites may offer upgrades for an affordable fee, including Socrative **(socrative.com)**, AnswerPad **(theanswerpad.com)**, AnswerGarden **(answergarden.ch)**, Quizlet **(quizlet.com)**, and Annotate **(annotate.net)**.

### Keeping Up with Students' State Assessments

Although your students will not be tested in K–2, it is important to understand what they will face beginning in third grade. As of 2018, twenty-three states use either PARCC or Smarter Balanced tests to assess their students. The rest use state-created or other tests to assess students. Your students may be tested more than once a year depending on their grade level and what test is given in your state. Many of these assessments are computerized and have certain technology requirements, but they allow traditional paper-and-pencil versions when necessary. (Teachers should be aware that traditional versions may be phased out eventually.)

We will not address the specifics of network requirements; just know that your school or district will need to meet certain operating system and networking specifications whether they are using the Smarter Balanced, PARCC, or state-created assessment. Additionally, your network must be able to address security requirements to keep student information safe. Following are informational sites to help you find what you will need.

- PARCC technical requirements: **(tinyurl.com/y8vknzrk)**

- Smarter Balanced technical requirements: **(tinyurl.com/yddyof89)**

## How Do We Overcome Software and Hardware Roadblocks?

You cannot benefit from technology if you don't have it. It is also difficult to share it if you don't have enough of it. You need it on time and easily accessible if you truly want to use it seamlessly. This may be the biggest roadblock. We discussed how you might use different configurations of new or existing hardware in your school. The more pervasive the technology, the easier it is for you to achieve the goals set forth by the CCR standards.

## Sources of Funding

If you don't have enough equipment and/or software, apply for grants. While there are more grants available for economically disadvantaged districts, some are accessible to all districts. State and federal grants are available especially if you can link your needs to the Common Core. The Bill & Melinda Gates Foundation and big companies like Google, Target, and Staples give to schools. Ask your Parent Teacher Association (PTA) or Parent Teacher Organization (PTO) for money. Many districts have foundations that fund grants for teachers. You could even do a fundraiser for new technology. Following is a list that is by no means complete but offers a great place to start.

### GOVERNMENT

- **21st Century Community Learning Centers (tinyurl.com/7nx37vb):** This funding is designed to get parents and the community to actively support your work in the classroom.

- **Individuals with Disabilities Education Act (IDEA) (tinyurl.com/y5ue5o6d):** These funds are for students with disabilities.

- **Grants.gov (tinyurl.com/k8fybkt):** Search this site for all available federal grants. These grants include:

  - **Every Student Succeeds Act (ESSA)(ed.gov/ESSA):** This funding replacing the No Child Left Behind Act is designed to create equitable funding, support for the standards, and grow innovation in the classroom.

  - **Investing in Innovation Fund (i3) (tiny.cc/gj9o7y):** This program provides competitive grants to schools demonstrating improved student achievement and innovative practices.

- **Grants Funding Forecast (tinyurl.com/hkcrx74):** This resource offers an annual list of funding opportunities.

- **Computers for Learning (computersforlearning.gov):** This government program encourages agencies to transfer their used computers and related peripheral equipment directly to schools.

- **State Government (tinyurl.com/y9dfltpr):** Look for your state's educational website in this online index.

## FOUNDATIONS

Many private foundations offer grants. Following are just a few.

- **Bill & Melinda Gates Foundation (tinyurl.com/odwcrra):** This is the largest private foundation in the world. Its primary aim in the United States is to expand educational opportunities and access to information technology.

- **The Foundation Center (foundationcenter.org):** This independent, nonprofit information clearinghouse collects information on foundations, corporate giving, and related subjects.

- **Foundations.org (tinyurl.com/7sf3c):** This online resource provides an A–Z directory of foundations and grant makers.

- **The NEA Foundation (tinyurl.com/or2qc56):** This teacher association gives grants in several areas.

## COMPANIES

Many of the companies that manufacture the products we use every day have educational initiatives that offer grants for public schools. Following are just a few.

- **Target (tinyurl.com/cdt25kz):** Target offers grants in many areas, including education, the arts, and public safety.

- **Toshiba (toshiba.com/taf/k5.jsp):** Toshiba also offers math and science grants for Grades K–5.

- **Google (tinyurl.com/pm9gar4):** Google has several sites dedicated to corporate giving. Google for Nonprofits is a good place to start your search.

- **Microsoft Corporate Citizenship (tinyurl.com/p62et7u):** These grants are available for after-school programs.

- **Staples Foundation (tinyurl.com/yaysgbpo):** Staples Foundation educational giving teaches, trains, and inspires people from around the world by providing educational and job skill opportunities.

- **CenturyLink Clarke M. Williams Foundation's Teachers and Technology Program (tinyurl.com/otej8rl):** These grants are designed to help fund projects that advance student success through the innovative use of technology. Teachers in public or private PK–12 schools in CenturyLink's residential service areas are eligible to apply for a Teachers and Technology grant.

### OTHER RESOURCES

Microfunding through school- and classroom-specific grants can yield substantial results. Often donors are willing to fund projects whose impact they can directly observe.

- **Donors Choose (donorschoose.org)**: A crowd-sourced educational funding site that works with donors funding specific projects of various types.

- **ClassWish (classwish.org)**: Crowd-sourced educational funding that lets you raise money for any classroom project in the country.

- **Adopt-a-Classroom (adoptaclassroom.org)**: Facilitates individual donations to help teachers get the supplies they need.

- **National Charter School Resource Center (tinyurl.com/ph2ytng)**: This resource website has many links to funding opportunities.

- **eSchool News (eschoolnews.com)**: This is a great grant resource for K–12 and higher education.

- **Internet@Schools (tinyurl.com/nnh5n9d)**: This online magazine for education provides a vast list of free resources, grants, and funding.

- **Scholastic (tinyurl.com/nd3t97t)**: This educational mainstay has many great grant resources.

## Free Software and Apps

Software and app purchases are a challenging roadblock, especially if your district or school doesn't provide enough funding. Fortunately, there are many free resources. Search app stores for free apps. Free sites, such as Google Docs, are also great places to start. In addition, there are entire sites with free services geared toward the standards.

If you are in a small district or a private school, or if you live in a state where funding is limited, follow the money. Go to websites in states and at schools that do have the funds. Look at websites in wealthier school districts near you. Do they have lessons, activities, and technology ideas that match your standards and are free to anyone on the internet?

Many states have CCSS resources posted for free! Take advantage of them. For example, New York has many helpful suggestions at EngageNY.org **(tinyurl.com/npc7q58)**. Utah has also published a very resourceful standards site that can be found at the Utah Education Network (UEN) **(tinyurl.com/l2e532)**.

Free software and apps are also available from private companies. These sites usually have ads, or they may want you to purchase add-ons; you and your district will have to judge their value for yourselves. More examples of free applications and websites are given in the Practical Ideas chapters (8–13) of this book.

# What Other Roadblocks Must We Solve?

Systemic educational roadblocks can take many forms, which are often unintended or unavoidable. Following are three common challenges teachers face.

## Misguided Policies

Some districts or schools require that all classrooms have the same apps or software. They don't allow teachers to choose what they prefer, and this can be frustrating. If your district wants all software to be the same, you might try explaining why each grade level and each teacher would benefit from using different software, apps, and equipment appropriate to their students' needs.

Some districts implement policies that do not allow teachers to use technology as a tool. Instead, they force teachers to use technology when other mediums or tools make more sense. For example, we discovered a district that required teachers to teach with a tablet 85% of their instructional time. This district even required students to bring tablets to gym class and physical education teachers to use tablets in every class period. School leaders who enforce this kind of policy know very little about infusing technology into the classroom. It would be better to achieve higher technology use through staff development and individual coaching (e.g., through the use of this book) than by generating untenable policies that don't actually affect meaningful student learning.

To counter these policies, speak to your principal, go to a technology meeting, or attend a board meeting! Explain that technology is a tool and that meeting the CCSS does not require you to use technology every second of the day. There is a time and place for technology just as there is a time and place for math manipulatives, a calculator, a book, and even a pencil. Balance is the key. If anything is overused, it (and your effort) is set up for failure.

### Parents

Parents will ask the question, "Why do we need new or more technology?" Have a discussion at PTA/PTO meetings, open house nights, and board meetings about what you will be doing or would like to do with technology. Explain that the standards require everyone to integrate technology, and this is important for today's students. Please refer to the chapter on parent education (Chapter 2), which has specific suggestions about many of the issues that become parental roadblocks.

### Staff Development

Teacher training is so important. You need to have professional development in the area of technology for yourself as well as for your students. If you have a technology or instructional coach, great! Spend a lot of time with this coach—set up weekly meetings. A coach can help you as well as model or co-teach with you. There are many professional development opportunities online as well as off-site in the area of technology. Refer to Chapter 4 to learn how to get staff development outside your district and how to best get around these roadblocks!

## How Do You Get the Help You Need?

One of the key components of using technology is getting help. It is very difficult to manage a class of young students who are all trying to use technology at the same time. This is also the case when teachers try to work with a small group while the rest of the class is doing something else on tablets. Inevitably, something goes wrong with someone's computer or students are not sure what to click next. You can teach them to use a few apps or programs if you do it consistently, especially in a self-contained classroom center where students are engaged in independent and self-directed learning activities. However, when you want to expose them to something new or want to change the routine in any way, it is extremely helpful to have another set of hands.

Most elementary classrooms are not fortunate enough to have a full-time aide with them. Therefore, you will need to get more creative. If you have assistants who come to you on a regular basis to help in the classroom, this is a great resource. You can schedule technology use for when they are in the room. This allows you greater freedom to work with the whole class—assuming you have enough equipment. You can teach and your assistant can go around the room problem solving. If you work in small groups or at a media center, you each can take a group, doubling your efforts.

If you do not have access to assistants, you might try using parent volunteers. The worst part of using volunteers is inconsistent attendance. However, if you can find parents who are willing to come in on a regular basis, they can be a great help. You will need to find time to train your volunteers, of course, but once you do, most will be savvy enough to pick up what they need to do in class.

Another option is to work with your fellow teachers. Consider arranging your schedules so that you each take extra students while the other uses technology with a smaller group. Overseeing fewer students makes technology use much easier to manage.

If you don't have access to assistants or volunteers, training students is an option. When you are working with a group, have tech-savvy students problem solve technical issues. When you are setting up, they can help other students prepare. We have successfully had student experts as young as first grade. Four or five students can be used to help with small tasks, such as printing or finding an app. Training them is fairly easy, too. You can do so at recess or during one of their free periods, and it is helpful to have a checklist for them that outlines what you want them to learn. Following are examples of what to put on your checklist.

- How to save a document

- How to print a document or webpage

- How to find and open software

- How to open apps

- How to carefully handle the equipment

- How to charge devices

- How to distribute equipment (as well as understanding of usage policies)

- How to check internet connectivity

- How to use search engines

Make sure that you post passwords where it is easy for students to find them. Forgotten passwords are an annoying occurrence, so having them easily accessible will help you manage the situation comfortably.

Create peer groups that have a mix of tech-savvy students and those who struggle with technology. Arrange a time when older students can work with your younger students. Older students like to work with younger ones, and older students can be a big help in classroom management of technology. Even kindergarten classrooms can use technology; it's all in the management.

Although there can be many roadblocks that prohibit you from using classroom technology the way that you would like, there are ways to overcome these challenges. By using the suggestions given in this chapter, we hope you will overcome any roadblocks that lie in your way and that you have most everything you need at your fingertips.

# Staff Development

> When technology integration is at its best, a child or a teacher doesn't stop to think that he or she is using a technology tool—it is second nature. And students are often more actively engaged in projects when technology tools are a seamless part of the learning process. —"What Is Successful Technology Integration?" (Edutopia, 2007)

Without a doubt, today's students come to school with strong backgrounds and understandings of technology. This generation of tech-savvy students is interested, motivated, and even driven by technology. As you will see, CCSS have explicit technology standards within grade levels. But technology, as a tool, needs to be infused in all other CCSS as well. Having a tech-savvy classroom for today's students is the best way to create a digital age learning environment.

Truly integrated technology is ever present but invisible. You can use technology as a tool for instruction–as a way to vary the way you present information. You can also provide technology options for students as a way for them to engage in content skills. Students in your class should be given opportunities to create and share their new learning with a myriad of technology tools. The standards are not just about presenting information to students; today's students need to be able to plan, reason, analyze, evaluate, and create. Technology integration in today's classroom will do just that–it will not only allow your students to become more engaged in the learning process but empower them to gain a deeper understanding of their learning.

A plethora of articles have been written about the success of how to succeed with CCSS standards and how good professional development for teachers and staff is a significant key to its success. Technology plays a very valuable role in guiding and fostering this effective professional development, as well as helping to boost current professional-development resources and practices. And technologies that make tools available to teachers on an ongoing basis present a solid jumping-off point for successful classroom integration.

Research has found that sending teachers to workshop-based professional development alone is not very effective. Approximately, 90–100% of teachers participate in workshop-style or in-service training sessions during a school year and through the summer. While workshops can be informational and timely, teachers need opportunities to implement new teaching techniques, not just learn about them. Thus, professional development needs to be ongoing and meaningful to your own professional circumstances. The most effective professional development also uses peer coaches, educational coaches, and mentors to implement new learning in class.

# How Do You Create a Technology Plan?

You need lots of support and tools to utilize and sustain technology in your classroom. If you do not have a district or school technology director or coach, how do you develop a plan to get yourself (as well as your fellow colleagues) what is needed? You can be the pioneer to get the technology ball rolling.

Following are suggestions to help you begin the journey of infusing technology in your classroom. Although this should not be your task alone, sometimes it falls to a single individual to blaze the trail. Fortunately, there are many online resources that can assist you with creating a technology plan. Edutopia is a well-known place to start, offering (among other things) "Ten Steps to Effective Technology Staff Development" by Barbara Bray **(tinyurl.com/oesjsmn)**.

The first step is to put together a technology committee with as many representatives from different buildings and grade levels as you can find. It would be great to include administration staff as well as a district office representative. Parents, students, and outside technology experts can only enhance your committee. Next, come up with some ways to show how you and your students can use technology in the classroom. Providing specific examples of students working with technology to address the ISTE Standards and the CCSS would be powerful!

Develop a detailed questionnaire for teachers to express their classroom needs, frustrations, and fears. This questionnaire can also serve as a place for teachers to describe what they hope to learn from professional development, including technology goals they would like students to pursue in class.

Ask students to describe the ideal state of technology in their classroom in one year, two years, five years, and so on. Then place the ideas from this brainstorming session in a public document so everyone on the committee and in the community can see and refer to it.

Lastly, conduct a teacher survey using the ISTE Standards for Educators as a guide (iste.org/standards). These standards outline what educators should know and be able to apply in order to teach effectively and grow professionally. ISTE has organized them into the following seven categories:

1. **Learner:** Educators continually improve their practice by learning from and with others and exploring proven and promising practices that leverage technology to improve student learning.

2. **Leader:** Educators seek out opportunities for leadership to support student empowerment and success and to improve teaching and learning.

3. **Citizen:** Educators inspire students to positively contribute to and responsibly participate in the digital world.

4. **Collaborator:** Educators dedicate time to collaborate with both colleagues and students to improve practice, discover and share resources and ideas, and solve problems.

5. **Designer:** Educators design authentic, learner-driven activities and environments that recognize and accommodate learner variability.

6. **Facilitator:** Educators facilitate learning with technology to support student achievement of the ISTE Standards for Students.

7. **Analyst:** Educators understand and use data to drive their instruction and support students in achieving their learning goals.

Each standard has performance indicators that provide specific, measurable outcomes. You can use them to ascertain teachers' technology comfort level, attitude, and integration use in your school. Answers could be on a scale, such as "proficient enough to teach someone else," "able to hold my own," "a little knowledge," or "scared to death to even try." It may even be helpful to have teachers identify

**Figure 4.1.** ISTE Standards for Educators

three-to-five areas that they feel are most important to improving technology within the year. Providing a space for them to write an explanation is also important, as they may not be able to rank themselves on a scale when they can't quantify what they don't know. Writing a paragraph about where they stand with technology might be easier for them. The data you gain from this survey should be shared with your building, other participating schools, the administration, and the district office. And you may want to consider repeating this comfort-level survey several times throughout the year.

Once you've determined the proficiency of staff members, you can enlist their help to create a digital folder of suggested lesson plans, activities, and projects for all to access and use. Your colleagues will be able to implement the folder's learning opportunities in their classrooms and add to the folder as they try new things.

Something you may want to consider having is a reflection page to accompany any lesson, activity, or project posted. This will help others learn from and refine the ideas as they implement them on their own.

Additionally, your meetings, questionnaires, and survey results will identify teachers, staff members, parents, and administrators who have expertise in specific technology areas. Talk to your principal or district administrators to see if funding is available to pay for the planning time and workshops your experts may wish to lead. (As a general rule, every hour of professional-development class time takes at least two hours of planning.) Opportunities also need to be offered to your experts to advance their professional development. Perhaps you can even find a way to tap into the technology expertise of students, parents, and/or community members by having them lead some of your professional-development workshops. If possible, build in this professional-development/collaboration time at least once a week. Carrying on conversations about the workshops at team meetings, staff meetings, even lunch, is a great way to foster and gain interest in what you and your committee are doing.

Even if you are not willing or able to head up a technology committee, there are many things you can do to prepare your classroom for digital age learning.

## What Are Some Staff Development Ideas?

Be creative in your pursuit of ongoing staff development. If you are pressed for time, observe other teachers who use technology in their classrooms. (Ask your principal, department head, or coach to find someone to cover your classroom so you can do this.) If you are fortunate enough to have a coach or staff-development person in your building or district, ask them to set up a weekly meeting with you to work on technology goals. If you do not have a coach, partner up with another teacher or two. Peer coaching, team teaching, peer modeling, or even conferring with other teachers is a great way to advance your goals, objectives, and outcomes.

There are many conferences and workshops offered throughout the year. Check to see if your district will cover the expenses and provide substitutes so you and your colleagues can attend. Check out the Bureau of Education & Research (BER) **(ber.org)**; it is a sponsor of staff-development training for professional educators in the United States and Canada, offering many technology workshops and seminars about how to implement technology with the CCSS. There are also many technology grants offered by businesses. The magazines *Innovation & Tech Today* **(inno-techtoday.com)** and *Tech & Learning* **(techlearning.com)** are good places to look for these opportunities, as well as our "Sources of Funding" section in Chapter 3.

Ask your principal to provide grade-level time for teachers to review standards and plan how technology can be used. As a group, develop activities, projects, and lessons that include technology; come up with management strategies for using technology; and (perhaps most important) decide how you are going to assess and evaluate students' learning. This team time is important for you to brainstorm, share and develop ideas, and gather materials. Summer is also a good time for you and your colleagues to collaborate and develop projects. Check with your district to see if they will provide paid time for your summer work.

Don't forget to share your successes and those of others. Share disappointments as well so that others can learn from them. Take pictures, write press releases, post on your school's website, use social media—both the school and your own accounts—and include what you are doing in your parent newsletters and emails. If possible, make a short presentation at a school board meeting. Who knows? You may gain the moral and financial support you're looking for! Share your successes any way you can.

Because needs continually change, keep planning and reevaluating where you are and where you want to be. Encourage teachers to reach for the stars with their technology needs. Ask students how they feel about using technology and how it has affected their learning. These suggestions will help you and your colleagues get the technology you need.

# Where Can You Learn about Staff Development?

There are a multitude of professional-development opportunities out there for technology, either in the workshop/conference format or online (accessible from the comfort of your home or classroom). Some opportunities are free and some come with a membership fee to use the website or attend organization events. Others are priced per event. Following are a few suggestions.

- **ISTE (iste.org)** has several fantastic staff-development resources, including its Professional Learning Networks (PLNs), which allow you to instantly connect with experts in your field from around the globe **(community.iste.org/home).** There are many different networks to join (depending on your professional interests) where you can ask questions, learn from colleagues, and get access to exclusive events and professional learning opportunities. ISTE also offers free Strategic Learning Programs with partners like NASA and Verizon, which can be brought to your school or district **(bit.ly/1PeJ97t).** In addition, ISTE may have affiliate organizations in your area that provide professional development at seminars and conferences **(iste.org/affiliates).**

- **EdTechTeacher (edtechteacher.org)** is another organization that provides help to teachers and schools wishing to integrate technology to create student-centered, inquiry-based learning environments. They offer keynote presentations, hands-on workshops, online courses, and live webinars for teachers, schools, and school districts—all from your computer! What is nice about EdTechTeacher is that they understand teachers and students because the people leading the professional development have been or still are in the classroom.

- **Education World (educationworld.com)** is a complete online resource that offers high-quality lesson plans, classroom materials, information on how to integrate technology in the classroom, as well as articles written by education experts—a great place for you to find and share ideas with other teachers.

- **Discovery Education (discoveryeducation.com)** supplies a plethora of digital media that is immersive and engaging, bringing the world into the classroom to give every student a chance to experience fascinating people, places, and events. All of its content is aligned to standards that can be adjusted to support your specific curriculum and classroom instruction, regardless of what technology you have in your room. Discovery Education can help you transition to a digital age environment and even replace all of your textbooks with digital resources, if that is your ultimate goal.

Because you are reading this book, you have already started your technology journey! And you are not alone in this nationwide endeavor to harness what you didn't know about technology. Kristi Meeuwse is an Apple distinguished educator and offers sage advice at her blog, iTeach with iPads **(iteachwithipads.net).** You can also read about "How Kristi Meeuwse Teaches with iPad" at Apple.com **(tinyurl.com/ybv9esou).** Following is just a taste of her guidance.

> Wherever you are in your classroom journey, it's important to reflect on where you are and where you've been. It's important to celebrate your successes, no matter how small, and then be willing to move forward and try new things. Daring to imagine the possibilities and being willing to change is not just transforming to your own teaching, it will transform your classroom in ways you never thought were possible. Today we will do exciting new things. Let's get to it. (Meeuwse, 2013)

We provide additional resources for staff development in the Practical Ideas chapters (8-13) of this book. To learn about staff development in grades other than K-5, look for the 6-12 title in this series. Before we dive into lesson ideas for your specific grade and subjects, however, we will discuss how to effectively read, understand, and use CCSS in the next three chapters.

# Organization of the Standards

When discussing standards in this section, we will be focusing on the CCSS Initiative, which is the basis for the CCR standards in this book, and we will be referring to Common Core State Standards as CCSS. These were adopted by the National Governors Association in 2009 and the timeline for review and voluntary adoption individually by states was by 2013. Common Core State Standards was fully underway by 2014. So Common Core has been the standard most states have used or based their standards on for several years now. While reading this chapter, you might want to explore "Read the Standards" on the CCSS website **(tinyurl.com/p9zfnwo)** as we discuss the details.

## How Are the ELA Standards Organized?

The K–5 English language arts (ELA) standards are divided into six parts (see Figure 5.1), five of which are comprehensive K–12 sections (grey boxes). Then there is one specific content area section for foundational skills in Grades K–5 (white box). The CCSS website's introduction to the ELA standards has its own "How to Read the Standards" section **(bit.ly/1ZgEHIa)** that gives more information about organization as well as three appendices of supplemental material.

Each section is divided into strands. At the beginning of each strand is a set of CCR anchor standards, which are the same across all grades and content areas. Take, for example, the first anchor standard illustrated in Figure 5.2. It is the same in kindergarten as it is in second grade, but the grade-level standard is refined by what the student at each grade level is expected to accomplish within the anchor standard.

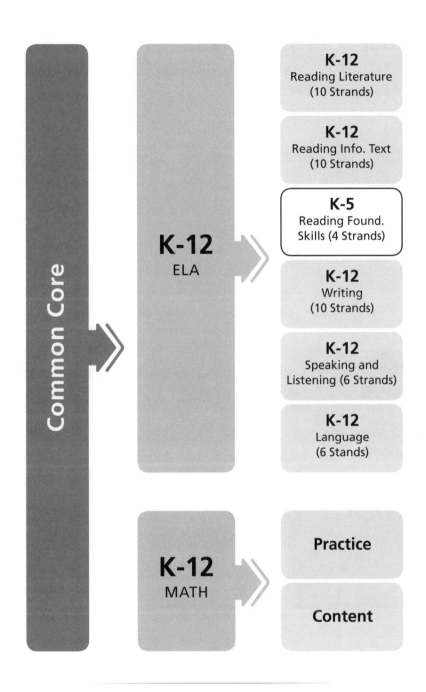

**Figure 5.1.** The CCSS ELA standards

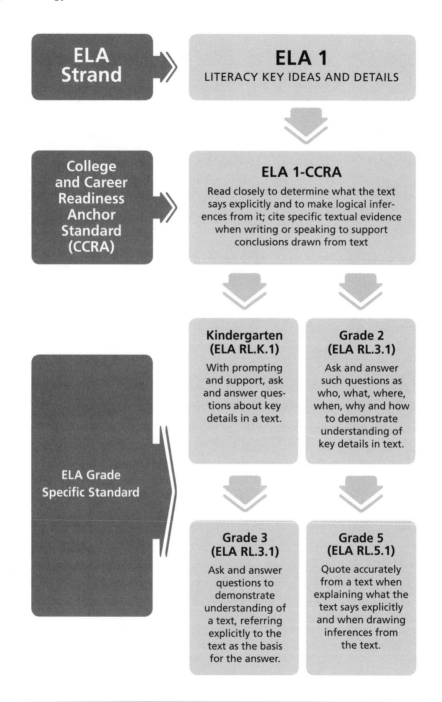

**Figure 5.2.** College and Career Readiness (CCR) anchor standard ELA 1 (CCSS.ELA- Literacy.CCRA.R.1) with grade-specific standards for Grades 9–12

**ELA 1 Anchor Standard**: Read closely to determine what the text says explicitly and to make logical inferences from it; cite specific textual evidence when writing or speaking to support conclusions drawn from the text.

**ELA 1 Standard in Kindergarten**: With prompting and support, ask and answer questions about key details in the text.

**ELA 1 Standard in Grade 2**: Ask and answer such questions as who, what, where, when, why, and how to demonstrate understanding of key details in the text.

**ELA 1 Standard in Grade 3**: Ask and answer questions to demonstrate understanding of a text, referring explicitly to the text as the basis for the answer.

**ELA 1 Standard in Grade 5**: Quote accurately from a text when explaining what the text says explicitly and when drawing inferences from the text.

These anchor standards complement the specific grade-level standards and define the skills and knowledge base that students should have by the end of each grade. The CCR standards are broad, while the grade-level standards are specific.

ELA standards focus on the following four areas:

1. Reading

2. Writing

3. Speaking and Listening

4. Language

The reading standards focus on text complexity (the difficulty of what students read), as well as the growth of their comprehension skills. Along with fictional stories and informational text, the CCSS focuses on poetry and dramas, too. The writing standards delve into specific text types, reading response, and research. Some writing skills, such as the ability to plan, revise, edit, and publish, can be applied to most types of writing. Other writing skills are more specific: opinion and argumentation, informational explanatory texts, and narratives. Speaking and listening standards deal with collaboration and flexible communication. In this area, students acquire and refine their oral communication and interpersonal skills, and perhaps demonstrate these skills through formal presentations.

The language standards concentrate on vocabulary, conventions, and effective use. This strand not only incorporates the essential "rules" of standard written and spoken English but also helps students to understand how language functions in different contexts. Making effective choices in meaning and style leads to better comprehension when reading and listening. The vocabulary part of this strand clarifies and/or determines the meaning of unknown and multiple-definition words and phrases by using the appropriate context clues and/or reference materials as needed. This strand also helps students demonstrate an understanding of figurative language, word relationships, and nuances in word meanings. In addition, students will be able to acquire and accurately use a range of general and domain-specific words and phrases in any academic area. (We'll talk more about domains later in this chapter, in the math standards section.)

With the organization in mind, let's learn how you, as an individual teacher, use the CCSS in ELA.

## How Do You Find ELA Standards by Subject and Grade?

Since most elementary teachers teach just one grade level, the standards are organized so you can focus on your specific area, but it is very helpful to put your grade-level curriculum in context. Look back at the level before the one you teach, and look ahead to the standards that come next. (If you would like to review a grade not included in this book, please refer to the other title in this series.)

Using the main "English Language Arts Standards" page on the CCSS website is probably the most efficient way to find your grade- and subject-level standards **(tiny. cc/w1vn3y).** If you know what you are looking for, the corresponding reference numbers are useful. Here is a quick introduction:

All standards that relate to literature, informational text, writing, speaking, listening, language, history/social studies, and science and technical begin with "CCSS. ELA-Literacy." The difference comes at the end, with the numbering system.

Let's use the following as examples.

• CCSS.ELA-Literacy.RL.2.1

- CCSS is the abbreviation for Common Core State Standard.

- ELA-Literacy identifies this as an English language arts standard.

- RL stands for "reading literature."

- 2 is the grade.

- 1 is the strand.

• CCSS.ELA-Literacy.SL.K.5

- CCSS.ELA-Literacy represents the same information as in the previous example.

- SL stands for "speaking and listening."

- K is the grade.

- 5 is the strand.

But there are standards within standards that are not easily apparent at first glance. For instance, there may be a reading standard that uses historical or science text, or a speaking and listening standard that has a technology component. This book focuses on where technology is required in the CCSS, and there is plenty of technology to discuss in ELA and math!

You may be wondering how you will be able to keep all of this straight. After all, we haven't even started talking about math! We invite you to view the math standards online **(tiny.cc/wrvn3y)** as you read this next section.

# How Does the Organization of Math Standards Differ?

When you look at the math standards, you will see immediately that they were written by a different group of individuals; they do not integrate other subjects like the ELA standards. Even the mathematical technology standard is separate. The system of organization is different, too. The authors of the math standards also state that the grade-level order can be changed. After the following overview, we will help you sort it all out.

Long before CCSS was implemented, it was widely reported that math curricula in the United States was not even close to being on the same level as math education in high-performing countries. The consensus: U.S. math education needed to be substantially more focused and coherent to improve. To solve this, the CCSS were written to be clear, specific, and rigorous. Not only do the Common Core math standards stress conceptual understanding of key ideas, but they continually return to the main organizing principles (place value and properties of operations) to structure those ideas. It is important to note that these standards address what students should understand and be able to do in their study of mathematics. But asking a student to understand something also means asking a teacher to assess whether a student understands it. Therefore, we need to break apart these standards to enhance readability and gauge what Common Core math comprehension looks like—so your students will be able to understand and you will be able to assess their learning.

First, you need to understand that in Grades K–5, the CCSS provide a solid foundation in whole numbers, addition, subtraction, multiplication, division, fractions, and decimals. Also, instead of covering a myriad of topics, your students will be required to immerse themselves in deep comprehension by applying mathematics to problems they have not encountered previously.

The CCSS for math begin with eight Standards for Mathematical Practice (SMP), **(tiny.cc/wrvn3y),** which apply to all grades, K–12. These standards represent ways in which students will engage with math content, processes, and proficiencies—longstanding, important practices. The eight SMP are:

1. Make sense of problems and persevere in solving them.

2. Reason abstractly and quantitatively.

3. Construct viable arguments and critique the reasoning of others.

4. Model with mathematics.

5. Use appropriate tools strategically.

6. Attend to precision.

7. Look for and make use of structure.

8. Look for and express regularity in repeated reasoning.

For kindergarten through eighth grade, there are also grade-specific standards. Each contains a number of domains. Domains are larger groups of related standards that are sometimes broken into clusters. Clusters are summarized groups of related standards that fall under the main standard (see the cluster that follows the standard in Table 5.3). Due to the connected nature of math, you may see closely related clusters in other domains as well. You can read more about this on the "How to Read the Grade-Level Standards" page **(bit.ly/1sPykwd)** of the CCSS website's math standards introduction.

The grade-specific domains for K-2 are the following, although for your background information we have indicated that some go beyond the K-2 level:

- Counting and Cardinality (kindergarten only)

- Operations and Algebraic Thinking (K-5)

- Number and Operations in Base Ten (K-5)

- Measurement and Data (K-5)

- Geometry (K-8)

Here is an example of how domains are used to organize the math standards:

- CCSS.Math.Content.1.NBT.B.2

    ○ CCSS is the abbreviation for Common Core State Standard.

    ○ Math.Content identifies that this is a math standard.

    ○ 1.NBT is the domain (Grade 1—Number and Operations in Base Ten).

    ○ B.2 is the identifier for a related standard (or cluster) under the main standard—in this case, "Understand Place Value" (see Table 5.3).

Now that you know how to identify a math standard and its numbering system, let's look at Table 5.3 to see the way in which this standard is actually presented in this domain.

The standard in Table 5.3 defines what your students should know and be able to do after you have taught and assessed that standard. Reading and familiarizing

| | | Table 5.3 |
|---|---|---|
| **Example of a standard in the first-grade domain of number and operations in base ten.** | | |
| GRADE | STANDARD | CLUSTER |
| 1 | **Understand Place Value** | CCSS.Math.Content.1.NBT.B.2: Understand that the two digits of a two-digit number represent amounts of tens and ones. Understand the following as special cases:<br><br>• CCSS.Math.Content.1.NBT.B.2.A: 10 can be thought of as a bundle of ten ones—called a "ten."<br><br>• CCSS.Math.Content.1.NBT.B.2.B: The numbers from 11 to 19 are composed of a ten and one, two, three, four, five, six, seven, eight, or nine ones.<br><br>• CCSS.Math.Content.1.NBT.B.2.C: The numbers 10, 20, 30, 40, 50, 60, 70, 80, 90 refer to one, two, three, four, five, six, seven, eight, or nine  tens (and zero ones). |

yourself with all the standards will go a long way in helping you teach the standards later.

There are also SMPs that are part of the CCR anchor standards of the ELA. These standards are not overtly assessed but are necessary for you to include in your instruction. SMP will not be the focus of this book except when they involve technology.

As you can see, math and ELA standards are written and organized very differently. We have tried our best to guide you through these differences, but we do recommend that you explore the resources we have provided below as well as others that we have referenced on our website **(tinyurl.com/y9dfltpr).** Here are two great resources that will explain the standards of mathematical practices:

• State of California CCSS Mathematics Resources: **tinyurl.com/l3zzsae**

• ASCD's Implementing the Common Core Mathematical Practices: **tinyurl. com/ybfdgtwr**

In the next chapter, we discuss technology and how it relates to the CCSS.

# CHAPTER 6
# Technology in the Common Core

This chapter focuses on the CCSS in ELA and math that have technology-related components written into them, first identifying and then analyzing these standards. This will prepare you for the later chapters, where we offer practical examples of how you can integrate these standards into your curriculum.

As instructional coaches, we know that there are those of you who are excited about technology, those of you who think it is an annoyance, and those of you who still fear it. These standards affect all of you because they force your districts and you, as teachers, to use technology more pervasively. Schools feel pressure to address areas that may have been avoided in the past due to cost or apprehension. If you are a fan of technology, you welcome this focus; if you are not, you still need to become proficient. You simply cannot avoid technology in your classroom.

## Where Is Technology in the ELA Standards?

The CCSS are designed to prepare students for college, the workforce, and a technology-rich society. And as you learned in the last chapter, the ELA standards have the CCR anchor standards—reading, writing, speaking and listening, and language—at their core. Following is a summary of those CCR standards that are embedded with technology in Grades K–5.

# Where Is Technology in the Math Standards?

As mentioned in Chapter 5, the math standards are written differently, and the technology standard in math (yes, only one standard) is separate from the rest of the math standards. However, this technology standard is meant to be used ubiquitously. Though many math standards do not overtly say that technology is required, if there is a need for a calculator or statistical analysis using a computer then that is what students should use. In math, the understanding is that these technology tools are used across grade levels and throughout the math standards even though there

---

## ELA Standards (Grades K-5) in Which Technology Appears

**READING (K–5)**

- CCR Reading (R) Standard 7 **(tinyurl.com/h9n9ek9)**

    - Reading Literature (RL)

    - Reading Informational Text (RI)

- CCR Reading (R) Standard 5 **(tinyurl.com/z7cqpqj)**

- Note: We will get into more detail about related anchor standard R.5 later in this chapter.

**WRITING (K–5)**

- CCR Writing (W) Standard 2 **(tinyurl.com/zt6kysv)**

- CCR Writing (W) Standard 6 **(tinyurl.com/zmxfdp8)**

- CCR Writing (W) Standard 8 **(tinyurl.com/jercjbv)**

**SPEAKING AND LISTENING (K–5)**

- CCR Speaking and Listening (SL) Standard 2 **(tinyurl.com/gvdrr3g)**

- CCR Speaking and Listening (SL) Standard 5 **(tinyurl.com/hrw3bdu)**

**LANGUAGE (K–5)**

- CCR Language (L) Standard 4 **(tinyurl.com/hmu54nx)**

---

is only one written standard. (Note: This math standard is presented in detail after the grade-specific ELA standards at the end of this chapter.)

## What about Using Technology in All Subjects?

Because technology is integrated throughout the CCSS, we should discuss in more depth what this actually means as you go about implementing the curriculum day to day. Though the standards give you specific language, the use of technology has been left wide open. They use terms like "digital tools," "other media," and "both print and digital" to let you choose what is appropriate to the lesson. The standards are trying to infuse technology into everyday classroom use, as opposed to having a separate period in a computer lab or someplace you send the students while you are meeting, planning, or collaborating with colleagues. Technology must become like the pencil: simply another tool to choose when students need to find the most appropriate one to complete the task at hand.

CCSS strongly encourage project-based lessons and are designed to be cross-curricular. Also, the standards are looking for higher-level thinking, learning, and application. All of these things lead to technology as the most appropriate tool in many situations. They fit very well into the Partnership for 21st Century Learning (P21) Framework for 21st Century Learning (**tinyurl.com/nzvwyen**) and the ISTE Standards for Students (**iste.org/standards**). If you have been working for some time on lessons that integrate technology and you think you will have to begin again, you will be relieved to know that the technology-embedded standards are not so different.

## How Do You Put ELA Technology Standards into Context?

When you look at the patterns of technology use in the standards, you improve your integration planning and learning achievements with these standards. Let's take a quick look at the technology patterns in the related K–5 standards.

**R.7:** Although R.7 does not state standards that include technology until tGrade 2, earlier grades can use it both in preparation for successive grade levels and  differentiation. The standard then continues to develop in subsequent grades comparing text and illustrations in various formats that include technology.

**RL.7:** This standard begins in kindergarten, comparing illustrations and text, and then grows through the grades, using all types of media to compare, support, and analyze the story's meaning. Essentially, the purpose of the standard is to get meaning from more than the text. Meaning can also come from all the accompanying media and even the format of the story.

**RI.7:** This is similar to RL.7 but refers to informational text, history, science, and technology. Thus, you must keep in mind informational graph-ics—maps; photographs; diagrams; charts; and other media in history, science, and technical subjects—and the way in which they augment information or help to solve a problem.

**RI.5:** Beginning in kindergarten with learning the parts of a book, this stan-dard grows through third grade to an analysis of text structure. Of course, informational text in the digital age is not only in book form. Get-ting meaning through the use of electronic menus and graphics in digital media is an important skill that must also be taught.

**W.2:** From drawing, writing, and telling about a topic in kindergarten, this standard evolves into producing a thesis in high school. It is your basic research paper that now includes an expectation to use any and all media that is appropriate for conveying the information.

**W.6:** This is one of the few anchor standards that is solely technology-driven. From kindergarten through high school, students are required to use technology to collaborate with others when writing. Of course, this requires keyboarding skills, but they are not mentioned in the standard until Grade 3.

**W.8:** Although not explicitly stated in grades K–2, primary teachers should know that CCR W.8 does state technology be used. Digital sources could be taught to younger students who are ready. Technology in this standard is expected from Grade 3 through high school. This writing standard is keying in on the gathering of information, analyzing the information, and avoidance of plagiarism using multiple sources, digital as well as text when writing informative or explanatory works.

**SL.2:** This standard expects the use of technology from kindergarten through Grade 12. It is a listening standard, but in today's world, all kinds of diverse media are constantly available. Students need to be able to analyze and make decisions about this content.

**SL.5:** Beginning with the use of pictures when speaking in kindergarten, this standard builds to making strategic use of digital media for presentations in high school. Learning to use media in presentations is critical for college and career readiness.

**L.4:** This is a very straightforward standard that clarifies the meaning of words at all grade levels. Starting in second grade, students need to know how to find word meanings using not just print but digital dictionaries, glossaries, and thesauruses.

## What about Assessment?

You don't begin a trip without an end in mind, and the end that must always be kept in mind with the CCSS is the standardized test your state administers. Even though students in K–2 will not be taking part in the national assessments, it is important to prepare them for its eventuality. Whether it is the PARCC, Smarter Balanced assessment, or some other assessment your state is developing, it will certainly involve technology.

This, of course, depends on your state and district. In fact, the tests that are being developed will expect students to write short passages using the computer starting in third grade. This is just one example of an assessment (keyboarding) that is not overtly stated as a standard in kindergarten, first grade, or second grade but is expected as a performance outcome in third grade. Educators know you can't start teaching keyboarding in Grade 3 and expect students to be proficient in Grade 3. So it is important to start with the end in mind.

The tests will require some level of competence in selecting and highlighting text, dragging and dropping text, and moving objects on the screen. In the math areas of the test, tools that might be needed for the exam (calculators, rulers, a slide rule) will be available on the screen. Students may need headphones for text-to-speech features. To find a full list of technology skills needed for the PARCC computer-based assessment go to **tinyurl.com/y8ge25a4.** For Smarter Balanced requirements, visit **tinyurl.com/y8wvrcqj**.

The best way to prepare students is to know in advance the scope of technology they will need to master. Many things about the tests that your state is using are continually changing. The changes mean your students may not be as fully prepared as you would like them to be. However, your preparation—giving students opportunities to use a myriad of technologies as often as possible—will help them to be as ready as they can be for the assessments.

# What Are the ELA Standards with Technology?

The following is a listing of where technology appears in the CCSS. The first section contains the anchor standards, and the second section has the more specific grade-level standards. The standards are ordered by level so that you can find those related to the grade you teach more quickly. The part of the standard that pertains to technology is in boldface type. It is always helpful to look at the standards above and below your level to see where the students have come from and where they are going on their educational journey. Please refer to the second book in this series if you would like to see other grade levels.

## Reading

CCSS.ELA-Literacy.CCRA.R.7

> **R.7:** Integrate and evaluate content presented in diverse media and formats, including visually and quantitatively, as well as in words.
>
> Note **R.5** as well: Analyze the structure of texts, including how specific sentences, paragraphs, and larger portions of the text (e.g., a section, chapter, scene, or stanza) relate to each other and the whole.

The **R.5** anchor standard does not have any multimedia but does overtly include technology in its informational-text (RI) strand concerning the use of electronic text from Grades 1–3 **(RI.1.5, RI.2.5, RI.3.5)**. It has a non-technical focus in **RI.4.5** and **RI.5.5**.

## Writing

CCSS.ELA-Literacy, CCRA.W.2, CCSS.ELA-Literacy.CCRA.W.6, and CCSS.ELA-Literacy.CCRA.W.8

**W.2:** Write informative/explanatory texts to examine and convey complex ideas and information clearly and accurately through the effective selection, organization, and analysis of content.

Note: Anchor standard W.2 does not have multimedia but does include technology in its strand starting in Grade 4 (**W.4.2.a**).

**W.6:** **Use technology, including the internet**, to produce and publish writing and to interact and collaborate with others.

**W.8:** Gather relevant information from multiple print and **digital sources**, assess the credibility and accuracy of each source, and integrate the information while avoiding plagiarism.

## Speaking and Listening

CCSS.ELA-Literacy.CCRA.SL.2 and CCSS.ELA-Literacy.CCRA.SL.5

**SL.2:** Integrate and evaluate information presented in **diverse media and formats**, including visually, quantitatively, and orally.

**SL.5:** Make strategic use of **digital media** and **visual displays** of data to express information and enhance understanding of presentations.

Even when your grade does not have a technology standard included in these main anchor strands **(R.7, W.6, W.8, SL.2, SL.5, L.4)**, it is implied that it be used. We have listed here only those that state a technology use. For instance, the first time that **RI.7** overtly states the use of technology is in Grade 4 **(RI.4.7)**; but because it is in the anchor standard, it is implied that technology be used in **RI.7** in Grades 1–3 **(RI.1.7, RI.2.7, RI.3.7)** whenever it is appropriate to use it.

# What Are the ELA Grade-Level Standards with Technology?

Following is where ELA grade-level standards appear in the CCSS (listed by grade). Note the following abbreviations: reading literature (RL), reading informational text (RI), writing (W), speaking and listening (SL), and language (L). We are including Grade 3 to give the technology standards some context. Please refer to the other books in this series to get a sense of the full scope of technology standards, Grades K–12. (Note: as in the preceding section, the part of the standard that pertains to technology is in boldface type.)

## Kindergarten

**W.K.6:** With guidance and support from adults, explore a variety of **digital tools** to produce and publish writing, including collaboration with peers.

**SL.K.2:** Confirm understanding of a text read aloud or information presented orally or through **other media** by asking and answering questions about key details and requesting clarification if something is not understood.

**SL.K.5:** Add drawings or other **visual displays** to descriptions as desired to provide additional detail.

## Grade 1

**RI.1.5:** Know and use various text features (e.g., headings, tables of contents, glossaries, **electronic menus, icons**) to locate key facts or information in a text.

**W.1.6:** With guidance and support from adults, use a variety of **digital tools** to produce and publish writing, including in collaboration with peers.

**SL.1.2:** Ask and answer questions about key details in a text read aloud or information presented orally or through **other media**.

**SL.1.5:** Add drawings or other **visual displays** to descriptions when appropriate to clarify ideas, thoughts, and feelings.

## Grade 2

**RL.2.7:** Use information gained from the illustrations and words in a print or **digital text** to demonstrate understanding of its characters, setting, or plot.

**RI.2.5:** Know and use various text features (e.g., captions, bold print, subheadings, glossaries, indexes, **electronic menus, icons**) to locate key facts or information in a text efficiently.

**W.2.6:** With guidance and support from adults, use a variety of **digital tools** to produce and publish writing, including in collaboration with peers.

**SL.2.2:** Recount or describe key ideas or details from a text read aloud or information presented orally or through **other media**.

**SL.2.5:** Create **audio recordings** of stories or poems; add drawings or other **visual displays** to stories or recounts of experiences when appropriate to clarify ideas, thoughts, and feelings.

**L.2.4.e:** Use glossaries and beginning dictionaries, both print and **digital**, to determine or clarify the meaning of words and phrases.

## Grade 3

**RI.3.5:** Use text features and search tools (e.g., **key words, sidebars, hyperlinks**) to locate information relevant to a given topic efficiently.

**W.3.6:** With guidance and support from adults, **use technology** to produce and publish writing (using **keyboarding skills**) as well as to interact and collaborate with others.

**W.3.8:** Recall information from experiences or gather information from print and **digital sources**; take brief notes on sources and sort evidence into provided categories.

**SL.3.2:** Determine the main ideas and supporting details of a text read aloud or information presented in **diverse media and formats**, including visually, quantitatively, and orally.

**SL.3.5:** Create engaging **audio recording**s of stories or poems that demonstrate fluid reading at an understandable pace; add **visual displays** when appropriate to emphasize or enhance certain facts or details.

**L.3.4.d:** Use glossaries or beginning dictionaries, both print and **digital**, to determine or clarify the precise meaning of key words and phrases.

## Grade 4

**RL.4.7:** Make connections between the text of a story or drama and a **visual** or oral **presentation** of the text, identifying where each version reflects specific descriptions and directions in the text.

**RI.4.7:** Interpret information presented visually, orally, or quantitatively (e.g., in charts, graphs, diagrams, time lines, **animations**, or **interactive elements on webpages**) and explain how the information contributes to an understanding of the text in which it appears.

**W.4.2.a:** Introduce a topic clearly and group related information in paragraphs and sections; include formatting (e.g., headings), illustrations, and **multimedia** when useful to aiding comprehension.

**W.4.6:** With some guidance and support from adults, use **technology, including the internet**, to produce and publish writing as well as to interact and collaborate with others; demonstrate sufficient command of **keyboarding skills** to type a minimum of one page in a single sitting.

**W.4.8:** Recall relevant information from experiences or gather relevant information from print and **digital sources**; take notes and categorize information, and provide a list of sources.

**SL.4.2:** Paraphrase portions of a text read aloud or information presented in **diverse media and formats**, including visually, quantitatively, and orally.

**SL.4.5:** Add **audio recordings and visual displays** to presentations when appropriate to enhance the development of main ideas or themes.

**L.4.4.c:** Consult reference materials (e.g., dictionaries, glossaries, thesauruses), both print and **digital**, to find the pronunciation and determine or clarify the precise meaning of key words and phrases.

## Grade 5

**RL.5.7:** Analyze how visual and **multimedia elements** contribute to the meaning, tone, or beauty of a text (e.g., graphic novel, **multimedia presentation** of fiction, folktale, myth, poem).

**RI.5.7:** Draw on information from multiple print or **digital sources**, demonstrating the ability to locate an answer to a question quickly or to solve a problem efficiently.

**W.5.2.a:** Introduce a topic clearly, provide a general observation and focus, and group related information logically; include formatting (e.g., headings), illustrations, and **multimedia** when useful to aiding comprehension.

**W.5.6:** With some guidance and support from adults, use **technology, including the Internet**, to produce and publish writing as well as to interact and collaborate with others; demonstrate sufficient command of **keyboarding skills** to type a minimum of two pages in a single sitting.

**W.5.8:** Recall relevant information from experiences or gather relevant information from print and **digital sources**; summarize or paraphrase information in notes and finished work, and provide a list of sources.

**SL.5.2:** Summarize a written text read aloud or information presented in **diverse media and formats**, including visually, quantitatively, and orally.

**SL.5.5:** Include **multimedia components (e.g., graphics, sound) and visual displays** in presentations when appropriate to enhance the development of main ideas or themes.

**L.5.4.c:** Consult reference materials (e.g., dictionaries, glossaries, thesauruses), both print and **digital**, to find the pronunciation and determine or clarify the precise meaning of key words and phrases.

## Grade 6

**RL.6.7:** Compare and contrast the experience of reading a story, drama, or poem to **listening to or viewing an audio, video,** or live version of the text, including contrasting what they "see" and "hear" when reading the text to what they perceive when they listen or watch.

**RI.6.7:** Integrate information presented in **different media or formats** (e.g., visually, quantitatively) as well as in words to develop a coherent understanding of a topic or issue.

**W.6.2.a:** Introduce a topic; organize ideas, concepts, and information using strategies such as definition, classification, comparison/contrast, and cause/effect; include formatting (e.g., headings), graphics (e.g., charts, tables), and **multimedia** when useful to aiding comprehension.

**W.6.6:** Use **technology, including the internet**, to produce and publish writing as well as to interact and collaborate with others; demonstrate sufficient command of **keyboarding skills** to type a minimum of three pages in a single sitting.

**W.6.8:** Gather relevant information from multiple print and **digital sources**; assess the credibility of each source; and quote or paraphrase the data and conclusions of others while avoiding plagiarism and providing basic bibliographic information for sources.

**SL.6.2:** Interpret information presented in **diverse media and formats** (e.g., visually, quantitatively, orally) and explain how it contributes to a topic, text, or issue under study.

**SL.6.5:** Include **multimedia components (e.g., graphics, images, music, sound) and visual displays** in presentations to clarify information.

**L.6.4.c:** Consult reference materials (e.g., dictionaries, glossaries, thesauruses), both print and **digital**, to find the pronunciation of a word or determine or clarify its precise meaning or its part of speech.

# What Is the Math Standard with Technology?

The Standards for Mathematical Practice (SMP) are skills that all of your students should look to develop. As you learned in Chapter 5, there are eight SMP, which are designed to overlay the math content standards. In other words, the math practice standards apply to every one of the math content standards. So, although MP5 is the only standard that includes technology, it actually means that every math content standard should use the appropriate tools, including tools that use technology.

Following is MP5, taken verbatim from the CCSS website. As in the preceding two sections, any text that pertains to technology is in boldface type.

## CCSS.MATH.PRACTICE.MP5

**MP5:** Use **appropriate tools** strategically.

Mathematically proficient students consider the available tools when solving a mathematical problem. These tools might include pencil and paper, concrete models, a ruler, a protractor, **a calculator, a spreadsheet, a computer algebra system, a statistical package, or dynamic geometry software**. Proficient students are sufficiently familiar with tools appropriate for their grade or course to make sound decisions about when each of these tools might be helpful, recognizing both the insight to be gained and their limitations. For example, mathematically proficient high school students analyze graphs of functions and solutions generated using a **graphing calculator**. They detect possible errors by strategically using estimation and other mathematical knowledge. When making mathematical models, they know that **technology** can enable them to visualize the results of varying assumptions, explore consequences, and compare predictions with data. Mathematically proficient students at various grade levels are able to identify relevant external mathematical resources, such as **digital content located on a website**, and use them to pose or solve problems. They are able to use **technological tools** to explore and deepen their understanding of concepts.

It is important to note the standard's emphasis on using technology pervasively. Keep technology in mind, not only when teaching the standards but in the assessment as it creates a learning advantage for your students.

We hope you have taken away important information on where technology can be found in the CCSS. In the next chapter, we discuss practical strategies and offer helpful resources so you can begin teaching the CCR standards with technology right away.

# Implementing Practical Ideas

Our world and education are changing rapidly. Without question, one size does not fit all in teaching. We know you work hard to personalize the learning in your classroom to reflect the individual needs, capabilities, and learning styles of your students so they have opportunities to reach their maximum potential. With this in mind, why not create tech-savvy classrooms for today's students?

In this chapter, we address practical ways to use new technology ideas within your classroom. Most of your students already come to school with a strong background in, and understanding of, technology. They are interested, motivated, and even driven by technology. Having a tech-savvy classroom for today's students is the best way to create a digital age learning environment.

## How and Where Do I Begin?

Whether you are a new teacher, a teacher in the middle of a career, or a veteran teacher with only a few years before retirement, you will begin at the same place in respect to technology. To bring technology into your classrooms and your students into the digital age, you must give up your role at the front of class and let technology be a primary source of information. This journey calls for no longer teaching in the way you've been teaching and instead becoming a facilitator of your classroom and the information presented there. Embrace all of the devices you have ignored or struggled to keep out of your classroom. Introduce yourself to new concepts that may not have existed when you were in school.

First, sign up for as many technology teaching blogs and websites as you can find. One website definitely worth a look is PowerMyLearning **(powermylearning.org).**

There are many free activities for you to explore, and you can search for lessons by standards. This website also allows you to build classes, assign and monitor student work, and customize playlists for your classroom.

Blogs are becoming an increasingly pervasive and persistent influence in people's lives. They are a great way to allow individual participation in the marketplace of ideas around the world. Teachers have picked up on the creative use of this technology and put the blog to work in the classroom. The education blog can be a powerful and effective tool for students and teachers. Edutopia has a wonderful technology blog **(tinyurl.com/p33sd7b)**. Scholastic also offers a blog for teachers PK–12 **(tinyurl.com/oaaycar),** and on a wide variety of educational topics.

Edmodo **(edmodo.com)** is a free and easy blog for students and teachers to communicate back and forth. We have given you links to all of these resources on our website **(tinyurl.com/y9dfltpr).** Teachers can post assignments, and students can respond to the teacher, as well as to each other, either in the classroom or at home. Students also have the ability to post questions to the teacher or one another, if they need help.

# What Strategies Can I Use?

Get a routine going. Engage students in independent and self- directed learning activities. This is a great way to begin integrating technology in your classroom. All centers can be tied to your curriculum targets, and a couple of them can be technology based. There are a plethora of computer-based games that you can bring to an educational center or learning station. **ScootPad (scootpad.com)** and **DreamBox Learning (dreambox.com)** are two programs that support CCR standards and can be used on computers or tablets.

Differentiated math instruction meets the needs of all learners. It consists of whole group, minilessons, guided math groups, and independent learning stations with a wide variety of activities, and ongoing assessment. Independent learning is a great way to infuse technology into your centers. One station with computers and another with games make great rotation centers and are easy to plan for, as well as a great way for students to practice math fluency and target-related games. For more information on how to set up a guided math classroom, check out the book *Guided*

*Math: A Framework for Mathematics Instruction* (2009) by Laney Sammons, or view her guided math slide presentation online **(tiny.cc/5btg2y).**

Guided reading is a key component of balanced literacy instruction. The teacher meets with a small group of students, reading and instructing them at their level. Other students are involved in small groups or independent practice that involves reading, writing, or vocabulary. **Reading A-Z (readinga-z.com)** offers many literacy-based books and games that can be used in reading centers. Students can use recording devices to record and listen to themselves reading. You can also listen to their recordings for quick assessment purposes. Reading A-Z also offers Vocabulary A-Z and Science A-Z. There are many games and activities for these content areas, and this offers you additional rotations for your literacy centers.

Programs and apps, such as **Google Docs, Puppet Pals, and Comic Life,** are just a few resources you can use to meet standards and bring writing into your literacy rotations. Your students are using technology to be creative.

Flipping the classroom is another great way to integrate technology into your classroom. This teaching model, which uses both online and face-to-face instruction, has been transforming education for the last several years. Flipping is an educational strategy that provides students with the chance to access information within a subject outside of the classroom.

Instead of students listening in class to content and then practicing that concept outside of the school day, that traditional practice is flipped. Students work with information whenever it best fits their schedule, and as many times as necessary for learning to occur. Inside the flipped classroom, teachers and students engage in discussion, practice, or experiential learning. By creating online tutorials of your instruction, using some of the tools mentioned in this book, you can spend valuable class time assisting students with homework, conferencing about learning, or simply being available for student questions.

Pick an app or program you are interested in bringing into your classroom. Play and explore. See what the possibilities are for using this technology in your classroom. You and your students can be technology pioneers. Allow your students to problem solve and seek new knowledge on their own, and then have them share with you. A great resource is **Teaching with iPad (tiny.cc/jdtg2y),** where you can learn more about how to teach with and use digital tablets in your classroom. This site from Apple gives you lots of information about what the iPad is capable of, connects you to examples of iPad lessons done by other teachers, and matching apps!

# How Do I Determine What Works Best?

Perhaps the next place to look is the ISTE Standards for Students **(iste.org/standards)**. These standards are a great framework to help you plan lessons and projects to support the CCR technology standards in literacy, math, and critical thinking skills.

P21 developed The Framework for 21st Century Learning. This framework identifies key skills known as the 4C's: Critical Thinking, Collaboration, Communication, and Creativity. Table 7.1 takes those four skills and overlays them with digital resources that you can use in ELA. For instance, if you are a second-grade teacher and want to use Collaboration in your lesson, you might try any of the seven digital resources suggested to plan your lesson: Google Docs, Popplet, GarageBand, Wixie, Edmodo, or Google Sites. These are suggestions, but there are many more apps and sites that might also fit well. You might notice that the 4C's mirror many of the ISTE Standards. This table is included to get you to think about how you can include the 4C's and technology in your daily lesson planning. All of the resources listed

| Digital resources for teaching ELA Standards. | | | | Table 7.1 |
|---|---|---|---|---|
| GRADE | CRITICAL THINKING | COLLABORATION | COMMUNICATION | CREATIVITY |
| K-5 | BrainPop Jr. | Google Docs | Skype Edmodo | Puppet Pals |
| | Dreambox Learning | Popplet | Explain Everything | Comic Life Wixie |
| | ScootPad | Garage Band | Show Me | iMovie |
| | Reading/ Science A-Z | Wixie | Sock Puppets | Keynote |
| | | Edmodo | Puppet Pals | Sock Puppets |
| | | Google Sites | Garage Band | Garage Band |
| | | | Wixie | |

TABLE 7.1. Examples of Digital Resources for ELA that Fit into the 4C's.

in Table 7.1 are included in the following chapters to provide concrete examples of how you might implement critical thinking, collaboration, communication and creativity.

Being an expert on all of the apps or programs listed in Table 7.1 is not necessary. Start with one you know, or find out which ones your students are familiar with and start there. Think about the target or lesson you want to teach. What is the goal? What technology device or app or program will support your teaching? Create an end product to show your students what you expect. Instead of step-by-step teaching of the technology, it is important to let the students explore and discover for themselves, as long as your end product and expectations have been met.

You can also teach yourself about many of the apps or programs available by searching for them online. YouTube has step-by-step how-to videos for many tech apps and programs. Have your students show what they know by creating samples for you. Save everything you, your colleagues, or your students create, and keep it all in a digital portfolio so you can share it with your new students for years to come.

Watch the difference you will make as learning in your classroom skyrockets when using an active learning environment and providing the tools your students need for digital age learning. All of this technology is transforming today's classrooms.

Social networking and mobile learning are just a few tech-related activities that students and teachers are embracing. The website for this book **(tinyurl.com/y9dfltpr)** contains further lists of resources for how to incorporate the technology you have (or want to have) and ways for your students to learn and interact with it. In the following chapters, we further explore the CCSS for K–5 that incorporate technology, suggest specific applications and strategies, and provide lessons to help students successfully achieve those standards.

# CHAPTER 8
# Practical Ideas for Kindergarten

We realize that you will want to focus on your particular grade or subject when you are planning your lessons and implementing CCSS, so we have organized the Practical Ideas chapters by grade level and subject. Each grade starts with an overview followed by ELA technology standards with accompanying apps, software, and websites that you can use to help your students succeed with that standard. We then continue with the math standard for the grade level, and review appropriate resources. Finally, we have included sample lessons for each grade level in various subject areas. Although we have organized the book so you can find your specific grade and subject easily, please do not disregard other sections of this chapter. It is often helpful to see what the standards require before and after the grade you teach. To see grades other than K–5, look for the second book in this series covering grades 6–12, as it provides information to help you differentiate for students at all levels of your class.

Students entering kindergarten come with a variety of skills, and you will need to establish a baseline of technology proficiency. In the kindergarten standards, technology appears in two areas: writing and speaking/listening. Students will need to begin working with computers, audio recording, video, and tablets to write, listen to stories, watch videos, read, and create pictures using technology. Something for you to keep in mind: Other grades will require your students to have many varied experiences with technology so they are ready for greater challenges.

# Writing Resources

## W.K.6. • WRITING

> With guidance and support from adults, explore a variety of **digital tools** to produce and publish writing, including collaboration with peers.

When you look at the kindergarten writing standard 6, you realize your students won't be expected to do this on their own. Your class is meant to explore and begin using digital tools with your direct help. The standard specifies "a variety of digital tools." That would mean any and all digital tools at your disposal, from older technology such as videos and tape recorders to newer technologies such as tablets, MP3 players, computers, and whiteboards. Your class should have a good base on which to build. Any word-processing software can be used to produce writing and to publish, such as **Microsoft Office (office.com), Pages (apple.com/mac/pages),** and **Google Docs (google.com/docs/about).**

Collaboration is another key in this standard. All of the resources in the following list can be used collaboratively. With traditional word-processing software, collaboration would be thought of as students partnering, but working independently. Online applications, such as blogs or Google Docs, allow interactive collaboration where students can work together on a piece of writing in real time, whether they are in close proximity or miles apart. You may also want to try something geared more to your younger students. **Table 8.1** shares some software options that are more user-friendly for the primary grades.

**Table 8.1: Writing Resources**

SOFTWARE

| | |
|---|---|
|  **Kid Pix**<br>kidpix.com<br><br> **Tux Paint**<br>tuxpaint.org | This software is not free, but students can use it to publish collaborative writing that uses pictures and text. There is a new version called Kid Pix 3D that features more animation. For an alternative, try **Tux Paint (tuxpaint.org)**. It is a free online download that is also for primary students and has similar features. |

**Wixie**
wixie.com

**Pixie**
tech4learning.com/pixie

This software for purchase uses multimedia, pictures, sound, video, and text to create presentations and stories stored in the cloud for mobile access. The apps are free, but there are online versions with more features available with educational pricing.

**Fakebook**
tinyurl.com/y64bog5v

**My Fakewall**
tinyurl.com/jhrslv6

These websites use the popularity of Facebook to encourage writing by creating a Fakebook page or My Fakewall posting to write about characters or historical figures. The sites are free.

**Storybird**
storybird.com

This free website uses art to inspire storytelling. Students can write, read, share, and print short books.

**Little Bird Tales**
littlebirdtales.com

This website is free. Students can draw original artwork and import pictures to create and write stories. You must pay to download as a digital movie, but you can print stories for free.

**StoryJumper**
storyjumper.com

This free site gives your students a fun set of tools for writing and illustrating stories that can be shared online. You must pay for a hardbound book.

**Tikatok**
tikatok.com

On this website, there are story starters for Grades K–6 in ELA, science, and social studies that inspire students to write their own books with artwork to share and print. Tikatok StorySpark is the app version, also available for purchase.

**Google Earth**
google.com/earth

This is a free program and can be used for many purposes at this age level. Students can map their homes, find national symbols, and find places about which they are reading, writing, or sharing.

**Table 8.1: Writing Resources**

| | | |
|---|---|---|
| | **Explain Everything**<br>explaineverything.com | This app uses text, video, pictures, and voice to help students present a variety of possible creations. The company offers educational pricing. |
| | **StoryBuddy 2**<br>tapfuze.com/<br> storybuddy2 | This app is easier to use than Explain Everything, but not as versatile. You can use it to create stories with pictures that can be recorded, printed, and read aloud. There is a cost. |
| | **Educreations**<br>educreations.com | This free app is used primarily for teachers to create presentations for their whiteboards, but students can use it to create expository or narrative writing. |

# Speaking and Listening Resources

## SL.K.2 • SPEAKING AND LISTENING

Confirm understanding of a text read aloud or information presented orally or through **other media** by asking and answering questions about key details and requesting clarification if something is not understood.

## SL.K.5 • SPEAKING AND LISTENING

Add drawings or other **visual displays** to descriptions as desired to provide additional detail.

What are some practical ideas for using technology in kindergarten speaking and listening? One idea is to have your students read to themselves and record their voices using a tape recorder, smart phone, MP3 player, tablet, or computer. Your class will need to practice asking and answering questions, not only when you read a story or they read to each other, but when they hear or see a story in another format, such as an audio recording, video recording, or visual display on a computer. Many websites and apps are free and serve as great storytelling tools (see Table 8.2). There are also some wonderful resources that you may want to buy, have your school/district acquire, or purchase with help from your PTO/PTA.

There are several options for audiobooks on CD or ebooks. Program sites such as **Follett (tiny.cc/cb2q3y), TeachingBooks** (**teachingbooks.net**), and **TumbleBooks** (**tumblebooks.com**) must be purchased but allow you to have access to multiple ebooks that include fiction and nonfiction. You can also check out ebooks at your local library or purchase them from booksellers such as Amazon or Barnes & Noble (especially if you have e-readers). There are some free ebooks out there. **Storyline Online (storylineonline.net)** is a free site, donated by the Screen Actors Guild Foundation, with videos of books read by famous people (including *Harry the Dirty Dog* read by Betty White and *Brave Irene* read by Al Gore). The websites **FreeReadFeed (freereadfeed.com)** or **Freebook Sifter (freebooksifter.com)** are additional possibilities. There are adult titles on these sites, too, so choose carefully. Of course, pay sites offer a much better selection. On **YouTube (youtube.com)**, there are many short, free videos that your students can listen to, including folktales, science, and people reading popular books that are in your classroom. Your students can listen and then ask and answer questions.

**Table 8.2: Storytelling Resources**

| | | |
|---|---|---|
|  | **Toontastic**<br>tiny.cc/lv9e3y | Students use visuals to tell stories that they can collaborate on and share with others. The app Toontastic Jr. is free with a few backgrounds. Upgrade for a price or purchase a classroom set, discounted depending on the number of students. |
|  | **Explain Everything**<br>explaineverything.com | This app uses text, video, pictures, and voice to help students present a variety of possible creations. The company offers educational pricing. |
|  | **StoryBuddy 2**<br>tapfuze.com/storybuddy2 | This app is easier to use than Explain Everything, but not as versatile. You can use it to create stories with pictures that can be recorded, printed, and read aloud. There is a cost. |
| | **Google Earth**<br>google.com/earth | This is a free program and can be used for many purposes at this age level. Students can map their homes, find national symbols, and find places about which they are reading, writing, or sharing. |

**APPS**

**Table 8.2: Storytelling Resources**

| | | |
|---|---|---|
| **APPS** |  **Puppet Pals** <br> tinyurl.com/btxmr9b | This app allows students to create a puppet production using familiar characters to tell or retell a story. It is free, but see the website for add-on pricing. |
| |  **Felt Board** <br> softwaresmoothie.com | This app is a virtual felt board that students can use for storytelling. The app is available to purchase. |
| |  **Sock Puppets** <br> tinyurl.com/luznt6n | This free app allows you to create a play with sock puppets, recording your students' voices and automatically syncing them to the puppets. Get all the extras for a price. |
| |  **iBook Author** <br> apple.com/ibooks-author | This free app is an amazing way for teachers and students to create iBooks. There are galleries, videos, interactive diagrams, 3D objects, mathematical expressions, and much more! |
| **SOFTWARE** |  **Kid Pix** <br> kidpix.com | This software must be purchased, but it can be used to publish and collaborate on students' writing using pictures and text. The new version, Kid Pix 3D, features more animation. For an alternative, try **Tux Paint (tuxpaint.org).** It is a free online download that is also for primary students and has similar features. |
| |  **Prezi** <br> prezi.com | You can sign up for a free educational account, and your students can create and share presentations online. Prezi has mind-mapping, zoom, and motion, and it can import files. Presentations can be downloaded. A Prezi viewer app is available. |
| |  **Wixie** <br> wixie.com <br><br>  **Pixie** <br> tech4learning.com/pixie | This software for purchase uses multimedia, pictures, sound video, and text to create presentations and stories stored in the cloud for mobile access. The apps are free, but there are online versions with more features available with educational pricing. |

| | | |
|---|---|---|
| | **Little Bird Tales**<br>littlebirdtales.com | This website is free. Students can draw original artwork and import pictures to create and write stories. You must pay to download as a digital movie, but you can print stories for free. |
| | **Miro**<br>realtimeboard.com | This endless whiteboard allows you to enhance your classroom lessons, create school projects, work collaboratively with team members, and so much more. There is a free education version; you'll need to use a school email address. Upgrades are also available. |
| | **Seesaw**<br>web.seesaw.me | Seesaw is a student-driven digital portfolio and presentation tool. Students can create, reflect, collaborate, and share. Family members are also able to keep up-to-date with their child's learning and easily communicate between school and home. Free. Upgrade available for a fee. Educational pricing available. There is also an app. |

# Math Resources

## MP5 • MATH

Use appropriate **tools** strategically.

There are two main sets of standards for the Common Core math standards: processes and practices. First, you have the math targets, written similarly to ELA (Counting and Cardinality; Operations and Algebraic Thinking; Number and Operation in Base Ten; Measurement and Data; and Geometry). While you work with kindergarten students on mathematical processes, such as counting and cardinality, you need to teach them how to apply the SMP (which include problem solving and precision) to those processes. One practice, the only one that includes technology, is mathematical practice 5: "Use appropriate tools strategically." Following is the explanation CCSS provides for **MP5.** As this is the standard explanation for Grades K–12, it does include references to higher grades:

Mathematically proficient students consider the available tools when solving a mathematical problem. These tools might include pencil and paper, concrete models, a ruler, a protractor, **a calculator, a spreadsheet, a computer algebra system, a statistical package, or dynamic geometry software**. Proficient students are sufficiently familiar with tools appropriate for their grade or course to make sound decisions about when each of these tools might be helpful, recognizing both the insight to be gained and their limitations. For example, mathematically proficient high school students analyze graphs of functions and solutions generated using a **graphing calculator.** They detect possible errors by strategically using estimation and other mathematical knowledge. When making mathematical models, they know that technology can enable them to visualize the results of varying assumptions, explore consequences, and compare predictions with data. Mathematically proficient students at various grade levels are able to identify relevant external mathematical resources, such as **digital content located on a website**, and use them to pose or solve problems. They are able to use **technological tools** to explore and deepen their understanding of concepts.

Because this description does not give examples for all grades, we have provided lists of appropriate apps, websites, software, and lessons that will help translate this standard for kindergarten.

Your students will need to begin using technology as a tool to help them become better at math. That is essentially what this math standard—the only one that explicitly includes technology—states. Using technology as a mathematical practice tool can be interpreted in many different ways. In any case, students should use technology as a math tool as much as possible. Fortunately, there are many math programs, websites, and apps available. The best of them have students learning in creative ways and are not merely electronic worksheets. They automatically adapt to the students' skill levels and tell you where students are in their learning and what they need to advance. **Table 8.3** lists many good math resources. Some are free and some are not. The free resources (many with ads) are often less interesting to students and not as well organized. They don't give you the feedback you need. However, you must make the decision about what is best for your circumstances and budget.

**Table 8.3: Math Resources**

 **ScootPad**
scootpad.com

This web-based math site is totally customizable for individual students. It adapts to the student and keeps the teacher in the loop with multiple reports. It is completely aligned to the CCR standards. Pricing is available on the website.

 **BrainPOP Jr.**
jr.brainpop.com

This site offers top-notch educational videos for elementary school teachers. There are great animations, and it comes with a question-and-answer section. Most videos use Adobe Flash and don't work for iPad unless you have an additional Flash player app. This is an expensive program, but it is well worth it, if you can find the funds.

 **IXL Math**
ixl.com/math

This site features adaptive individualized math through gameplay, including data and graphing problems. It gives students immediate feedback and covers many skills, despite its emphasis on drills. Levels range from prekindergarten to Grade 8. Class pricing is available on the website.

**BBC Schools: Numeracy**
tinyurl.com/y9k7xj

This free site has great online interactive math products that are free (without ads!) and organized by skill, although you won't be able to track your students' progress.

 **PBS LearningMedia**
pbslearningmedia.org

This site is a great source for classroom-ready, free digital resources. There are resources here for every subject, including math.

 **Starfall**
starfall.com

This free website has a few clever activities for early literacy and math exploration, but you can purchase a membership for a full range of activities.

**Table 8.3: Math Resources**

 **PrimaryGames**
tinyurl.com/72ojhan

offer free games that cover all math topics at each grade level. However, these sites have ads, are not able to track a student's success rate, and are not generally self-adaptive to a student's skill level.

 **Coolmath Games**
coolmathgames.com

 **SoftSchools**
softschools.com

 **Sheppard Software**
tinyurl.com/ccrxoa

 **ABC Count Us In**
abc.net.au/countusin

This is a free website by ABC Australia that has some great primary activities and resources for your students, but it is not self-adaptive.

 **Kindersite**
kindersite.org

A free site without ads, but you will need to search through the games to find those appropriate to the skill you need. Moreover, it will not track students' success rates. The games are not adaptive to skill level.

 APPS  **Explain Everything**
explaineverything.com

This app uses text, video, pictures, and voice to help students present a variety of possible creations. It is very useful for explaining math concepts and creating visual math. The company offers educational pricing.

 **Bugs and Bubbles**
tinyurl.com/hdr3bxe

Fascinating graphics engage PK–1 students as they practice prereading and STEM skills. This app also adapts to users' level of math skill.

 **Todo K–2 Math Practice**
tinyurl.com/y5rgq26f

This one arithmetic app fulfills the needs of many learners in K–2, and is free.

 **Moose Math**
tinyurl.com/lfqz9wm

A well-done free app by Duck Duck Moose on number sense, skip counting, shapes, addition, and subtraction. Five math minigames come together in a little town that kids help build. For example, kids enter Moose Juice, the smoothie shop, to practice counting, addition, and subtraction.

 **Elmo Loves 123s**
tinyurl.com/na72o4b

This app is for iPad and Android. Sesame Street sets the standard for teaching numbers with characters kids love.

 **Love to Count by Pirate Trio**
tinyurl.com/jwvvjtp

Built for PK–2 students, this app has hundreds of tasks and swashbuckling fun for new math learners.

 **Motion Math, Hungry Fish**
tinyurl.com/pnulzgc

Six games build mental math skills and promote fact fluency with a fish hungry for numbers.

 **Sumdog**
sumdog.com

This is an online adaptive set of math games. In addition, there are apps available for tablets and minis. It is free, but you can get more programs, reports, and so on if you purchase an upgrade. It is not necessary to upgrade to use the site.

 **DreamBox Learning**
dreambox.com

Individualized, adaptive game-based math program that keeps kids coming back for more. Available online or through an app. Check out the website for pricing information. Educational pricing is available if purchasing for a class or school.

**WEB APPS**

## Digital Math Games

Many studies in recent years have shown how math games can increase student learning. An annual Speak Up survey in 2016 found that "teachers' use of game-based environments and online apps has doubled in the last six years. . . . In 2010, 47 percent of teachers said they used online videos, and that jumped to 68 percent of teachers in 2015" (qtd. in Devaney, 2016).

With this research and study in mind, the week of the 100th day of school is a perfect time for your students to do some fun activities on the computer that are related to the number 100. First, watch the BrainPOP Jr. video "One Hundred" on the interactive whiteboard. Then, have students try to identify the mystery word on a hundred chart and a mystery picture by connecting the dots from 1 to 100. **Table 8.4** includes some websites that offer fun 100th day of school activities to try at the computer.

Table 8.4: Digital Math Game Resources

| | | |
|---|---|---|
| | **Splat Square** tinyurl.com/38exsd | This is a hundred grid game, which can be played electronically or on paper. The teacher "calls out" a specific number as the target and students find the number and "splat" it. |
| | **Mathwire** mathwire.com | Many standards-based math activities for the 100th day of school! |
| | **Give the Dog a Bone** tinyurl.com/y6cce8jq | An interactive game where students try to find the ten hidden bones on the hundreds chart in less than a minute. |
| | **100 Snowballs** tinyurl.com/6jyuvuk | An interactive activity that gives students the chance to play and have fun in the snow! Students click-and-drag snowballs in the snow, creating any scene they desire—as long as they use only 100 snowballs! |
| | **TVO Kids** tvokids.com/school-age | Many 100th day of school interactive math games, and perfect for differentiating! Games are separated into two categories: 2–5 years of age, and 11 and under. Many other math and reading games are also available. |

# Literacy Lessons

Cross-curriculum planning is encouraged with the CCSS by using ELA standards in history, science, and technical subjects. Getting through all of the standards you need in kindergarten is very difficult in the time given. The key to planning with the CCSS is to teach multiple standards in one lesson, when you can. We hope the following list of sample lessons for kindergarten will inspire you to become an effective technology lesson planner. The following two sample lessons address CCR ELA standards.

## Sentence Writing

This first lesson uses Puppet Pals or Sock Puppets on the iPad. The students' assignment is to write a narrative sentence. Using Puppet Pals or Sock Puppets, students choose their characters and backdrop. Next, they record their narrative while moving the puppets. Students choose from one of three writing prompts:

1. Write about your favorite family vacation. Where did you go? Who was there? Why was it your favorite?

2. Write about your favorite birthday party. How old were you? Why was it your favorite?

3. Write about your favorite holiday that you and your family celebrate. Why is it your favorite? What are your family traditions?

The students' digital puppet shows can then be presented and shared in class. This simple lesson's primary focus satisfies **W.K.6,** which explores a variety of digital tools to produce and publish writing, including collaboration. Also satisfied are **SL.K.2** by asking and answering questions in text read in other media and **SL.K.5** by including visual displays.

### ISTE STUDENT STANDARDS

Students will use these ISTE Standards in this lesson.

- **Empowered Learner 1.d.** by understanding fundamental concepts of technology operations, demonstrating the ability to choose, use, and troubleshoot current technologies.

- **Creative Communicators 6.a. and 6.d.** with their presentations, choosing the appropriate platform. and publishing and presenting customized content.

## Class Mascots

Kindergarten teachers we know each have a class mascot (the cow class, the penguin class, etc.). One teacher uses the class mascot (other objects can be used as well) to demonstrate that a preposition is anywhere the class mascot can go. The teacher used a digital camera to take pictures of the mascot on the table, in a lunch box, sitting by the computer, sitting with a friend, and so on. Choose any favorite media tool for composing a digital book about your class mascot and its adventures with prepositions. Students help create the book by dictating sentences for each picture and preposition. One particular teacher chose iBook Author to compose the book. She has the class book stored on her tablets. During center time, students work with this book and record themselves (on the tablet) echo reading the preposition pages. Other teachers loved this idea so much they copied it, but they used different media tools for composing a book. One used Puppet Pals, while another used Wixie. There are many possibilities. The primary focus for this lesson satisfies **W.K.6,** which explores a variety of digital tools to produce and publish writing, and collaboration. Also satisfied is **SL.K.2,** by choral reading the preposition sentences. Confirming understanding is checked by having students record their choral reading. Teachers can then not only listen to the individual choral readings, but check for understanding individually or across the whole class.

### ISTE STUDENT STANDARDS

Students will use these ISTE Standards in this lesson:

- **Empowered Learner 1.d.** by understanding fundamental concepts of technology operations, demonstrating the ability to choose, use, and troubleshoot current technologies.

- **Knowledge Constructor 3.a., 3.b., and 3.d.** by employing research, evaluating, and building knowledge using digital resources.

## Creative Authors

Students entering kindergarten come with a variety of skills. This activity encourages emerging readers and writers by turning them into authors, and it can be adapted for all levels in your classroom. Students also practice their retelling literacy skills while using technology! Students will be creating their own versions of popular books (we have provided some examples to get you started). In the beginning of the year, model what you are looking for, using your whiteboard. Students can create a single page for a class book, work collaboratively to create an adaptation of a classic, or design their own books. Try **Kid Pix (kidpix.com), Tux Paint (tuxpaint.org), Wixie (wixie.com), Pixie (techforlearning.com/pixie),** or any of our other resources for writing mentioned at the beginning of this chapter, or choose your own favorite!

## SUGGESTED BOOKS FOR ACTIVITY

*Brown Bear, Brown Bear, What Do You See?* or *Polar Bear, Polar Bear, What Do You Hear?* by Eric Carle. These repetitive texts are great for students to describe an environment, habitat, community, animal, or holiday.

*Mary Wore Her Red Dress and Henry Wore His Green Sneakers* by Merle Peek. Have students draw pictures of themselves and write descriptively about their dress, features, family, hobbies, and more.

*In the Tall, Tall Grass* by Denise Fleming. Students are given the story starter "In the tall, tall grass" with space provided for a noun and a verb. Or provide the story starter and let the children finish it as they see fit.

*I Love You, A Rebus Poem* by Jean Marzollo. "Every bird loves a tree, every flower loves a bee, every lock loves a key, and I love you." Students create their own "backwards poem" or a book of "backwards poems." This is also a great activity for Valentine's Day.

*Diary of a Worm* by Doreen Cronin. Have students create a diary of an animal, a famous person, a life cycle, a landmark, and so on. Discuss in class the definition of first-person narrative and have students write theirs in that same format.

*This Is the Way We Go to School* by Edith Baer. Students explain how they do an activity at school or at home. They can draw pictures to go with their explanations or use a digital camera to take pictures of the activity being performed. Students will need help learning how to upload and insert their graphic into the program they are using.

*How to Read a Story* by Kate Messner. Have students create their own "how-to" books.

*The Important Book* by Margaret Wise Brown. Students practice descriptive writing. "The important thing about grass is that it is green. It's soft and feels squishy. But the important thing ..."

*Cloudy With a Chance of Meatballs* by Judi Barrett. Have students forecast the weather with their ideas of strange items falling from the sky, such as cats and dogs, peanut butter sandwiches, or candy bars.

There are many possibilities and adaptations for this activity. Use it as a center throughout the year, and challenge students to make their stories more elaborate and difficult each time they try one. The primary focus for this activity is **W.K.6,** which explores a variety of digital tools to produce and publish writing, as well as collaboration with their classmates. Also satisfied is **SL.K.2** by having students read their stories aloud and answering questions about key details. Students should also request clarification if something in the story is not understood. Have authors work on their stories if there are parts that need clarification. They can then share the story again and ask the audience if it is clearer. Also satisfied is **SL.K.5,** as students choose from a variety of digital resources to add their drawings or other visual displays to their writing, providing additional detail when needed or asked by the audience.

### ISTE STUDENT STANDARDS

Students will use these ISTE Standards in this lesson.

- **Empowered Learner 1.d.** by understanding fundamental concepts of technology operations, demonstrating the ability to choose, use, and troubleshoot current technologies.

- **Creative Communicator 6.a. and 6.d.** by choosing the appropriate platform for their presentations and publishing and presenting customized content.

# Social Studies and Science Lessons

The following sample lessons address CCSS ELA standards and teach lessons based on national standards in social studies and science:

## Using Digital Tools

Kindergarten teachers tell us they love to use Google Earth to reinforce classroom learning whenever possible. For example, when the class is discussing American symbols (like the White House or the Statue of Liberty), they visit them via Google Earth. Images are often in 3D, which really gets the students' interest. The teachers then have students use Puppet Pals to illustrate their learning. With help from an adult, students pick a background and find the symbols they were learning. Next, they narrate a brief description of what the symbol is and where it is located. Students can then take a picture of one of their Puppet Pal pages using a tablet, as well as print a page to hang in the hall. Using a reader like **i-nigma Reader (tiny.cc/vxdf3y)** or **QR Code Generator (qr-code-generator.com),** the teacher assigns a QR code to the printed page. Students' work can be hung in the hallway. People passing by can use their smartphones with a QR reader to see the students' entire projects. This lesson also satisfies **W.K.6** by exploring a variety of digital tools to produce and publish writing, including collaboration, as well as **SL.K.2** by asking and answering questions in text read in other media, and **SL.K.5** by including visual displays.

### ISTE STUDENT STANDARDS

Students will use these ISTE Standards in this lesson:

- **Knowledge Constructor 3.a., 3.b., and 3.d.** by employing research, evaluating, and building knowledge using digital resources.

- **Global Collaborator 7.a. and 7.b.** by using digital tools to broaden their perspectives and enrich their learning by collaborating with others and working effectively in teams locally and globally.

## Weather Activities

Most kindergarten teachers discuss weather during daily calendar time. Several times a year, teachers guide students in a discussion about the seasons of the year, as well as types of clothing to wear. During the discussion, students name clothing associated with each season. The teacher lists clothing words on the interactive whiteboard as students name them. Students are then led in a discussion of how to sort the words into categories, and they are asked to explain their choices. The teacher writes the word on a chart divided into four sections labeled fall, winter, spring, and summer. Following the sorting activity, students write about their favorite season using words from the interactive whiteboard. Teachers can choose their favorite media tool (Wixie, Pixie, Kid Pix, Little Bird Tales, etc.) to have students write their story about their favorite season. Students include drawings and phonetically spelled words to add meaning to their writing. Students then record themselves reading their stories to the class. Student presentations can also be done in front of the class. This activity can be done several times a year. Students can see and compare what they wrote previously by storing presentations on desktops or in classroom ebook shelves. This activity can also be differentiated in many ways. For example, phonetically spelled words can become simple sentences, pictures can be labeled, and students can work collaboratively or individually. This simple lesson's primary focus satisfies **W.K.6**, which explores a variety of digital tools to produce and publish writing, including collaboration. Also satisfied is **SL.K.2** by reading aloud (and recording) about their favorite season, and **SL.K.5** by including visual displays to describe and add detail to their story

### ISTE STUDENT STANDARDS

Students will use these ISTE Standards in this lesson:

- **Empowered Learner 1.d.** by understanding fundamental concepts of technology operations, demonstrating the ability to choose, use, and troubleshoot current technologies.

- **Creative Communicator 6.a. and 6.d.** with their presentations choosing the appropriate platform, and publishing and presenting customized content.

- **Global Collaborator 7.a., 7.b., 7.c., and 7.d.** by using digital tools to broaden their perspectives and enrich their learning by collaborating with others and working effectively in teams locally and globally.

## Math Lessons

The following two sample lessons address the CCSS math standard **MP5:**

### Shapes

A math example when the class is discussing shapes has students use technology tools to explore and deepen understanding of concepts. With adults, students venture around the school finding examples of squares, circles, and triangles. Students draw them using Explain Everything. Next, they record what shape they saw and how they know it is a particular shape. Depending on how savvy students are with a tablet, they can take a picture of what they find, import to Explain Everything, and record information about a shape (four equal sides, etc.). A colleague reported that her kindergarten students are able to snap pictures using a tablet and upload them to Explain Everything. However, students needed time to practice this task.

This is a great way to satisfy standard **MP5**. In addition, this lesson satisfies **SL.K.2** by asking and answering math questions in text read in other media and **SL.K.5** by including visual displays.

ISTE STUDENT STANDARDS

Students will use these ISTE Standards in this lesson:

- **Empowered Learner 1.d.** by understanding fundamental concepts of technology operations, demonstrating the ability to choose, use, and troubleshoot current technologies.

- **Knowledge Constructor 3.a., 3.b., and 3.d.** by employing research, evaluating, and building knowledge using digital resources.

## Itchy, Itchy Chicken Pox

To help teach counting and cardinality, teachers start this project by reading *Itchy, Itchy Chicken Pox* by Grace Maccarone. Teachers lead students through the book, counting the chicken pox on each page. You can read the book and count for several days, each day discussing how you can represent seven chicken pox (seven red dots, four dots plus three dots, etc.). Next, take a digital picture of each student's face in your classroom. Remind them you will be making a book of them with chicken pox. Did the boy look happy in the story? Choose any favorite media tool for composing a digital book (Wixie, eBook, iBook Author, etc.) and download the individual pictures of your class. Each student's face will be one page. Under each face, type the sentence, "Look at me! I have chicken pox!" Make sure the media tool you choose allows students to write/draw on their picture. Discuss with your students the range of chicken pox on the boy's face in the book. Discuss with them the possibilities for drawing chicken pox on their faces. Each student will then have a turn to draw a number of red chicken pox dots on their face. In the blank, students write how many chicken pox they have. Below that, students can write their name. Encourage differentiation here! Any student who can write their number other than in numeral form should be encouraged to do so—for example, $4 + 3$, $3 \times 2$, VIII (yes, even Roman numerals), or in another language! To go one step further, you may wish to have students record their voices, saying how many chicken pox they have. The teacher can also show the digital book to the class and ask questions, such as, "How many chicken pox does ___ have? How do you know?" This digital book can then be stored on your desktop or ebook shelf for students to come back to all year long. This counting lesson satisfies **W.K.6,** exploring a variety of digital tools to produce and publish writing, including collaboration (individually and with the whole class); **SL.K.2** by asking and answering questions in text read in other media; and **SL.K.5** by including visual displays. This is a great way to satisfy standard **MP5.**

ISTE STUDENT STANDARDS

Students will use these ISTE Standards in this lesson:

- **Knowledge Constructor 3.a., 3.b., and 3.d.** by employing research, evaluating and building knowledge using digital resources.

- **Creative Communicator 6.a. and 6.d.** with their presentations choosing the appropriate platform, and publishing and presenting customized content.

## It's Pattern Time

Kindergarten students are just learning to recognize patterns. Tell your students that patterns are designs that repeat. First, model patterning by calling a few students to the front of the room. Demonstrate how to make a pattern by positioning students in various patterns. Start easy with: boy, girl, boy, girl. Have students tell you what comes next. Other ideas include:

- standing, standing, bending, bending

- hands up, hands down, hands down, hands up

- facing front, facing back, facing back, facing back, facing front

Once you have practiced this several times, demonstrate making patterns on your Smart Board or use **Miro (realtimeboard.com).** Model how students can use stamps or stickers to make a pattern. Work through this several times, having students explain the pattern each time.

Have students work in small groups of two or three. Have students use **Wixie (wixie.com), Pixie (tech4learning.com/pixie), Kid Pix (kidpix.com),** or **Little Bird Tales (littlebirdtales.com)** to create their own patterns to share with the class. Make sure students write the explanation for their pattern underneath their picture. Encourage students to continue this activity using different colors and different shapes or stickers. Once everyone has had ample time to practice, come together as a class and have students share their pattern creations.

To differentiate this activity, encourage students to make a pattern interactive game using Wixie, Pixie, Kid Pix, or Little Bird Tales. These games can be used by your students during center time. Each time students work on solving patterns, they should save their assignments using their names and in their digital portfolios, such as **Seesaw (seesaw.com).** You can review the student portfolios to assess this skill.

The primary focus for this activity is **MP5.** However, **W.K.6,** which explores a variety of digital tools to produce and publish their patterns, as well as collaboration with their classmates, is also satisfied. This activity satisfies **SL.K.2** by having students present and explain their patterns aloud and answer questions about key details. Students should request clarification if something in their pattern is not understood. Have students rework their patterns if there are parts that need clarification. Also satisfied is **SL.K.5,** as students add drawings (or stickers and stamps) to their pattern descriptions.

### ISTE STUDENT STANDARDS

Students will use these ISTE Standards in this lesson:

- **Computational Thinker** by creating patterns and explaining the reasoning behind them.

- **Knowledge Constructor 3.a., 3.b., and 3.d.** by employing research, evaluating, and building knowledge using digital resources.

- **Creative Communicators 6.a. and 6.d.** with their presentations choosing the appropriate platform and publishing and presenting customized content.

## Cardinal Directions

This activity was adapted from one we used when teaching elementary school. It can be used in first, second, and third grade with more enhancements. This lesson allows students to take a virtual field trip while learning about cardinal directions.

For this lesson, start by reading *Me on the Map* by Joan Sweeney. There are many places to obtain a digital copy or ebook. Try **Follet (tinyurl.com/oux56og), Teaching-Books (teachingbooks.net), TumbleBooks (tumblebooks.com), Storylineonline (storylineonline.net), FreeReadFeed (freereadfeed.com),** or **Freebook Sifter (freebooksifter.com).** You can also view the video on **YouTube (tinyurl.com/ybynjghk).** Next, review the compass rose and cardinal directions. Everyone probably knows "Never

Eat Soggy Waffles," the mnemonic device for directions. Discuss with students what it means, and have them repeat the chorus several times.

Using your Smart Board or **Miro (realtimeboard.com),** bring up **Google Earth (google.com/earth)** and enter your school's location. Students love when you zoom in from space and show them the roadside view as well as an aerial view.

Next, pick a destination; start with places in the United States. Disney World or Disneyland are good places to start. Have the students tell you which direction(s) to travel to get to your school. "Fly" down to the destination. Turn on the 3D feature and zoom in. Have students call out directions to navigate the 3D maps to find various rides. A very neat feature on Google Earth is the thirty-second video clip, once you locate an attraction.

You can repeat this with cities, states, countries, continents, or major tourist attractions around the world. Using your Smart Board or Miro, take notes of the places you visited and the directions you took to get there. **Evernote (evernote.com)** is a good note-taking app.

With support from adults, have your students use **KidPix (kidpix.com), Tux Paint (tuxpaint.org), Wixie (wixie.com),** or **Pixie (tech4learning.com/pixie)** to draw a picture of the favorite place they visited. With help, they should write a sentence using cardinal directions to describe how they got there. These can be presented and shared in class. The entire class artwork and sentences can be assembled into a digital class book or ebook for students to view all year. Their individual projects can also be shared to their digital portfolio (Seesaw is one example).

There are so many possibilities and adaptations for this activity. The primary focus for this activity is **W.K.6,** which explores a variety of digital tools to produce and publish writing. Also satisfied is **SL.K.2** by having students read their stories aloud and answering questions about key details. Students should request clarification if something in the story is not understood. Have students work on their pictures and sentences if there are parts that need clarification. They can then share the story again and ask the audience if it is clearer. Also satisfied is **SL.K.5,** as students choose from a variety of digital resources to add their drawings or other visual displays to their writing, providing additional detail when needed, or asked by the audience.

ISTE STUDENT STANDARDS

Students will use these ISTE Standards in this lesson:

- **Computational Thinker** by solving problems in ways that leverage the power of technological methods to develop and test solutions technologies.

- **Knowledge Constructor 3.a., 3.b., and 3.d.** by employing research, evaluating and building knowledge using digital resources.

- **Creative Communicator 6.a. and 6.d.** with their presentations choosing the appropriate platform and publishing and presenting customized content.

# A Final Note

As students progress through the grades, they establish their baseline of proficiency in technology. This will definitely enhance their experiences with technology in the upper grades, as well as satisfy the CCSS performance standards at the K–5 levels. We hope that you find the resources and lesson ideas presented in this chapter useful and that they are easy to adapt to your class.

You will find more resources on our website **(tinyurl.com/y9dfltpr)**, which may be helpful as you look to differentiate your instruction. Visit our online site for updated information about this book. To learn more about meeting technology standards found within the CCSS in other grades, look for our additional title in this series.

# Practical Ideas for First Grade

We realize that you will want to focus on your particular grade or subject when you are planning your lessons and implementing CCSS, so we have organized the Practical Ideas chapters by grade level and subject. Each grade starts with an overview followed by ELA technology standards with accompanying apps, software, and websites that you can use to help your students succeed with that standard. We then continue with the math standard for the grade level and review appropriate resources. Finally, we have included sample lessons for each grade level in various subject areas. Although have organized the book so you can find your specific grade and subject easily, please do not disregard other sections of this chapter. It is often helpful to see what the standards require before and after the grade you teach. To see grades other than K–5, look for the second book in this series, covering grades 6–12, as it provides information to help you differentiate for students at all levels of your class.

Students in first grade are expected to accomplish many of the same standards as kindergarteners. Three of the four standards are very similar. Therefore, your students coming into first grade should have a background in many of the standards that feature technology in your first-grade classroom. The only difference is the first standard, listed next **(RI.1.5).** The reading standard has added a technology component to first grade (electronic menus, icons) that in kindergarten had only basic text features (headings, tables of contents, glossaries).

# Reading Resources

## RI.1.5 • READING INFORMATIONAL TEXT

Know and use various text features (e.g., headings, tables of contents, glossaries, **electronic menus, icons**) to locate key facts or information in a text.

This may be your students' first foray into using specific features in informational text that might be digital. In kindergarten, your students were taught common parts of a book. Now they will be adding electronic menus and icons they might see in digital books, internet pages, and software. Students will need to learn how to navigate and interpret software and internet menus. Additionally, you will need to make sure they know the function of most major icons. Unfortunately, there are few resources currently available that specifically teach this concept. That does not mean you will have a problem teaching this standard. It is easily included in every-day lessons. When you are introducing a new piece of software or app to the class, make this a part of the lesson. When you look at a website, email, or word-processing document as a class, discuss the common menu choices and what each does.

### TEACHING DIGITAL TEXT FEATURES

Following are some practical ideas for teaching digital text features in first-grade informational text.

Every time you introduce a new app or piece of software, you should point out the similarities in the menu options, such as where Open, Print, Save, and so on, are usually found.

Many icons have become standardized in software. How do the following help students find information on a page more easily?

A printer icon for print

A magnifying glass for search and zoom

Arrows for next or forward, last, or backspace

Rounded arrows for undo and redo

Discuss why these icons were chosen, discuss their meaning, and make a game of finding them in new programs.

Tell students how to find and use the spelling help in many programs.

Discuss what *cut* and *paste* are in digital terms.

Discuss text features and formats, such as font types, boldfacing, underlining, resizing text, and why they would use different sizes and boldness for headings and subheadings. How do these help students find information on a page more easily?

You may want to differentiate for your more capable students by discussing tabs and paragraphs.

# Writing Resources

## W.1.6 • WRITING

With guidance and support from adults, use a variety of **digital tools** to produce and publish writing, including in collaboration with peers.

Your first-graders will be coming to you with some background in writing using digital resources. To continue this, and augment their learning, you should provide those experiences with as many varied digital tools as possible. This would include computers, tablets, and minis using the internet, software, and apps. Even if you have only one type of digital tool, you can still vary activities with some of the free sites listed in **Table 9.1**. Please remember that part of this standard includes collaboration, which the resources we share help to facilitate.

Table 9.1: Writing Resources

| SOFTWARE |  **Kid Pix** kidpix.com | This software is not free, but students can use it to publish collaborative writing that uses pictures and text. There is a new version called Kid Pix 3D that features more animation. For an alternative, try Tux Paint (**tuxpaint.org**). It is a free online download that is also for primary students and has similar features. |

**Wixie**
wixie.com

**Pixie**
tech4learning.com/pixie

This software for purchase uses multimedia, pictures, sound, video, and text to create presentations and stories stored in the cloud for mobile access. The apps are free, but there are online versions with more features available with educational pricing.

**Fakebook**
tinyurl.com/y64bog5v

**My Fakewall**
tinyurl.com/jhrslv6

These websites use the popularity of Facebook to encourage writing by creating a Fakebook page or My Fakewall posting to write about characters or historical figures. The sites are free.

**PebbleGo**
pebblego.com

This website from the publisher Capstone has taken their books and made them digital. They include print, pictures, video, and audio and are great for researching at the K–3 levels. Articles are leveled, and the site is interactive. The cost is steep, depending on what package you choose.

**Storybird**
storybird.com

This free website uses art to inspire storytelling. Students can write, read, share, and print short books.

**StoryJumper**
storyjumper.com

This free site gives your students a fun set of tools for writing and illustrating stories that can be shared online. (You must pay for a hardbound book.)

**Tikatok**
tikatok.com

On this website, there are story starters for Grades K–6 in ELA, science, and social studies that inspire students to write their own books with artwork to share and print. Tikatok StorySpark, is the app version, also available for purchase.

**Little Bird Tales**
littlebirdtales.com

This website is free. Students can draw original artwork and import pictures to create and write stories. You must pay to download as a digital movie, but you can print stories for free.

**Google Earth**
google.com/earth

This is a free program and can be used for many purposes at this age level. Students can map their homes, find national symbols, and find places about which they are reading, writing, or sharing.

**Explain Everything**
explaineverything.com

This app uses text, video, pictures, and voice to help students present a variety of possible creations. The company offers educational pricing.

**StoryBuddy 2**
tapfuze.com/storybuddy2

This app is easier to use than Explain Everything, but not as versatile. You can use it to create stories with pictures that can be recorded, printed, and read aloud.

**Educreations**
educreations.com

This free app is used primarily for teachers to create presentations for their whiteboards, but students can use it to create expository or narrative writing.

**Puppet Pals**
tinyurl.com/btxmr9b

This app allows students to create a puppet production using familiar characters to tell or retell a story. It is free, but see the website for add-on pricing.

# Speaking and Listening Resources

## SL.1.2 • SPEAKING AND LISTENING

Ask and answer questions about key details in a text read aloud or information presented orally or through **other media**.

## SL.1.5 • SPEAKING AND LISTENING

Add drawings or other **visual displays** to descriptions when appropriate to clarify ideas, thoughts, and feelings.

Your first-grade students have many opportunities for speaking and listening when partnered in different activities, including reading to each other, but this section focuses on using technology. The standards require your students to be able to share through media and create digital pictures or drawings to help them explain something. The simplest way to help them meet this standard is to have your students read to themselves and record their voices using a tape recorder, smart phone, MP3 player, tablet, or computer. Then have other students listen to the recordings and ask and answer questions.

There are several options for audiobooks on CD or ebooks: Program sites such as **Follett (tinyurl.com/oux56og), TeachingBooks (teachingbooks.net), and TumbleBooks (tumblebooks.com)** must be purchased but allow you to have access to multiple ebooks that include both fiction and nonfiction. You can also check out ebooks at your local library or purchase them from booksellers such as Amazon or Barnes & Noble (especially if you have e-readers). There are some free ebooks out there. **Storyline Online (storylineonline.net)** is a free site, donated by the Screen Actors Guild Foundation, with videos of books read by famous people (including *Harry the Dirty Dog* read by Betty White and *Brave Irene* read by Al Gore). The websites **Project Gutenberg (gutenberg.org), FreeReadFeed (freereadfeed.com)** or **Freebook Sifter (freebooksifter.com)** are additional possibilities. There are adult titles on these sites, too, so choose carefully. Of course, pay sites offer a much better selection.

**Table 9.2** shares resources that can be used to incorporate technology in first-grade speaking and listening.

**Table 9.2: Speaking and Listening Resources**

| | | |
|---|---|---|
|  | **YouTube**<br>youtube.com | There are many short, free videos that your students can listen to, including folktales, science, and people reading popular books that are in your classroom. Your students can listen and then ask and answer questions. |
|  | **BrainPOP Jr.**<br>jr.brainpop.com | This site offers top-notch educational videos for elementary school teachers. There are great animations, and it comes with a question-and-answer section. Most videos use Adobe Flash and don't work for iPad unless you have an additional Flash player app. This is an expensive program, but it is well worth it if you can find the funds. |

SOFTWARE

**Table 9.2: Speaking and Listening Resources**

| | | |
|---|---|---|
|  | **Wixie**<br>wixie.com | This software for purchase uses multimedia, pictures, sound, video, and text to create presentations and stories stored in the cloud for mobile access. The apps are free, but there are online versions with more features available with educational pricing. |
|  | **Pixie**<br>tech4learning.com/pixie | |
|  | **Miro**<br>realtimeboard.com | This endless whiteboard allows you to enhance your classroom lessons, create school projects, work collaboratively with team members, and so much more. There is a free education version; you'll need to use a school email address. Upgrades are also available. |
|  | **Prezi**<br>prezi.com | You can sign up for a free educational account, and your students can create and share presentations online. Prezi has mind-mapping, zoom, and motion, and it can import files. Presentations can be downloaded. A Prezi viewer app is available. |
|  | **Seesaw**<br>web.seesaw.me | Seesaw is a student-driven digital portfolio and presentation tool. Students can create, reflect, collaborate, and share. Family members are also able to keep up-to-date with their child's learning and easily communicate between school and home. Free. Upgrade available for a fee. Educational pricing available. There is also an app. |

| | | |
|---|---|---|
|  | **Toontastic**<br>tiny.cc/lv9e3y | Students use visuals to tell stories that they can collaborate on and share with others. The app Toontastic Jr. is free with a few backgrounds. Upgrade for a price or purchase a classroom set, discounted depending on the number of students. |
|  | **Explain Everything**<br>explaineverything.com | This app uses text, video, pictures, and voice to help students present a variety of possible creations. The company offers educational pricing. |

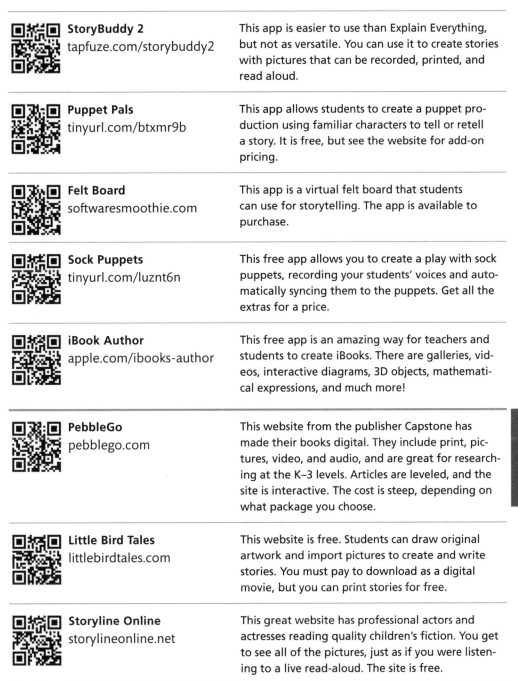

**StoryBuddy 2**
tapfuze.com/storybuddy2

This app is easier to use than Explain Everything, but not as versatile. You can use it to create stories with pictures that can be recorded, printed, and read aloud.

**Puppet Pals**
tinyurl.com/btxmr9b

This app allows students to create a puppet production using familiar characters to tell or retell a story. It is free, but see the website for add-on pricing.

**Felt Board**
softwaresmoothie.com

This app is a virtual felt board that students can use for storytelling. The app is available to purchase.

**Sock Puppets**
tinyurl.com/luznt6n

This free app allows you to create a play with sock puppets, recording your students' voices and automatically syncing them to the puppets. Get all the extras for a price.

**iBook Author**
apple.com/ibooks-author

This free app is an amazing way for teachers and students to create iBooks. There are galleries, videos, interactive diagrams, 3D objects, mathematical expressions, and much more!

**PebbleGo**
pebblego.com

This website from the publisher Capstone has made their books digital. They include print, pictures, video, and audio, and are great for researching at the K–3 levels. Articles are leveled, and the site is interactive. The cost is steep, depending on what package you choose.

**Little Bird Tales**
littlebirdtales.com

This website is free. Students can draw original artwork and import pictures to create and write stories. You must pay to download as a digital movie, but you can print stories for free.

**Storyline Online**
storylineonline.net

This great website has professional actors and actresses reading quality children's fiction. You get to see all of the pictures, just as if you were listening to a live read-aloud. The site is free.

**WEBSITES**

**Table 9.2: Speaking and Listening Resources**

|  **We Give Books**<br>wegivebooks.org | This website has hundreds of ebooks available for kids to read free. You only need to sign up. In addition, the foundation donates books to kids in need around the world for all of your time spent on this site. |
| --- | --- |

# Math Resources

There are two main sets of standards for the Common Core math standards: processes and practices. First, you have the math targets, written similarly to ELA (Counting and Cardinality; Operations and Algebraic Thinking; Number and Operation in Base Ten; Measurement and Data; and Geometry). While you work with first-grade students on mathematical processes, such as counting and cardinality, you need to teach them how to apply the SMP (which include problem solving and precision) to those processes. One practice, the only one that includes technology, is mathematical practice 5: "Use appropriate tools strategically." Following is the explanation CCSS provides for **MP5**. As this is the standard explanation for Grades K–12, it does include references to higher grades.

### MP5 • MATH

Use appropriate **tools** strategically.

Mathematically proficient students consider the available tools when solving a mathematical problem. These tools might include pencil and paper, concrete models, a ruler, a protractor, **a calculator, a spreadsheet, a computer algebra system, a statistical package, or dynamic geometry**. Proficient students are sufficiently familiar with tools appropriate for their grade or course to make sound decisions about when each of these tools might be helpful, recognizing both the insight to be gained and their limitations. For example, mathematically proficient high school students analyze graphs of functions and solutions generated using a **graphing calculator**. They detect possible errors by strategically using estimation and other mathematical knowledge. When making mathematical models, they know that **technology** can enable them to visualize the results of varying assumptions, explore consequences, and compare predictions with data. Mathematically proficient students at various grade levels are able to identify relevant external mathematical resources, such as **digital content** located on a website, and use them to pose or solve problems. They are able to use **technological tools** to explore and deepen their understanding of concepts.

Because this description does not give examples for all grades, we have provided a list of appropriate apps, websites, software, and lessons that will help translate this standard for first grade.

Your students will be using technology as a tool to help them become better at math. That is essentially what this math standard—the only one that explicitly includes technology—states. Using technology as a mathematical practice tool can be interpreted in many different ways. In any case, students should use technology as a math tool as much as possible. Many math programs, websites, and apps allow students to explore and deepen their understanding of math concepts. The

**Table 9.3: Math Resources**

| | | |
|---|---|---|
| | **XtraMath**<br>xtramath.org | A free site that lets you practice math facts. It tracks student progress, it's easy to pick what you want your students to work on, and it's easy for kids to use independently. |
| | **ScootPad**<br>**scootpad.com** | This web-based math site is totally customizable for individual students. It adapts to the student and keeps the teacher in the loop with multiple reports. It is completely aligned to the CCR standards. Pricing is available on the website. |
| | **PBS LearningMedia**<br>pbslearningmedia.org | This site is a great source for classroom-ready, free digital resources. There are resources here for every subject, including math. |
| | **Prodigy**<br>prodigygame.com | This is an adaptive math practice site wrapped in role-playing adventure from Canada. The base price is free; optional paid upgrades are available with membership. |

WEBSITES

**Table 9.3: Math Resources**

 **Starfall**
starfall.com

This free website has a few clever activities for early literacy and math exploration, but you can purchase a membership for a full range of activities.

 **PrimaryGames**
tinyurl.com/72ojhan

These sites offer free games that cover all math topics at each grade level. However, these sites have ads, are not able to track a student's success rate, and are not generally self-adaptive to the student's skill level.

 **Coolmath Games**
coolmathgames.com

 **SoftSchools**
softschools.com

 **Sheppard Software**
tinyurl.com/ccrxoa

 **IXL Math**
ixl.com/math

This site features adaptive individualized math through gameplay, including data and graphing problems. It gives students immediate feedback and covers many skills, despite its emphasis on drills. Levels range from prekindergarten to Grade 8. Class pricing is available on the website.

 **Sumdog**
sumdog.com

This is an online adaptive set of math games. In addition, there are apps available for tablets and minis. It is free, but you can get more programs, reports, and so on if you purchase an upgrade. It is not necessary to upgrade to use the site.

 **BrainPOP Jr.**
jr.brainpop.com

This site offers top-notch educational videos for elementary school teachers. There are great animations, and it comes with a question-and-answer section. Most videos use Adobe Flash and don't work with iPad unless you have an additional Flash Player app. This is an expensive program, but it is well worth it, if you can find the funds.

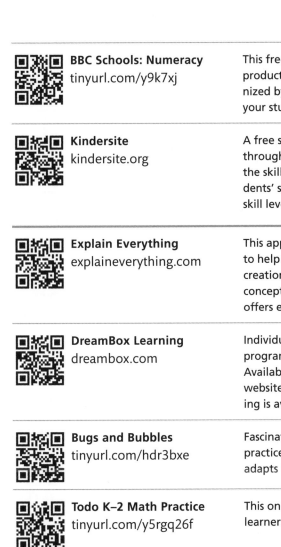

**BBC Schools: Numeracy**
tinyurl.com/y9k7xj

This free site has great online interactive math products that are free (without ads!) and organized by skill, although you won't be able to track your students' progress.

**Kindersite**
kindersite.org

A free site without ads, but you will need to search through the games to find those appropriate to the skill you need. Moreover, it will not track students' success rates. The games are not adaptive to skill level.

**Explain Everything**
explaineverything.com

This app uses text, video, pictures, and voice to help students present a variety of possible creations. It is very useful for explaining math concepts and creating visual math. The company offers educational pricing.

**DreamBox Learning**
dreambox.com

Individualized, adaptive game-based math program that keeps kids coming back for more. Available online or through an app. Check out the website for pricing information. Educational pricing is available if purchasing for a class or school.

**Bugs and Bubbles**
tinyurl.com/hdr3bxe

Fascinating graphics engage PK–1 students as they practice prereading and STEM skills. This app also adapts to users' level of math skill.

**Todo K–2 Math Practice**
tinyurl.com/y5rgq26f

This one arithmetic app fulfills the needs of many learners in K–2, and the app is free.

**Moose Math**
tinyurl.com/lfqz9wm

A well-done free app by Duck Duck Moose on number sense, skip counting, shapes, addition, and subtraction. Five math minigames come together in a little town that kids help build. For example, kids enter Moose Juice, the smoothie shop, to practice counting, addition, and subtraction.

**Jungle Time**
jungleeducation.com

Students learn to tell time in this customizable app. The clocks are easy to read, and there are eight different languages available within the app.

**Table 9.3: Math Resources**

| | | |
|---|---|---|
| | **Elmo Loves 123s**<br>tinyurl.com/na72o4b | This app is for iPad and Android. Sesame Street sets the standard for teaching numbers with characters kids love. |
| | **Mystery Math Town and Mystery Math Museum**<br>artgigapps.com | Fun, well-designed, customizable app with a clever storyline. Students solve a mystery while they solve math problems that require strategy and critical thinking. For Grades 1–6. Allow multiple users. |
| | **Love to Count by Pirate Trio**<br>tinyurl.com/jwvvjtp | Built for PK–2 students, this app has hundreds of tasks and swashbuckling fun for new math learners. |
| | **Motion Math, Hungry Fish**<br>tinyurl.com/pnulzgc | Six games build mental math skills and promote fact fluency with a fish hungry for number. |

best of them have students learning in creative ways and are not merely electronic worksheets. They automatically adapt to the students' skill levels and tell you where the students are in their learning and what they need to advance. Of course, these usually do not come free. **Table 9.3** lists many good math resources. Some are free; some are not. The free resources (many with ads) are often less interesting and not as well organized. They don't give you the feedback you need. It is up to you to decide what is best for your circumstances and budget.

# Literacy Lessons

Cross-curriculum planning is encouraged with the CCSS by using ELA standards in history, science, and technical subjects. How will you ever get through everything if you teach standard by standard? The key to planning with the CCSS is to teach multiple standards in one lesson, when you can. We hope the following list of sample lessons for first grade will inspire you to become an effective technology lesson planner.

## Narrative Writing

A first-grade teacher recently shared a lesson with us that uses Puppet Pals. The assignment was to write a narrative story. Using Puppet Pals, students created a project to share with the class. When the students shared, they took the time to ask and answer questions about their projects. This simple lesson satisfies **RI.1.5** to teach electronic menus and icons, if you take the time to teach those skills when you introduce Puppet Pals to the class. This lesson's primary focus is satisfying **W.1.6,** which uses digital tools to produce and publish writing collaboratively. Also satisfied is **SL.1.2** by having students ask and answer questions in text read in other media, as well as **SL.1.5,** by including visual displays.

After the students completed and presented their projects, the teacher took a single picture from each of the Puppet Pals projects and assigned a QR code to each project using a reader like **i-nigma Reader (tiny.cc/vxdf3y)** or **QR Code Generator (qr-code-generator.com).** A picture from student work in Puppet Pals hangs in the hall with the QR code, allowing anyone to scan QR codes and view the Puppet Pals projects through any camera-enabled smart device.

### ISTE STUDENT STANDARDS

Students will use these ISTE Standards in this lesson:

- **Empowered Learner** by understanding fundamental concepts of technology operations, demonstrating the ability to choose, use, and troubleshoot current technologies.

- **Creative Communicator** with their presentations, choosing the appropriate platform and publishing and presenting customized content.

## Recount Stories

Many teachers in first grade use The Daily 5 during their literacy block. Students choose a book they have practiced reading to themselves or a friend. Using Sock Puppets, students record their recount of the chosen book. A suggestion might be to help students organize their thoughts by providing a simple storyboard graphic organizer so students can plan their recount or retell scenes before they begin their work on Sock Puppets. The primary focus for this lesson satisfies **W.1.6,** which uses digital tools to produce and publish writing collaboratively. Also satisfied is **SL.1.2,** by asking and answering questions in text read in other media, and **SL.1.5,** by including visual displays.

ISTE STUDENT STANDARDS

Students will use these ISTE Standards in this lesson:

- **Empowered Learner** by understanding fundamental concepts of technology operations, demonstrating the ability to choose, use, and troubleshoot current technologies.

- **Creative Communicator** by choosing the appropriate platform for their presentations and publishing and presenting customized content.

## Digital Retelling

A first-grade teacher shared this lesson with us. Kids love to hear their own voices and watch themselves! Using iPads, let your students record themselves reading a book, passage, or sentence. They can replay it to hear what they sound like when they read. This will help with fluency. You can also pair them up with a partner and have them take videos of each other reading. Not only do they hear themselves reading, but they can see their body language and facial expressions while reading.

Once your students get used to the idea of being videotaped while reading, move into retelling a story. This is a great idea for first-graders to report monthly on a book they have been reading, and it is an excellent way for them to practice their retelling skills! This is very effective in reading groups. Have students pick a book they have been reading (or you can use what you are reading in your groups). Students work together in partners or small groups. They retell their books, showing the covers, titles, and important pictures. The retellings should then be saved and dated.

Next, students can retell their stories using drawings they have created. They should be encouraged to use a program such as **Kid Pix (kidpix.com),** or **Wixie (wixie.com)** to both draw and label key parts of their stories. They are then videotaped retelling their stories. This works with student creative writing, too. Encourage students to share with their classmates. Allow a question-and-answer session after each retelling, so students can ask and/or answer key questions about their story's details. Allow students to edit their retellings based on feedback from their peers.

This tool is useful when you conference with them. Encourage students to use a program such as **Seesaw (web.seesaw.me)** to digitally upload their retellings to a digital portfolio. By the end of the year, students will have a nice representation of their retelling videos. They can watch themselves and see their progress! This is also a great feature for children to share with their parents at conference time or at an end of year learning celebration. Peers, parents, and teachers can leave comments on the digital portfolio, and students can listen and make changes based on feedback.

This lesson's primary focus is satisfying **W.1.6,** which uses digital tools to produce and publish writing collaboratively. Also satisfied is **SL.1.2** by having students ask and answer questions about their text, as well as **SL.1.5** by including digital visual displays. If students include various text features (headings, table of contents, etc.) in their retellings, then **RI. 1.5** is also satisfied by this activity as students prove they are able to locate key facts or information in a text.

### ISTE STUDENT STANDARDS

Students will use these ISTE Standards in this lesson:

- **Empowered Learner** by understanding fundamental concepts of technology operations, demonstrating the ability to choose, use, and troubleshoot current technologies.

- **Creative Communicator** with their presentations choosing the appropriate platform, and publishing and presenting customized content.

# Social Studies and Science Lessons

The following example lessons address CCR ELA standards and teach lessons based on national standards in social studies and science:

## Animals

This lesson plan idea has students using PebbleGo to research animals and how they survive. Using Wixie, students draw the animal, including habitat, predators, and adaptations of body parts that help them survive, and so on. Students narrate their pictures. All pictures are put together into a class zoo ebook. Student books can be saved as a class book on the class ebook shelf. You can be creative and use this for any primary science topic. This lesson satisfies **RI.1.5** to teach electronic menus and icons, especially if you point out to students, when using PebbleGo, how they can navigate the site's menus and icons. This lesson's primary focus satisfies **W.1.6**, which uses digital tools to produce and publish writing collaboratively. Also satisfied is **SL.1.2** by asking and answering questions in text read in other media, and **SL.1.5** by including visual displays.

ISTE STUDENT STANDARDS

Students will use this ISTE Standard in this lesson:

- **Knowledge Constructor** by employing research, evaluating and building knowledge using digital resources.

## Famous Americans

To enhance a social studies lesson, a teacher shared that she uses Puppet Pals during the months of January and February. Students make a slideshow to explain and illustrate what they learned about Martin Luther King Jr., Abraham Lincoln, and George Washington. Student work can be compiled into one slideshow and displayed for parents. Once again, the primary focus for this lesson satisfies **W.1.6**, which uses digital tools to produce and publish writing collaboratively. Also satisfied is **SL.1.2** by narrating what they learned about the famous men, and **SL.1.5** by including visual displays. Students can have the characters moving around and even include speech bubbles to bring their characters to life.

ISTE STUDENT STANDARDS

Students will use these ISTE Standards in this lesson:

- **Knowledge Constructor** by employing research, evaluating and building knowledge using digital resources.

- **Creative Communicator** with their presentations choosing the appropriate platform and publishing and presenting customized content.

# Math Lessons

The following two sample lessons address CCR math standard MP5:

## Geometry Activity

To help teach geometry, a teacher uses this activity to enhance her lessons on shapes. The classroom has a "shape of the day." Students (working individually or with partners) use iPads or digital cameras to take pictures of the shape, which they look for around the classroom or school. Using a favorite media-publishing tool (Wixie, eBook, iBook Author, etc.), students download their pictures. Each shape becomes a chapter in their digital shape book. Students write a sentence or two about each picture taken. For example, "The hall floor tiles are squares. There are forty-five squares from our room to the cafeteria." To differentiate, some students may record all they have learned about squares. For example, "Squares have four sides. The sides of squares are all equal. A square is a quadrilateral." Students then share their finished shape books with the class. Books can be checked out and read by other classmates during center time. This activity satisfies **W.1.6**, to produce and publish writing, including collaboration with peers. Furthermore, **SL.1.5** is addressed, as students are adding their digital photos (visual displays) to descriptions of their shapes. This also covers the **MP.1.5** by using digital tools to enhance mathematical learning.

### ISTE STUDENT STANDARDS

Students will use these ISTE Standards in this lesson:

- **Knowledge Constructor** by employing research, evaluating and building knowledge using digital resources.

- **Creative Communicator** with their presentations choosing the appropriate platform and publishing and presenting customized content.

- **Global Collaborator** by using digital tools to enrich learning and to collaborate with peers.

## Class Addition Strategies

After teaching addition strategies, ask each student to make a page for the class ebook that explains their favorite method for adding. Using your favorite media-publishing tool (Wixie, ebook, iBook Author, etc.), pair students to write and illustrate their favorite addition strategy. There will be duplicates—and that is OK, as every illustration and explanation will be different. Encourage students to make their own drawings to go with their strategies. They may need your help to locate and download pictures from the internet. Simply search the terms to find pictures for strategies such as "Ten Frame" or "Rekenrek."

Following are some additional strategies for teaching addition:

- Doubles
- Split numbers
- Draw a picture
- Count on fingers
- Counters
- Use a number line

Each page should include a heading for the strategy. As a class, making a table of contents as well as a glossary will help students learn and apply text features to math and thus satisfy **RI.1.5**. Finished books can be shared with the class, placed on a class ebook shelf, or shared with students in their electronic math folders. Encourage students to frequently refer to this electronic book to view different strategies. Making a similar book with subtraction strategies is a great way to ensure that your students are learning addition and subtraction strategies all year. Students should also be encouraged, as they learn and/or find new strategies, to add them to the electronic addition and subtraction books.

This activity satisfies **W.1.6**, to produce and publish writing, including collaboration with peers. Furthermore, **SL.1.5** is addressed, as students are adding their digital photos (visual displays) to descriptions of their addition or subtraction strategies. This meets **MP.1.5** by using digital tools to enhance math learning. Projecting the book, as well as having a class discussion where students answer questions about the material presented in the strategy book, would satisfy **SL.1.2**.

### ISTE STUDENT STANDARDS

Students will use these ISTE Standards in this lesson:

- **Knowledge Constructor** by employing research, evaluating and building knowledge using digital resources.

- **Creative Communicator** with their presentations choosing the appropriate platform and publishing and presenting customized content.

- **Global Collaborator** by using digital tools to enrich learning and to collaborate with peers.

## Exploring Symmetry

Symmetry is taught in the lower grades. This lesson can be adapted for kindergarten or second grade. Start with your Smart Board or **Miro (realtimeboard.com)**. Write the word *symmetry* on your board. Ask students if they know what the word means. Show them pictures of objects with symmetry: a strawberry cut in half, the Eiffel Tower, a pair of scissors, and so on. See if drawing a line of symmetry through these items helps students define symmetry. Remind them, if needed, that symmetry is when you draw a line (imaginary or real) and have both halves match exactly. Go back to the objects you previewed and demonstrate the line of symmetry by drawing a line through each object.

Next, read Loreen Leedy's book, *Seeing Symmetry,* with your students. You can find online copies at **FreeClassicAudioBooks (freeclassicaudiobooks.com), Follet (tinyurl. com/oux56og),** or **TeachingBooks (teachingbooks.net). BrainPOP Jr. (jrbrainpop.com)** also has great videos and activities on symmetry.

Have students practice by using your Smart Board or Miro, and type the capital letters of the alphabet. Call students up to draw the line of symmetry (if any). Discuss why there is or is not a line of symmetry.

Give students a chance to practice recognizing symmetry. Divide students into groups of three or four. Using a digital camera, tablet, or smartphone, students take pictures of symmetrical objects. Help each team transfer their images to the computer. Have students import their images into a program such as **Wixie (wixie.com).** They should use the line tool to draw the line (or lines) of symmetry on each image.

Butterflies are common symmetrical objects. Share several images of butterflies and have students discuss their symmetry. Make sure they can identify the line of symmetry that runs directly through the body of the butterfly. Using **Wixie (wixie. com), Pixie (tech4learning.com/pixie),** or **KidPix (kidpix.com),** have your students paint a butterfly with a vertical body and one wing. To make a complete butterfly, select half the butterfly, copy, and paste on the other side. Next, use the flipping tool and move it into position. Have students write about their symmetrical butterfly, explaining why it is symmetrical, and so on.

Next, test students' ability to think symmetrically by having them use the mirroring feature of the paintbrush tool to draw another butterfly. Have students choose the paintbrush tool, check the mirror box on the editing panel, and choose 2 for line of symmetry painting. Starting in the middle of the page, have them paint one wing; the other wing will paint at the same time. If they need to start again, have them click the undo button. Encourage students to continue this activity, drawing and painting other objects with symmetry. Again, encourage students to use the typing feature to write one or two sentences describing their symmetrical pictures.

You can print and post students' artwork or compile all of the symmetry drawings into an online classroom book, using **iBook Author (apple.com/ibooks-author)** or **Project Gutenberg (gutenberg.org).** Don't forget to have students save their symmetrical creations into their digital portfolios, such as **Seesaw (seesaw.com).**

The primary focus for this activity is **MP5.** However, **W.1.6,** which explores a variety of digital tools to produce and publish their symmetrical works of art, as well as collaboration with their classmates, is also satisfied. Also satisfied is **SL.1.2** by having students present and explain their symmetry pictures aloud and answering questions about key details. Students should also request clarification if something in their pictures is not understood. Have students rework their pictures if there are parts that need clarification. Also satisfied is **SL.1.5,** as students use drawings and descriptions to explain their symmetrical pictures.

ISTE STUDENT STANDARDS

Students will use these ISTE Standards in this lesson:

- **Empowered Learner** by understanding fundamental concepts of technology operations, demonstrating the ability to choose, use, and troubleshoot current technologies.

- **Knowledge Constructor** by employing research, evaluating, and building knowledge using digital resources.

- **Creative Communicator** with their presentations, choosing the appropriate platform and publishing and presenting customized content.

# A Final Note

As students progress through the grades, they establish their baseline of proficiency in technology. This will definitely enhance their experiences with technology in the upper grades, as well as satisfy the CCSS performance standards at the K–5 levels. We hope that you find the resources and lesson ideas presented in this chapter useful and that they are easy to adapt to your class.

You will find more resources on our website **(tinyurl.com/y9dfltpr)**, which may be helpful as you look to differentiate your instruction. Visit our online site for updated information about this book. To learn more about meeting technology standards found within the CCSS in other grades, look for our additional title in this series.

Technology in the classroom has afforded me the opportunity to differentiate instruction as well as provide individual feedback to each student. In first grade, the CCSS **RL.1.2** requires students to retell stories, including key details, and demonstrate understanding of their central message. Meeting with students 1:1 can be very challenging and time consuming. However, with technology, students are able to record their retellings, and I am able to listen to each student and provide meaningful feedback. Web-based learning applications enable students to use games and videos to learn independently, and students in first grade are motivated to learn.

— **Kathy Angel, teacher**

# Practical Ideas for Second Grade

We realize that you will want to focus on your particular grade or subject when you are planning your lessons and implementing CCSS, so we have organized the Practical Ideas chapters by grade level and subject. Each grade starts with an overview followed by ELA technology standards with accompanying apps, software, and websites that you can use to help your students succeed with that standard. We then continue with the math standard for the grade level and review appropriate resources. Finally, we have included sample lessons for each grade level in various subject areas. Although we have organized the book so you can find your specific grade and subject easily, please do not disregard other sections of this chapter. It is often helpful to see what the standards require before and after the grade you teach. To see grades other than K–5, look for our additional title in this series, 6–12, as it provides information to help you differentiate for students at all levels of your class.

Your second-grade students will increasingly be asked to use technology in their learning. One second-grade standard that includes technology is exactly the same as its first-grade counterpart (**W.2.6**). Other second-grade standards have slight to significant variations (**RI.2.5, SL.2.2, SL.2.5**), and two are completely new tech standards for the students coming into second grade (**RL.2.7, L.2.4e**). Although it is not stated in the second-grade standards that you should teach typing, by third grade, students will need to be learning to type. In addition, by fourth grade, students will be expected to type one page in a single sitting. As students will be typing more this year, it is important to start teaching them proper typing skills so they do not form bad habits. You don't need to spend too much extra time on this skill. Even the basics would really help when they become third-graders. Have an introduction showing students how to use home key positioning, how to use the shift and space key, and discuss proper posture. During writing time, monitor students who are using keyboards as you walk around the room.

# Reading Resources

## RL.2.7 • READING LITERATURE

Use information gained from the illustrations and words in a print or **digital text** to demonstrate understanding of its characters, setting, or plot.

Your students will already have some background in electronic menus and icons from their first-grade experiences. Gaining information from digital texts will be a new addition to their previous standard in first grade, though they should have experience using digital tools in the previous year and a general understanding of character, plot, and setting. Luckily, there are some great apps, software, and internet sites that are perfect fits for standard **RL.2.7**. **Table 10.1** lists some practical tools for teaching and using digital text in second-grade reading.

**Table 10.1: Digital Text Resources**

APPS

| | |
|---|---|
|  **Toontastic**<br>tiny.cc/lv9e3y | Students use visuals to tell stories that they can collaborate on and share with others. The app Toontastic Jr. is free with a few backgrounds. Upgrade for a price or purchase a classroom set, discounted depending on the number of students. |
|  **Explain Everything**<br>explaineverything.com | This app uses text, video, pictures, and voice to help students present a variety of possible creations. The company offers educational pricing. |
|  **StoryBuddy 2**<br>tapfuze.com/storybuddy2 | This app is easier to use than Explain Everything, but not as versatile. You can use it to create stories with pictures that can be recorded, printed, and read aloud. |
|  **Puppet Pals**<br>tinyurl.com/btxmr9b | This app allows students to create a puppet production using familiar characters to create a setting and tell or retell a story. It is free, but see the website for add-on pricing. |

 **Felt Board**
softwaresmoothie.com

This app is a virtual felt board that students can use for storytelling. The app is available to purchase.

 **Sock Puppets**
tinyurl.com/luznt6n

This free app allows you to create a play with sock puppets, recording your students' voices and automatically syncing them to the puppets. Get all the extras for a price.

 **PebbleGo**
pebblego.com

This website from the publisher Capstone has made their books digital. They include print, pictures, video, and audio, and are great for researching at the K–3 levels. Articles are leveled, and the site is interactive. The cost is steep, depending on what package you choose.

 **Little Bird Tales**
littlebirdtales.com

This website is free. Students can draw original artwork and import pictures to create and write stories. You must pay to download as a digital movie, but you can print stories for free.

 **Storyline Online**
storylineonline.net

This great website has professional actors and actresses reading quality children's fiction. You get to see all of the pictures, just as if you were listening to a live read-aloud. The site is free.

 **Project Gutenberg**
gutenberg.org

This website has hundreds of ebooks available for kids to read free. You just need to sign up. In addition, the foundation donates books to kids in need around the world for all of your time spent on this site.

 **International Children's Digital Library**
en.childrenslibrary.org

This online resource has thousands of digital children's books free. There are many different levels and languages available.

WEBSITES

# Reading Ideas

## RI.2.5 • READING INFORMATIONAL TEXT

Know and use various text features (e.g., captions, bold print, subheadings, glossaries, indexes, **electronic menus, icons**) to locate key facts or information in a text efficiently.

There is not much available for teaching electronic menus and icons, but following are some suggestions. When you are introducing a new piece of software or app to your class, make this standard a part of the lesson. When you look at a web page, email, or word-processing document as a class, look at the common menu choices and what options are under each. This standard is primarily to find information in text, so students should also learn how to use search engines and online encyclopedias.

Every time you introduce a new app or piece of software, you should point out the similarities in the menu options, such as where open, print, save, and so on are usually located.

Many icons are standardized in software. Discuss how visual cues help people find information on a page more easily.

Discuss the following visual cues and ask students why they think these were chosen, what their meanings are, and make a game of finding them in new programs.

- The printer icon for print
- The magnifying glass for search or zoom in/out
- Arrows for next or forward, last or backward
- Rounded arrows for undo and redo, etc.
- A search box to find information on the page

Tell them how to find and use the spell check feature in different programs, and discuss what cut and paste are in digital terms. Following are some other suggestions for class discussion and exploration.

- Discuss fonts and formatting, such as bolding, underlining, and resizing. Ask why they would use different sizes and formatting for headings and subheadings, etc.

- What are the icons for formatting text? Are they the same in different applications?

- How do these visual cues help them find information on a page more easily?

- Discuss tabs, paragraphs, and how to format a page layout.

- Have students use the "Find" feature to zero in on a certain word or phrase on a digital page.

# Writing Resources

## W.2.6 • WRITING RESOURCES

With guidance and support from adults, use a variety of **digital tools** to produce and publish writing, including in collaboration with peers.

The second-graders in your class will be coming to you with two years of background in writing using digital resources. To continue this and augment their

**Table 10.2: Writing Resources**

**Kid Pix**
kidpix.com

This software is not free, but students can use it to publish collaborative writing that uses pictures and text. There is a new version called Kid Pix 3D that features more animation. For an alternative, try Tux Paint (tuxpaint.org). It is a free online download that is also for primary students and has similar features.

**Wixie**
wixie.com

**Pixie**
tech4learning.com/pixie

This software for purchase uses multimedia, pictures, sound, video, and text to create presentations and stories stored in the cloud for mobile access. The apps are free, but there are online versions with more features has available with educational pricing.

SOFTWARE

**Table 10.2: Writing Resources**

**Kidspiration**
tinyurl.com/dg2cxa

A mind-mapping software program that helps student organize their writing. It can be especially helpful for students who are learning to create paragraphs and organize big ideas into their smaller parts. Their web-based version is called Webspiration Classroom (tinyurl.com/bmop3nh). See the website for pricing; educational pricing is available.

**APPS**

**Popplet**
popplet.com

A wonderful online organizational tool for students' writing. A free app called Popplet Lite is also available. It is easy to use, and students can import pictures and text to create web maps.

**Book Creator**
redjumper.net/bookcreator

This versatile app can be used to have your students create their own ebooks with pictures, audio, drawing, text, video, and music. Easy for young students to use, but sophisticated enough for high school.

**Explain Everything**
explaineverything.com

This app uses text, video, pictures, and voice to help students create their own stories with character, setting, and plot. The company offers educational pricing.

**StoryBuddy 2**
tapfuze.com/storybuddy2

This app is easier to use than Explain Everything, but not as versatile. You can use it to create stories with pictures that can be recorded, printed, and read aloud.

**Educreations**
educreations.com

This free app is used primarily for teachers to create presentations for their whiteboards, but students can use it to create expository or narrative writing.

**Puppet Pals**
tinyurl.com/btxmr9b

This app allows students to create a puppet production using familiar characters to create a setting and tell or retell a story. It is free, but see the website for add-on pricing.

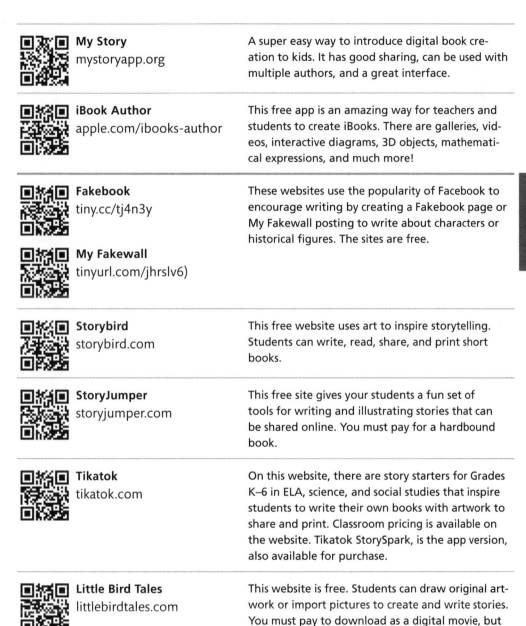

| | | |
|---|---|---|
| **My Story**<br>mystoryapp.org | A super easy way to introduce digital book creation to kids. It has good sharing, can be used with multiple authors, and a great interface. |
| **iBook Author**<br>apple.com/ibooks-author | This free app is an amazing way for teachers and students to create iBooks. There are galleries, videos, interactive diagrams, 3D objects, mathematical expressions, and much more! |
| **Fakebook**<br>tiny.cc/tj4n3y<br><br>**My Fakewall**<br>tinyurl.com/jhrslv6) | These websites use the popularity of Facebook to encourage writing by creating a Fakebook page or My Fakewall posting to write about characters or historical figures. The sites are free. |
| **Storybird**<br>storybird.com | This free website uses art to inspire storytelling. Students can write, read, share, and print short books. |
| **StoryJumper**<br>storyjumper.com | This free site gives your students a fun set of tools for writing and illustrating stories that can be shared online. You must pay for a hardbound book. |
| **Tikatok**<br>tikatok.com | On this website, there are story starters for Grades K–6 in ELA, science, and social studies that inspire students to write their own books with artwork to share and print. Classroom pricing is available on the website. Tikatok StorySpark, is the app version, also available for purchase. |
| **Little Bird Tales**<br>littlebirdtales.com | This website is free. Students can draw original artwork or import pictures to create and write stories. You must pay to download as a digital movie, but you can print stories for free. |

**Table 10.2: Writing Resources**

**Biblionasium**
biblionasium.com

This site makes reading and sharing books fun. It is a virtual bookshelf and review site for students. Teachers can set up free safe accounts for their class. Students rate and review books and keep track of their reading.

**CAST UDL Book Builder**
bookbuilder.cast.org

This free site lets you publish your ebook and see what others have published.

**Picture Book Maker**
culturestreet.org.uk

This website by culturestreet.org allows students to create six-page stories with background scenes, animals, and props and typing text. Text is limited to roughly two lines per page. Completed stories are displayed with simple page-turning effects. Stories created on Picture Book Maker can be printed. It is a UK funded site, but is currently free internationally.

**Google Earth**
google.com/earth

This is a free program and can be used for many purposes at this age level. Students can map their homes, find national symbols, and find places about which they are reading, writing, or sharing.

**BatchGeo**
batchgeo.com

This free (for basic) website works with Google Maps to locate places on a map using coordinates, addresses, and so on. You can upload a series of locations for the site to map and print or paste the map into any digital document.

**Dance Mat Typing**
bbc.co.uk/guides/z3c6tfr

This website by BBC schools teaches typing for in an easy format.

**Typing**
typing.com

This site has ads, but it does track student progress and allows reports. Free.

experiences, you should use as many varied digital tools as possible. Students should now be able to work more independently. They also will be able to collaborate in groups more effectively. **Table 10.2** includes some practical tools for using digital tools in second-grade writing.

# Speaking and Listening Resources

## SL.2.2. • SPEAKING AND LISTENING

Recount or describe key ideas or details from a text read aloud or information presented orally or through **other media**.

## SL.2.5 • SPEAKING AND LISTENING

Create audio recordings of stories or poems; add drawings or other **visual displays** to stories or recounts of experiences when appropriate to clarify ideas, thoughts, and feelings.

Your second-grade students have standards that require them to be able to share through media and create digital pictures or drawings to help them explain something. New to this grade level, along with stories, are poems with which to create audio recordings. Reading poems aloud is a great way to increase fluency with rhythmic pattern and rhyming. The simplest way to help students meet this standard is to have them read to themselves and record their voice using a tape recorder, smart phone, MP3 player, tablet, or computer. **Keynote (apple.com/mac/keynote)** is a great program to record voices and keep a yearlong documentation of reading. You can also buy digital books to use with tablets and minis that students can listen to and then recount or draw about the story or poem. There are many apps similar to Keynote in app stores.

Program sites such as **Follett (tinyurl.com/oux56og), TeachingBooks (teachingbooks. net),** and **TumbleBooks (tumblebooks.com)** must be purchased but allow you to have access to multiple ebooks that include both fiction and nonfiction. You can also check out ebooks at your local library or purchase them from booksellers such as Amazon or Barnes & Noble (especially if you have e-readers). There are some free ebooks out there. **Storyline Online (storylineonline.net)** is a free site, donated by the Screen Actors Guild Foundation, with videos of books read by famous people

**Table 10.3: Speaking and Listening Resources**

 **YouTube**
youtube.com

There are many short, free videos that your students can listen to, including folktales, science, and people reading popular books that are in your classroom. Your students can listen and then ask and answer questions.

 **BrainPOP Jr.**
brainpop.com

This site offers top-notch educational videos for elementary school teachers. There are great animations, and it comes with a question-and-answer section. Most videos use Adobe Flash and don't work for iPad unless you have an additional Flash Player app. This is an expensive program, but it is well worth it if you can find the funds.

 **Wixie**
wixie.com

 **Pixie**
tech4learning.com/pixie

This software for purchase uses multimedia, pictures, sound, video, and text to create presentations and stories stored in the cloud for mobile access. The apps are free, but there are online versions with more features available with educational pricing.

 **Toontastic**
tiny.cc/lv9e3y

Students use visuals to tell stories that they can collaborate on and share with others. The app Toontastic Jr. is free with a few backgrounds. Upgrade for a price or purchase a classroom set, discounted depending on the number of students.

 **PebbleGo**
pebblego.com

This web site from the publisher Capstone has made their books digital. They include print, pictures, video, and audio, and are great for researching at the K–3 levels. Articles are leveled, and the site is interactive. The cost is steep, depending on what package you choose.

 **PowerKnowledge**
pkearthandspace.com
pklifescience.com

This subscription website from Rosen Publishing is similar to PebbleGo, but for higher-level readers in Grades 3–5. It is useful for second-grade students who need a challenge.

**iMovie**
apple.com/ios/imovie

This app, which also comes as a program, has many uses in the classroom to create full edited videos or short one-minute trailers. The trailers can be very useful for recounting and presenting ideas to others. There is a free online site to create short videos called Animoto.

**Explain Everything**
explaineverything.com

This app uses text, video, pictures, and voice to help students present a variety of possible creations. The company offers educational pricing.

**Book Creator**
bookcreator.com

Students can use this versatile app to create their own ebooks with pictures, audio, drawing, text, video, and music. Easy for young students to use, but sophisticated enough for high school.

**StoryBuddy 2**
tapfuze.com/storybuddy2

This app is easier to use than Explain Everything, but not as versatile. You can use it to create stories with pictures that can be recorded, printed, and read aloud.

**Puppet Pals**
tinyurl.com/btxmr9b

This app allows students to create a puppet production using familiar characters to tell or retell a story. It is free, but see the website for add-on pricing.

**Little Bird Tales**
littlebirdtales.com

This website is free. Students can draw original artwork and import pictures to create and write stories. You must pay to download as digital movie, but you can print stories for free.

**Felt Board**
softwaresmoothie.com

This app is a virtual felt board that students can use for storytelling. This app is available to purchase.

**ChatterPix Kids**
tinyurl.com/ptwhtxd

This free app is for creating and sharing videos. Make anything talk! Just take a picture, draw a line to make a mouth, and record your voice. Great for reading aloud and poetry sharing. Sock Puppets (**tinyurl.com/luznt6n**). This free app allows you to create a play with sock puppets, recording your students' voices and automatically syncing them to the puppets. Get all the extras for a price.

**Table 10.3: Speaking and Listening Resources**

| | |
|---|---|
| **Story Builder**<br>tinyurl.com/poxc4rl | This app is designed to help students improve paragraph formation and integration of ideas and improve higher-level inferencing. Extensive use of audio clips promotes improved auditory processing, and it also has the ability to record narrative. |
| **Storyline Online**<br>storylineonline.net | This great website has professional actors and actresses reading quality children's fiction. You get to see all of the pictures, just as if you were listening to a live read-aloud. The site is free. |
| **Project Gutenberg**<br>gutenberg.org | This website has hundreds of ebooks available for kids to read free. You just need to sign up. In addition, the foundation donates books to kids in need around the world for all of your time spent on this site. |
| **Starfall**<br>starfall.com | This free website has a few clever activities for early literacy and math exploration, but you can purchase a membership for a full range of activities. |
| **Scene Speak**<br>tinyurl.com/qg55sej | Use it to create visual scene displays and interactive social stories. It allows images to be edited and scenes to be linked to create "books" by theme or area of interest. The app is available for a fee. |
| **Evernote**<br>evernote.com | This free app allows students to share notes as well as audio and video recordings. |
| **Poetry Idea Engine**<br>tinyurl.com/2cuowf | This Scholastic site allows students to use templates to make different forms of poetry—another great way technology gets kids writing. Better still, it is free! |
| **Seesaw**<br>web.seesaw.me | Seesaw is a student-driven digital portfolio and presentation tool. Students can create, reflect, collaborate, and share. Family members are also able to keep up-to-date with their child's learning and easily communicate between school and home. Free. Upgrade available for a fee. Educational pricing available. There is also an app. |

**Prezi**
prezi.com

You can sign up for a free educational account, and your students can create and share presentations online. Prezi has mind-mapping, zoom, and motion, and it can import files. Presentations can be downloaded. A Prezi viewer app is available.

**Miro**
realtimeboard.com

This endless whiteboard allows you to enhance your classroom lessons, create school projects, work collaboratively with team members, and so much more. There is a free education version; you'll need to use a school email address. Upgrades are also available.

(including *Harry the Dirty Dog* read by Betty White and *Brave Irene* read by Al Gore). The websites **Project Gutenberg (gutenberg.org), FreeReadFeed (freereadfeed.com)** or **Freebook Sifter (freebooksifter.com)** are additional possibilities. There are adult titles on these sites, too, so choose carefully. Of course, pay sites offer a much better selection. **Table 10.3** shares technology tools for second-grade speaking and listening activities.

# Language Resources

## L.2.4e • LANGUAGE

Use glossaries and beginning dictionaries, both print and **digital**, to determine or clarify the meaning of words and phrases.

Second grade is the first time this standard appears. There is no L.1.4e. So, using any dictionary will be a new standard for your students. There are fewer child-friendly digital dictionaries and glossaries out there than you might think; you will

Table 10.4: Language Resources

**Wordsmyth**
wordsmyth.net

This comes with three levels of a children's dictionary. When looking up a word, you'll find links to both a thesaurus and rhyming dictionary for that word. The site is free with ads.

**Table 10.4: Language Resources**

| | | |
|---|---|---|
|  | **Scholastic Storia**<br>tinyurl.com/j7awgkd | This is an ebook reading app that comes with five fiction/nonfiction titles free. There is a built-in glossary to help with difficult words. Storia offers both school-wide and classroom subscriptions to eBook libraries, with unlimited and simultaneous access from most devices with an internet connection. |
|  | **TumbleBooks**<br>tumblebooks.com | This pay site has many wonderful digital stories with accessible glossaries. Prices depend on the number of students. |

need to introduce these and assist your students with them. Digital glossaries can be found online through online content. You can also introduce students by using the spelling checkers within programs. Many sites, programs, and operating systems have features that allow the user to check the meaning of a word by right-clicking or command-clicking on it. Table 10.4 shares a few other practical resources that can help second-grade students gain understanding.

# Math Resources

## MP5 • MATH

Use appropriate **tools** strategically.

There are two main sets of standards for Common Core math standards: processes and practices. First, you have the math targets, written similarly to ELA (Counting and Cardinality; Operations and Algebraic Thinking; Number and Operation in Base Ten; Measurement and Data; and Geometry). While you work with second-grade students on mathematical processes, such as operations and algebraic thinking in second grade, you need to teach them how to apply the SMP (which include problem solving and precision) to those processes. One practice, the only one that includes technology, is mathematical practice 5: "Use appropriate tools strategically." Following is the explanation CCSS provides for **MP5**. As this is the standard explanation for Grades K–12, it does include references to higher grades.

Mathematically proficient students consider the available tools when solving a mathematical problem. These tools might include pencil and paper, concrete models, a ruler, a protractor, **a calculator, a spreadsheet, a computer algebra system, a statistical package, or dynamic geometry software**. Proficient students are sufficiently familiar with tools appropriate for their grade or course to make sound decisions about when each of these tools might be helpful, recognizing both the insight to be gained and their limitations. For example, mathematically proficient high school students analyze graphs of functions and solutions generated using a **graphing calculator**. They detect possible errors by strategically using estimation and other mathematical knowledge. When making mathematical models, they know that **technology** can enable them to visualize the results of varying assumptions, explore consequences, and compare predictions with data. Mathematically proficient students at various grade levels are able to identify relevant external mathematical resources, such as **digital content** located on a website, and use them to pose or solve problems. They are able to use **technological tools** to explore and deepen their understanding of concepts.

Because this description does not give examples for all grades, we have provided a list of appropriate apps, websites, software, and lessons that will help translate this standard for second grade.

Your students will be using technology as a tool to help them become better at math. That is essentially what this math standard—the only one that explicitly includes technology—states. Using technology as a mathematical practice tool can be interpreted in many different ways. Because technology grabs students' attention, supports long-term learning, and makes math fun, students should be encouraged

**Table 10.5: Math Resources**

| | | |
|---|---|---|
|  | **PBS LearningMedia**<br>pbslearningmedia.org | This site is a great source for classroom-ready, free digital resources. There are resources here for every subject, including math. |
|  | **XtraMath**<br>xtramath.org | A free site that lets you practice math facts. It tracks student progress, it's easy to pick what you want your students to work on, and it's easy for kids to use independently. |

WEBSITES

**Table 10.5: Math Resources**

 **ScootPad**
scootpad.com

This web-based math site is totally customizable for individual students. It adapts to the student and keeps the teacher in the loop with multiple reports. It is completely aligned to the CCR standards. Pricing is available on the website.

 **Prodigy**
prodigygame.com

This is an adaptive math practice site wrapped in role-playing adventure from Canada. The base price is free; optional paid upgrades are available with membership.

 **IXL Math**
ixl.com/math

This site features adaptive individualized math through gameplay, including data and graphing problems. It gives students immediate feedback and covers many skills, despite its emphasis on drills. Levels range from prekindergarten to Grade 8. Class pricing is available on the website.

 **BrainPOP Jr.**
jr.brainpop.com

This site offers top-notch educational videos for elementary school teachers. There are great animations, and it comes with a question-and-answer section. Most videos use Adobe Flash and don't work with iPad unless you have an additional Flash player app. This is an expensive program, but it is well worth it, if you can find the funds.

 **BBC Schools: Numeracy**
tinyurl.com/y9k7xj

This site has great online interactive math products that are free (without ads!) and organized by skill, although you won't be able to track your students' progress.

 **Starfall**
starfall.com

This free website has a few clever activities for early literacy and math exploration, but you can purchase a membership for a full range of activities.

**Math Blaster HyperBlast**
mathblaster.com

The classic game many teachers used when they were students, now updated. Pricing available on the website.

**PrimaryGames**
tinyurl.com/72ojhan

These sites offer free games that cover all math topics at each grade level. However, these sites have ads, are not able to track a student's success rate, and are not generally self-adaptive to the student's skill level.

 **Coolmath Games**
coolmathgames.com

 **SoftSchools**
softschools.com

 **Sheppard Software**
tinyurl.com/ccrxoa

 **Kindersite**
kindersite.org

A free site without ads, but you will need to search through the games to find those appropriate to the skill you need. Moreover, it will not track your students' success rates. The games are not adaptive to skill level.

 **Freckle**
freckle.com

This web-based math site has aligned its content with Common Core and is great for differentiation. It covers all the math topics from kindergarten through ninth grade. The basic plan is free to use. There are upgraded plans for schools and districts for a price.

 **A Maths Dictionary for Kids**
tinyurl.com/38vkvrs

A free animated, interactive, online math dictionary for students that explains over 630 common mathematical terms and math words in simple language with definitions, examples, activities, practice, and calculators.

 **Explain Everything**
explaineverything.com

This app uses text, video, pictures, and voice to help students present a variety of possible creations. It is very useful for explaining math concepts and creating visual math. The company offers educational pricing.

APPS

125

**Table 10.5: Math Resources**

| | | |
|---|---|---|
| | **DreamBox Learning**<br>dreambox.com | Individualized, adaptive game-based math resource that keeps kids coming back for more. Available online or through an app. Check out the website for pricing information. Educational pricing is available if purchasing for a class or school. |
| | **Todo K–2 Math Practice**<br>tinyurl.com/y5rgq26f | This one arithmetic app fulfills the needs of many learners from K–2, and the app is free. |
| | **Todo Telling Time**<br>tiny.cc/kg4g3y | Well-done time-telling app that covers time from minutes to months. |
| | **Sumdog**<br>sumdog.com | This is an online adaptive set of math games. In addition, there are apps available for tablets and minis. It is free, but you can get more programs, reports, and so on if you purchase an upgrade. It is not necessary to upgrade to use the site. |
| | **Moose Math**<br>tinyurl.com/lfqz9wm | A well-done free app by Duck Duck Moose on number sense, skip counting, shapes, addition, and subtraction. Five math mini-games come together in a little town that kids help build. For example, kids enter Moose Juice, the smoothie shop, to practice counting, addition, and subtraction. Free app. |
| | **Love to Count by Pirate Trio**<br>tinyurl.com/jwvvjtp | Built for PK–2 students, this app has hundreds of tasks and swashbuckling fun for new math learners. |
| | **Pet Bingo**<br>tiny.cc/gv5g3y | This app is adaptable to each individual's level and will have students practicing math facts, measurement, and geometry while enjoying it with their very own pets. There is progress monitoring. See the website for pricing. |
| | **Motion Math, Hungry Fish**<br>tinyurl.com/pnulzgc | Six games build mental math skills and promote fact fluency with a fish hungry for numbers. |

**Jungle Time**
jungleeducation.com

Students learn to tell time in this customizable app. The clocks are easy to read, and there are eight different languages available within the app.

**Jungle Coins**
tinyurl.com/y8gtzymt

Students use realistic coins to learn how to count money. There are eight different languages, and U.S. dollars, Euros, and Canadian coins are available within the app.

**Geoboard**
tinyurl.com/kzyxjv7

This free app is a digital recreation of a geoboard. It is simple to use, and the geometry activities are open-ended and endless.

**Swipea Tangram Puzzles for Kids**
tinyurl.com/nsnoazj

This is a digital version of tangrams where students can manipulate, flip, and rotate shapes to create different pictures. App is free. Full upgrade is available for a fee.

**BrainPOP Jr.**
jrbrainpop.com

This is a great resource to use for many areas of your curriculum, including videos and activities on both surveys and graphs. There are wonderful animations, and it comes with a question-and-answer section. This is an expensive program, but it is well worth it if you can find the funds.

**Wixie**
wixie.com

**Pixie**
tech4learning.com/pixie

This software for purchase uses multimedia, pictures, sound, video, text, or surveys to create presentations and stories stored on the cloud for mobile access. The apps are free, but there are online versions with more features available with educational pricing.

to use math tools as much as possible. There are many math programs, websites, and apps out there. The best have students learning in creative ways and are not just electronic worksheets. They automatically adapt to students' skill levels, and tell you where students are in their learning and what they need to advance. We list many good math resources in **Table 10.5**. Some are free; some are not. The free resources (many with ads) are often less interesting and not as well organized. They don't give you the feedback you need. However, you must make the decision about what is best for your circumstances and budget.

## Digital Math Games

Many studies in recent years have shown how math games can increase student learning. An annual Speak Up survey in 2016 found that "teachers' use of

**Table 10.6: Digital Math Games**

| GAMES | | |
|---|---|---|
| | **Splat Square**<br>tinyurl.com/38exsd | This is a hundred grid game, which can be played electronically or on paper. Teacher "calls out" a specific number as the target and students find the number and "splat" it. |
| | **Mathwire**<br>mathwire.com | Many standards-based math activities for the 100th day of school! |
| | **Give the Dog a Bone**<br>tinyurl.com/y6cce8jq | An interactive game where students try to find the ten hidden bones on the hundreds chart in less than a minute. |
| | **100 Snowballs**<br>tinyurl.com/6jyuvuk | An interactive activity that gives students the chance to play and have fun in the snow! Students click-and-drag snowballs in the snow, creating any scene they desire—as long as they use only 100 snowballs! |
| | **TVO Kids**<br>tvokids.com/school-age | Many 100th day of school interactive math games, and perfect for differentiating! Games are separated into two categories: 2–5 years of age; and 11 and under. Many other math and reading games are also available. |

game-based environments and online apps has doubled in the last six years. . . . In 2010, 47 percent of teachers said they used online videos, and that jumped to 68 percent of teachers in 2015" (qtd. in Devaney, 2016).

With this research in mind, the week of the 100th day of school is a perfect time for your students to do some fun activities on the computer that are related to the number 100. First, watch the BrainPOP Jr. video "One Hundred" at the interactive whiteboard. Then, have students try to identify the mystery word on a hundred chart and a mystery picture by connecting the dots from 1 to 100. **Table 10.6** shares some fun games to try at your computer.

# Literacy Lessons

Cross-curriculum planning is encouraged with the CCSS by using ELA standards in history, science, and technical subjects. However, we encourage you to go further and include the arts, math, and physical education in your planning. The key to planning with CCSS is to teach multiple standards in one lesson, when you can. We hope the following sample lessons for second grade will inspire you to become an effective technology lesson planner.

## Flat Stanley

Second-grade teachers love to use the book *Flat Stanley* by Jeff Brown to teach a variety of literacy and technology standards. After reading the book, students are encouraged to bring or send Flat Stanley to different places in the world as an adventure. After each Flat Stanley is returned to the class, students use Google Earth to locate and place mark at least five places these Flat Stanleys have traveled. Students choose a few states within the United States and a couple of countries on other continents. Have your students try this activity, and then determine the distance Flat Stanley traveled. See if students can calculate how long it would take to get to Flat Stanley's destinations from your school. Students can also explore those locations when finished.

Using the BatchGeo map, students can see all the locations your classroom's Flat Stanleys traveled to this year. This engaging lesson satisfies **RI.2.5**, as students will get to know and use various text features and to locate key facts or information in a text efficiently, specifically with the Google Earth app or program. Students can also recount or retell *Flat Stanley,* including where their Flat Stanley has traveled. This can be illustrated and narrated in a Wixie slideshow.

This activity satisfies **RL.2.7**. Wixie slideshows can be saved to a class ebook shelf and made available to other students. This would satisfy **SL.2.2** and **SL.2.5**.

### ISTE STUDENT STANDARDS

Students will use these ISTE Standards in this lesson:

- **Knowledge Constructor** by employing research, evaluating, and building knowledge using digital resources.

- **Computational Thinker**  students develop and use strategies for understanding and solving problems in ways that use technology to develop and test solutions.

## Retell/Recount Stories

Yet another activity second-grade teachers have shared with us involves students using Puppet Pals to recount or retell a story from a book. Students take pictures of scenes from the book using tablets. Next, they use the puppets provided in Puppet Pals or add their own pictures (by both taking and uploading their pictures with tablets). They can also use a character from the book by taking and uploading pictures with tablets and cropping them to fit, or they can take a picture of a friend using a tablet. Next, students record their recount/retell version. Teachers typically provide a simple graphic organizer for students to use, which helps students outline their thoughts before they record. All recounts/retells are saved, and the class can check out their classmates' recounts and retells.

This simple lesson satisfies **RI.2.5**, to teach electronic menus and icons, if you take the time to teach those skills when you introduce Puppet Pals to the class. This lesson's primary focus is satisfying **W.2.6**, which uses digital tools to produce and publish writing collaboratively. Also satisfied is **SL.2.2** by asking and answering questions in text read in other media and **SL.2.5** by including visual displays. Then, using a reader such as **i-nigma Reader (tiny.cc/vxdf3y)** or **QR Code Generator (qr-code-generator.com),** teachers can take a single picture from each of the Puppet Pals projects and assign a QR code to each project. A picture from student work in Puppet Pals hangs in the hall with a QR code, allowing anyone to scan QR codes and view the Puppet Pals projects through any camera-enabled smart device.

ISTE STUDENT STANDARDS

Students will use these ISTE Standards in this lesson.

- **Empowered Learner** by understanding fundamental concepts of technology operations, demonstrating the ability to choose, use, and troubleshoot current technologies.

- **Creative Communicator** with their presentations choosing the appropriate platform and publishing and presenting customized content.

## Book Recommendations

A second-grade teacher we know used this idea throughout the year. Students use Toontastic, Wixie, Explain Everything, Puppet Pals, or your favorite storytelling app or website to once a month retell and present to the class a book they would like to recommend. You could have a template available for students to use with suggestions for pages. In the beginning of the year, encourage them to have a name/title/author page, followed by a plot summary page. As the year goes on, encourage students to add pages, labeling each page (characters, setting, plot, resolution, etc.).

Each page should have text, retelling the story, and key points. Students should include illustrations to go with their retellings. As they become more proficient, encourage them to explore and use various text features from their book in their retellings (bold, captions, glossary, etc.). Later in the year, introduce hooks and endings that leave the listener wanting more! For example: *Checkout and read this book to discover other adventures the character experiences.* Or: *There are many other really interesting books by this author; which is your favorite?*

Using your whiteboard, encourage students to share with their classmates. They can video themselves ahead of time and then share with the class. Students should have a copy of the book when they present. Allow a question-and-answer section after each retelling, so students can ask and/or answer key questions about details from their stories. Allow students to edit their retellings based on feedback from their peers.

This is also a great tool to use with students when you conference individually. Encourage students to use a program such as **Seesaw (web.seesaw.me)** to digitally upload their retellings to a digital portfolio. By the end of the year, students will have a nice representation of their retelling videos. They can watch themselves and see their progress! This is also a useful feature for children to share with their parents at conference time or at the end-of-the-year learning celebration. Peers, parents, and teachers can leave comments on the digital portfolio, and students can listen and make changes.

This lesson's primary focus is satisfying **RL.2.7**, by using information gained to demonstrate understanding of a book's characters, setting, or plot. **RI.2.5** is also satisfied, if you encourage students to know and use various text features and then use them in their own retellings. Writing Resources **W.2.6** is also satisfied, as students will use a variety of digital tools to produce and publish their writing. When students present their retellings to the class, **SL.2.2** is satisfied, as well as **SL.2.5** when students clarify their thoughts and ideas when asked questions by their peers. If students are encouraged to include a glossary (as their last slide), or if they include and explain difficult vocabulary, then **L.2.4e** is also satisfied.

### ISTE STUDENT STANDARDS

Students will use these ISTE Standards in this lesson:

- **Empowered Learner** by understanding fundamental concepts of technology operations, demonstrating the ability to choose, use, and troubleshoot current technologies.

- **Creative Communicator** with their presentations choosing the appropriate platform and publishing and presenting customized content.

# Social Studies and Science Lessons

Sample lessons below address CCR ELA standards and teach lessons based on national standards in social studies and science.

## Earth Movie Trailer

For an integrated science activity, students can research an Earth event using PebbleGo. You will need to give your students a storyboard graphic organizer first, so they can organize their ideas. Using the iMovie Trailer app, students make a movie trailer for their Earth event using pictures they find on the internet or in a book. Make sure students include titles, subtitles, and keywords to describe their

Earth event. Students also select music to fit the event and import it into the iMovie Trailer. This highly motivating activity satisfies many standards, including **RL.2.7**, **RI.2.5**, **W.2.6**, and **SL.2.5**.

ISTE STUDENT STANDARDS

Students will use these ISTE Standards in this lesson:

- **Knowledge Constructor** by employing research, evaluating and building knowledge using digital resources.

- **Creative Communicator** with their presentations choosing the appropriate platform and publishing and presenting customized content.

## Economy Lesson

Another option is to teach a social studies lesson on the economy with technology. BrainPOP has several videos on the economy that explore needs, wants, goods, and services. Discuss the definitions and examples of each. Having students take notes in a flipbook or making an anchor chart for the classroom is beneficial. Using the BrainPOP vocabulary guide, or other online dictionaries, students can clarify the meanings of the vocabulary words: *needs, wants, goods,* and *services.* Having students look up words is a nice way to satisfy **L.2.4e** and help students determine or clarify meanings of words. Two of our former colleagues had different and unique ways to assess this lesson. The teachers had students use Explain Everything to write, draw examples, and record what they learned about goods, services, needs, and wants. **SL.2.2** is satisfied with this project by describing key ideas or details and presenting them through other media. **SL.2.5** is also satisfied by adding visual displays to clarify ideas, thoughts, and feelings.

ISTE STUDENT STANDARDS

Students will use these ISTE Standards in this lesson:

- **Knowledge Constructor** by employing research, evaluating and building knowledge using digital resources.

- **Creative Communicator** with their presentations choosing the appropriate platform and publishing and presenting customized content.

## Economy Definitions

Teachers we met from another district had students use QR codes to display what they had learned. Students divided their papers into fourths and had the definition (one in each quadrant) of *needs, wants, goods,* and *services.* Underneath each definition, students had 3–5 QR codes showing examples. Students can take digital pictures or draw pictures, scan, and upload to their tablets before converting to QR codes. This lesson's focus satisfies **W.2.6**, which uses digital tools to produce writing. Also satisfied is **SL.2.2**, by asking and answering questions in text read in other media, and **SL.2.5**, by including visual displays. This is a great project to hang in the hallway for conferences. Parents can scan the QR code through an app on their smartphones or digital devices.

### ISTE STUDENT STANDARDS

Students will use these ISTE Standards in this lesson:

- **Knowledge Constructor** by employing research, evaluating and building knowledge using digital resources.

- **Creative Communicator** with their presentations choosing the appropriate platform and publishing and presenting customized content.

# Math Lessons

The following two sample lessons satisfy the **MP5** math standard as well as ELA standards.

## Math Arrays

Another activity that a teacher suggested to us is for second-grade math. Using Wixie, students take a tablet around school, snapping pictures of any arrays they find. This can easily be done in a twenty-minute guided math station rotation. Once back in the classroom, students import their pictures into Wixie and make an arrays slide show.  They write the repeated number sentences under each array. All of the students' slides can be saved into a class collection of arrays. This can be a Wixie book so students can read one another's math collections. This activity satisfies **W.2.6,** to produce and publish writing, including collaboration with peers. Furthermore, if students write story problems to go along with their array number sentences, **SL.2.2** and **SL.2.5** will be addressed. This would also cover **MP.2.5** by using digital tools to enhance mathematical learning.

### ISTE STUDENT STANDARDS

Students will use these ISTE Standards in this lesson:

- **Computational Thinker** students develop and use strategies for understanding and solving problems in ways that use technology to develop and test solutions.

- **Creative Communicator** with their presentations choosing the appropriate platform and publishing and presenting customized content.

- **Global Communicator** by using digital tools to broaden their perspectives and collaborate with others.

## Money Activities

Second-grade teachers we know love this math activity for teaching students about money, specifically making change. This activity can span several days and it can be differentiated easily. Beforehand, identify several sites that sell children's toys. Divide your students into pairs or groups of three. Assign each team a toy site and $500 to "spend" as they "shop." Students keep track of what they buy and how much it costs, as well as subtracting it from their $500 so they know how much change is left. The team closest to $0 is the winner. However, the fun doesn't stop there! Teams must prove how they spent their money. Using your favorite presentation tool (Wixie, Pixie, Kid Pix, etc.) students design presentations showing how they spent their money. The presentations should include text features they have learned about, such as title pages and headings. This will satisfy **RI.2.5**, knowing and using various text features learned. Students can draw by hand or copy-and-paste pictures of their purchases from their site. You may need additional adults to help supervise this activity. Presentations are shown to the class by each team. Don't be surprised if you have some students "challenge" results!

Having students collaborate with others, as well as accept guidance and support from adults, satisfies **W.2.6**. Writing and presenting the account of how students spent their money addresses **SL.2.2** and **SL.2.5**, describing key ideas or details and presenting orally using other media. This also covers the **MP.2.5** by using digital tools to enhance mathematical learning.

ISTE STUDENT STANDARDS

Students will use these ISTE Standards in this lesson:

- **Empowered Learner** by evaluating and synthesizing information found online to meet their learning goals.

- **Innovative Designer** by designing and using presentations to illustrate their ideas and show their learning.

- **Creative Communicator** with their presentations choosing the appropriate platform and publishing and presenting customized content.

- **Global Communicator** by using digital tools to enrich their learning and collaborate with peers.

## Graph It

Graphing is taught throughout the grades. This lesson can be adapted for kindergarten and first grade. Enhance the lesson to teach in third, fourth and fifth grades. In this lesson, students work in small groups to choose a question and survey their classmates to collect data. Then, the teams create bar graphs of the data, analyze the results, and share their findings with the class. A bar graph is a simple way to present data to someone so it is easy to understand. Teaching students how to create and read a bar graph gets them thinking about information and builds a foundation of understanding for more complex data in the future.

With your Smart Board or **Miro (realtimeboard.com),** write the words *survey* and *graph*. Ask students if they know what either word means. According to **A Maths Dictionary for Kids (tinyurl.com/38vkvrs)**, a survey is "in statistics, a method of collecting a sample of data by asking people questions." Discuss this with your students to make sure they understand the meaning. Have they seen samples of surveys? Where?

Next, discuss the meaning of a graph, specifically a bar graph. According to **A Maths Dictionary for Kids (tinyurl.com/38vkvrs)**, a bar graph is "a graph using bars to show quantities or numbers so they can easily be compared." Discuss this definition with your students and ask them if they have ever seen a bar graph. Where? Using the dictionary with your students satisfies **L.2.4e** and encourages them to use it in the future to clarify words or phrases.

Depending on the time for your lesson, you may wish to include other graphs as well. Kindergarten and first grade may wish to include pictographs. Third, fourth, and fifth grades may wish to include line graphs.

Read Stuart J. Murphy's book, *Tally O'Malley*. You can find online copies at **FreeClassicAudioBooks (freeclassicaudiobooks.com), Follet (tinyurl.com/oux56og),** or **TeachingBooks (teachingbooks.net). BrainPOP Jr. (jr.brainpop.com)** also has great videos and activities on both surveys and graphs.

Show your students examples of graphs that can be found in their world. Newspapers often have daily graphs. BrainPOP Jr. will also have many samples. Or you can find samples at **Education.com (tinyurl.com/ybs2k6rd).** While you are looking at bar graphs, see if your students can interpret it and answer questions like:

- What is this graph about?

- Which is the most popular option?

- Which is the least popular option?

- Who would care about this information?

The last question may take some time for students to understand, as the answer is not in the graph. Help them to infer what this graph is about and who it might interest.

At this point in the lesson you may wish to review how to make tally marks on a survey. Using your Smart Board (or Miro), make a two- or three-option survey, such as: Which of these three books do you like? You can insert pictures of the books and titles. Have the students take turns coming to the board and placing their tally marks. Remind students that every fifth tally should be a cross tally. Review the survey results and discuss how to interpret the data that was gathered. Repeat this activity several times if you feel your students need more practice with tally marks and interpreting surveys. BrainPOP Jr., also has lesson and activities on surveys.

With the information from the survey you created, show students how to create a bar graph. **Wixie (wixie.com)** has several graphing templates you can use. Once the bar graph is finished, discuss the information generated by answering the questions (listed above).

Next, students will be working in small groups to create their own surveys and collect data, which they will display in bar graphs.

Students should collect data about something they want to know. For example: What is your favorite flavor of ice cream? What is your favorite animal? Talk with students about providing at least three or four choices. They also may want to have an "other" choice for those that like something not listed on the survey.

Ask students to help create a list of possible survey ideas. Put these on your Smart Board for all to see. Next, put students in small groups. Have them decide which topic they would like. As a topic is chosen, cross it off your board. When all topics have been chosen, students work in their small groups to create a survey. This can easily be done on **Explain Everything (explaineverything.com), Wixie (wixie.com), or Pixie (tech4learning.com/pixie).** You may want students to create surveys on their tablets so they get the practice. However, only one survey should be used to collect the data. When surveys are complete, have teams collect the data from each member of the class.

Each student should then create a bar graph to display the data collected. This makes it easier for you to assess individual understanding, as well as where to focus your reteaching.

Once the graphs are complete, have students present their bar graphs (using your Smart Board) and share it with the entire class. Encourage the students in the "audience" to ask questions about the data. Student presenters should also be encouraged to answer these questions about their graphs. You may wish to have the students select the top three or four graphs and then invite another class or your principal to see what your students have been working on.

You may wish to do this activity several times throughout the year, each time adding a few more details to the graphs (axis, more choices, etc.). Graphs can also be saved in students' digital portfolios, using programs such as **Seesaw (seesaw.com).**

The primary focus for this activity is **MP5.** However, **RI.2.5** is also satisfied when students practice reading graphs presented to them or work through survey and graphing activities on BrainPOP Jr. **W.2.6**, which explores a variety of digital tools to produce and publish their survey and graphing works as well as collaboration with their classmates, is also satisfied. Also satisfied is **SL.2.2** by having students present and explain their data and graphs aloud and answering questions about key details. Students should also request clarification if something in their graph is not understood. Have students rework their graphs if there are parts that need clarification. Also satisfied is **SL.2.5**, as students use their bar graphs to explain the data gathered. As we discussed earlier, **L.2.4e** is also satisfied when you use an online dictionary to look up the meanings of *survey* and *bar graph*.

### ISTE STUDENT STANDARDS

Students will use these ISTE Standards in this lesson:

- **Computational Thinker** by developing and using problem-solving strategies using technology tools.

- **Global Communicator** by using digital tools to enrich their learning and collaborate with peers.

# A Final Note

As students progress through the grades, they establish their baseline of proficiency in technology. This will definitely enhance their experiences with technology in the upper grades, as well as satisfy the CCSS performance standards at the K–5 levels. We hope that you find the resources and lesson ideas presented in this chapter useful and that they are easy to adapt to your class.

You will find more resources on our website **(tinyurl.com/y9dfltpr),** which may be helpful as you look to differentiate your instruction. Visit our online site for updated information about this book. To learn more about meeting technology standards found within the CCSS in other grades, look for our additional title in this series.

# 11 Practical Ideas for Third Grade

We realize that you will want to focus on your particular grade or subject when you are planning your lessons and implementing CCSS, so we have organized the Practical Ideas chapters by grade level and subject. Each grade starts with an overview followed by ELA technology standards with accompanying apps, software, and websites that you can use to help your students succeed with that standard. We then continue with the math standard for the grade level and review appropriate resources. Finally, we have included sample lessons for each grade level in various subject areas. Although we have organized the book so you can find your specific grade and subject easily, please do not disregard other sections of this chapter. It is often helpful to see what the standards require before and after the grade you teach. To see grades other than 3–5, look for our additional title in this series covering grades 6–12, as it provides information to help you differentiate for students at all levels of your class.

The standards expect third-graders to use technology to enhance their literacy skills. The literacy standards place an emphasis on information gathering and publishing of student writing. Students should also use technology to practice math skills. This includes the use of digital math tools in the form of software programs, apps, or websites. In this chapter, we list the third-grade standards that include technology. We also offer ideas and suggestions for which technologies to use and how to teach with them.

# Research Ideas

## RI.3.5 • READING INFORMATIONAL TEXT

Use text features and search tools (e.g., **keywords, sidebars, hyperlinks**) to locate information relevant to a given topic efficiently.

## W.3.8 • WRITING

Recall information from experiences or gather information from print and **digital sources**; take brief notes on sources and sort evidence into provided categories.

We have combined **RI.3.5** with **W.3.8** because search tools will be used when gathering information from digital sources. In third grade, students need to use search tools to find relevant information on the internet. They will need to be taught the features of webpages and how to navigate them. Understanding the layout of webpages, such as the functions of sidebars and hyperlinks, is also necessary. The best way to do this is to show various webpages (using websites from your literacy or science standards is a great way to integrate your curriculum with this technology standard), then model and explain the features and their functions by using an interactive whiteboard. Don't have an interactive whiteboard? Check out a free site called **Miro (realtimeboard.com).** All you need is a computer and a projector to run this virtual online whiteboard.

Teaching students which keywords to use and how to analyze search results will definitely help them find better sources and think more critically about any information they find on the internet. Following are some tips to help when teaching students to conduct a search.

- Choose your search terms carefully. Be precise about what you are looking for, but use phrases and not full sentences.

- Adding more words can narrow a search. Use Boolean searches to narrow your topic with quotation marks. There's a big difference between the search term "gopher" and "habitats of gophers in North America."

- Use synonyms! If students can't find what they're looking for, have them try keywords that mean the same thing or are related.

- Type "site:". Typing the word *site:* (with the colon) after your keyword and before a URL will tell Google to search within a specific website

- Add a minus sign. Adding a minus sign immediately before any word, with no space in between, indicates that you don't want that word to appear in your search results. For example, "Saturn-cars" will give you information about the planet, not the automobile.

## Kid-Friendly Search Engines

Browsing safe content is the most important reason for using search engines made specifically for kids. Allowing your students to have the run of the web using a search engine for young students helps you because it is difficult to monitor many students at once if your class is using unfiltered search engines. There is no guarantee that every search will be kid-safe. Many districts have filters on their networks, but if yours does not, we suggest you explore the following.

 **Cybersleuth Kids (cybersleuth-kids.com):** A comprehensive educational search engine, directory, and homework helper for K–12 students. Includes subject-specific videos, activities, printables, games, and more for all subjects. This site is free.

 **Safe Search Kids (safesearchkids.com):** This is a custom search engine using Google's Safe Search features with additional filtering to block more potentially harmful material than the typical Google search. It is fun, colorful, and easy for kids to use.

 **KidzSearch (kidzsearch.com):** This is another safe search engine powered by Google for Grades K–8. However, please be aware there are ads on this site.

 **Kiddle (kiddle.co):** This children's search site with images, news, video and a kid's encyclopedia. It does a decent job of filtering out most objectionable material, but what is good for 12-year-old may not be for a 5-year-old!

 **Ask Kids (ask.com):** This is a free, filtered search engine for Grades K–6.

Pay programs such as **PebbleGo (pebblego.com)** are great online sources for PK–3 students to find easy-to-read informational text that includes citation support, videos, and audio recordings, as well as games and activities on many science topics that are typically used at this level. **PowerKnowledge Earth & Space Science (pkearthandspace.com)** and **PowerKnowledge Life Science (pklifescience.com)** are programs that can be used with your third-grade science topics to find easy-reading science resources.

## Note-Taking Tools

Tried-and-true methods for note-taking and categorizing information found in books can still be used to gather and record information on websites. Teaching students to use data sheets, note cards, and Know, What, Learn (KWL) techniques still works; however, technology can make this easier. The **Kentucky Virtual Library (kyvl.org)** is an excellent resource for some of these techniques.

Mind-mapping tools will help your students organize their research when gathering information. Several wonderful software programs have been used for mind-mapping for many years. However, there are also free sites out there. **Table 11.1** shares some digital tools you can use to teach note-taking and categorizing.

**Table 11.1: Note-Taking Resources**

| | |
|---|---|
|  **Kidspiration** tinyurl.com/dg2cxa | A mind-mapping software program that helps students organize their writing. It can be especially helpful for students who are learning to create paragraphs and organize big ideas into smaller parts. See the website for pricing. The web-based version is called Webspiration Classroom (**tinyurl.com/bmop3nh**) and is available for purchase. |
|  **Bubbl.us** bubbl.us | This is a free (with limited use) mind-mapping website for Grades K–12. It can be shared by multiple students at a time and comes with an app. See the website for more options and to purchase a package. |

TOOLS

| | | |
|---|---|---|
| | **MindMeister**<br>tiny.cc/826i3y | This is a free, basic mind-mapping website for Grades 2–12. Upgrades are available and have a free trial period. See the website for details. |
| | **FreeMind**<br>tinyurl.com/5qrd5 | This is a free mind-mapping tool written in Java for Grades 2–12. Options for a basic or maximum install are available. |
| | **Evernote**<br>evernote.com | This free app allows you to import a worksheet, document, or picture, including a snapshot of a web-page, and then annotate it using tools common to interactive whiteboard software. You can highlight words, cut and paste, and add sticky notes. It also allows you to use voice recognition. You can then send your annotated sheet to someone else. |

Of course, students can also use word-processing tools, such as **Microsoft Office (office.com), Apple Pages (apple.com/mac/pages),** or **Google Docs (google.com/docs/about).** Some teachers make digital templates to help students find specific information and organize their notes.

Third-graders will also need to provide a list of sources. You could make a template for sources and have students fill it in using a word-processing program. However, there are websites students can use, such as **Easybib (easybib.com**), a free website and app for ages 5–12. You can use this site to generate citations in MLA, APA, and Chicago formats easily. Just copy and paste the URL or scan the book's barcode. Students can also cite a list of sources on their own by including URL, publisher or author, topic/title, and date a website was published. If the date published is not available, they should note the date retrieved from the internet.

# Writing Resources

## W.3.6 • WRITING

With guidance and support from adults, **use technology** to produce and publish writing (using **keyboarding skills**) as well as to interact and collaborate with others.

## Presentation Apps

**Microsoft PowerPoint (office.com)** is often the presentation tool of choice—even with young students—when using technology to produce and publish writing in a collaborative way. While this is still a great program, other presentation tools have emerged. Apple offers **Keynote (apple.com/keynote)** as part of its software package. Its features are similar to PowerPoint. **Google Slides (google.com/slides/about)** is geared toward business presentations, but it is free and web-based. It is easy to share a project that multiple users can work on at once, which makes this an especially useful program for interacting and collaborating remotely. You can add audio recordings to your slides, as well as visual displays such as pictures and short video clips. These can be used to enhance the development of the main ideas or themes of your presentations. **Table 11.2** includes some apps that can be used when beginning to produce writing.

**Table 11.2: Writing Resources**

| | | |
|---|---|---|
| | **Toontastic**<br>tiny.cc/lv9e3y | Students use visuals to tell stories that they can collaborate on and share with others. The app Toontastic Jr. is free with a few backgrounds. Upgrade for a price or purchase a classroom set, discounted depending on the number of students. |
| | **iMovie**<br>apple.com/ios/imovie | This app, which also comes as a program, has many uses in the classroom to create full, edited videos or short one-minute trailers. The trailers can be very useful for recounting and presenting ideas to others. See the website for pricing. |
| | **Animoto**<br>animoto.com | This website allows you to turn your photos and music into stunning video slideshows. Educational use is free for unlimited videos of twenty minutes. |

APPS

**Table 11.2: Writing Resources**

| | | |
|---|---|---|
| | **Explain Everything**<br>explaineverything.com | This app uses text, video, pictures, and voice to help students present a variety of possible creations. The company offers educational pricing. |
| | **StoryBuddy 2**<br>tapfuze.com/storybuddy2 | This app is easier to use than Explain Everything, but not as versatile. You can use it to create stories with pictures that can be recorded, printed, and read aloud. |
| | **Puppet Pals**<br>tinyurl.com/btxmr9b | This app allows students to create a puppet production using familiar characters to tell or retell a story. It is free, but see the website for add-on pricing. |
| | **Sock Puppets**<br>tinyurl.com/luznt6n | This free app allows you to create a play with sock puppets, recording your student's voices and automatically syncing them to the puppets. Get all the extras for a price. |
| | **Scene Speak**<br>tinyurl.com/qg55sej | Use it to create visual scene displays and interactive social stories. It allows images to be edited and scenes to be linked to create "books" by theme or area of interest. The app is available for a fee. |

## Publication Apps and Websites

Digital presentations are not limited to sharing with small or whole groups in the classroom. Blogging websites such as **Edmodo (edmodo.com)** and **Google Classroom (tiny.cc/9bbj3y)** are a way to share student writing in a safe, protected environment. Both Edmodo and Google Classroom allow teachers to set themselves up as administrators and add students to different groups. All student writing is secure in these groups. You can give assignments that ask all students to provide short answers, or you can give longer written assignments to individual students. They can then work on their writing and submit privately to you, or post on a website to share.

There are good software programs and sites that let you create books in both print and ebook formats. There are also sites that ask students to submit their work for possible publication. The resources in **Table 11.3** are only a few of our favorites.

Table 11.3: Writing and Publishing Resources

| | | |
|---|---|---|
| | **PBS Kids Writer's Contest** wtvp.org/writers-contest | This free site asks for student writing and serves as a nice incentive to get students to do their best. |
| | **Lulu** lulu.com | These sites allow you to create real books and publish them online. Parents can purchase the books as keepsakes. The site is free to use, but publishing requires a fee. |
| | **Lulu Junior** lulujr.com | |
| | **TikaTok** tikatok.com | This is another site that allows students to write, create, and publish stories as ebooks or hardcover books. Classroom pricing is available on the website. TikaTok Story Spark is the app version, also available for purchase. |
| | **Poetry Idea Engine** tinyurl.com/2cuowf | This Scholastic site allows students to use templates to make different forms of poetry—another great way technology gets kids writing. Better still, it is free! |
| | **LiveBinders** livebinders.com | Opens up new possibilities for collaboration, organization, and sharing. All your lessons and content are in one place, including documents, links, presentations, student portfolios, and more. Educational pricing available. |

## Keyboarding Sites

Exactly when you should teach keyboarding is a decades-old debate. Some teachers want students to begin formalized keyboarding as young as kindergarten. Others don't believe students' hands are developmentally ready until third grade. By fourth grade, students are expected to type a page in one sitting. Therefore, whether you think children's hands are ready or not, formalized keyboarding must begin in the primary grades. There are many keyboarding programs you can buy. **Table 11.4** features some tried and true programs that we have used.

Paying for a good typing program is worth the expense. A quality program tracks student progress and levels of accomplishment. If you can't buy a program, **Table 11.4** also shares some free sites that offer instruction and games.

**Table 11.4: Keyboarding Resources**

**PAID**

 **Mavis Beacon Keyboarding Kidz**
tinyurl.com/254v9on

Set words-per-minute goals; see what keys you need to practice and what keys you know well. Play games to practice what you've learned and to improve your speed and accuracy to become a typing pro. Check the website for pricing.

 **Type to Learn**
ttl4.sunburst.com

This typing program for Grades K–12 emphasizes both accuracy and words-per-minute speed, and it provides each student with individualized remediation and goals for success. Consult the website for various pricing options and to request a quote.

 **Typing Training**
typingtraining.com

This web-based program with apps (for Grades 3–12) allows access from any computer or handheld device. Animated coaches are available with a customizable curriculum. Students can play games or choose from more than 2,500 unique exercises while tracking progress with detailed reports and graphs. Consult the website for various options and to request a quote.

**FREE**

 **Dance Mat Typing**
bbc.co.uk/guides/z3c6tfr

This free website by BBC schools teaches typing in an easy format.

**Typing**
typing.com

This site has ads, but it does track student progress and allow reports. Free.

 **TypeRacer**
play.typeracer.com

Free website where you can race opponents by typing words in paragraph form. For experienced typists to bone up on accuracy and typing speed. There are ads.

Some districts send students to computer labs to practice keyboarding at given times, others fit it in where they can in the classroom, and still others have students practice and learn at home. We have found that the best way is to combine all three approaches. Students benefit from formal keyboarding instruction, but they need to practice both in the classroom and at home. When students are working at the computers in your classroom, they need repeated reminders to keep up good techniques such as sitting up straight, keeping hands in home row, holding wrists slightly curved, and moving the fingers instead of the hands.

# Speaking and Listening

## SL.3.2. • SPEAKING AND LISTENING

Determine the main ideas and supporting details of a text read aloud or information presented in **diverse media and formats**, including visually, quantitatively, and orally.

## SL.3.5 • SPEAKING AND LISTENING

Create engaging audio recordings of stories or poems that demonstrate fluid reading at an understandable pace; add **visual displays** when appropriate to emphasize or enhance certain facts or details.

The teacher, students, or even some programs can read text aloud. Sites such as **Follett** (**tiny.cc/cb2q3y**) and must be purchased but allow access to multiple ebooks that include both fiction and nonfiction. You can also check out ebooks at your local library or purchase them from booksellers such as Amazon or Barnes & Noble (especially if you have e-readers). There are some free ebooks out there.

**Storyline Online (storylineonline.net)** is a free site, donated by the Screen Actors Guild Foundation, with videos of books read by famous people (including *Harry the Dirty Dog* read by Betty White and *Brave Irene* read by Al Gore). The websites **Project Gutenberg (gutenberg.org), FreeReadFeed (freereadfeed.com)** or **Freebook Sifter (freebooksifter.com)** are additional possibilities. There are adult titles on these sites, too, so choose carefully. Of course, pay sites offer a much better selection.

## Apps to Support Main Idea

Using ebooks or a website with your interactive whiteboard (or free whiteboard sites) allows interaction when modeling or for student engagement. Informational text works especially well with standard **SL.3.2**, but fictional pieces can also be used. Working with the teacher or on their own, students need to understand the main idea of text and to state supporting details. Using ebooks with your interactive whiteboard tools (highlighting main ideas and supporting details or cutting and pasting) will allow you to work with the class as a whole or a small group to help them understand the main idea. Students can then work alone or with partners on a tablet or laptop to do what you have modeled.

Software programs can also be used to help extend thinking and learning with mind-mapping programs. **Table 11.5** shares some tool you can try.

**Table 11.5: Mind-Mapping Tools**

| Tool | Description |
|------|-------------|
| **Kidspiration** tinyurl.com/dg2cxa | A mind-mapping software program that helps students organize their writing. It can be especially helpful for students who are learning to create paragraphs and organize big ideas into their smaller parts. Their web-based version is called Webspiration Classroom (**tinyurl.com/bmop3nh**) and is available for purchase. |
| **Popplet** popplet.com | A wonderful online organizational tool for students' writing. A free app called Popplet Lite is also available. It is easy to use, and students can import pictures and text to create web maps. |
| **Bubbl.us** bubbl.us | This is a free (with limited use) mind-mapping website for Grades K–12. It can be shared by multiple students at a time and comes with an app. See the website for more options and to purchase a package. |
| **MindMeister** tiny.cc/826i3y | This is a free, basic mind-mapping website for Grades 2–12. Upgrades are available and have a free trial period. See the website for details. |
| **FreeMind** tinyurl.com/5qrd5 | This is a free mind-mapping tool using Java for Grades 2–12. Options for a basic or maximum install are available. |

**Puppet Pals**
tinyurl.com/btxmr9b

This app allows students to create a puppet production using familiar characters to tell or retell a story. It is free, but see the website for add-on pricing.

 **iFunFace**
ifunface.com

Students can create a read-aloud to show how the main idea and details flow by using a photo and audio recording to create an animation. It helps students visualize how to support details that branch off from the main ideas and how they flow together. The app is free but can be upgraded for a price.

## Sites to Support Fluency

Creating audio recordings and ebooks is a powerful and engaging way to demonstrate and perform fluid and accurate readings and satisfy **SL3.5**. Students can create their own audio recordings of stories or poems. You can use these recordings to check for fluency throughout the year.

Scanning finished book pages into **Microsoft PowerPoint (office.com), Keynote (apple.com/mac/keynote),** or **Google Slides (google.com/slides/about).** programs allow you to make ebooks for your classroom. Keynote allows you to speak directly into the program, and then stores ebooks for all students. Options include controlling the speed of page advancement, recording narration, adding action buttons, adjusting mouse-over and mouse-click actions, incorporating preset animation, and setting page transition effects.

Table 11.6: Fluency Resources

 **Evernote**
evernote.com

This free app allows you to import a worksheet, document, or picture, including a snapshot of a webpage, and then annotate it using tools common to interactive whiteboard software. You can highlight words, cut and paste, and add sticky notes. It also allows you to use voice recognition. You can then send your annotated sheet to someone else.

 **CAST UDL Book Builder**
bookbuilder.cast.org

This free site lets you publish your ebook and see what others have published.

WEBSITES

**Table 11.5: Mind-Mapping Tools**

| | | |
|---|---|---|
|  | **Prezi**<br>prezi.com | You can sign up for a free educational account, and your students can create and share presentations online. Prezi has mind-mapping, zoom, and motion, and it can import files. Presentations can be downloaded. A Prezi viewer app is available. |
|  | **WebQuest**<br>webquest.org | Webquests are good tools to use for presentations. The WebQuest site allows students to follow an already-created, project-based lesson where information is found solely on the internet. Students can create their own WebQuest if a website-building program or a website such as SiteBuilder (**sitebuilder.com**) is available. WebQuest.org is the original and most popular site, but if you search the internet, you will find more sites that you can use. |

# Resources

## L.3.4d • LANGUAGE

Use glossaries or beginning dictionaries, both print and **digital**, to determine or clarify the precise meaning of key words and phrases

**Merriam-Webster (merriam-webster.com**) is still the most commonly used digital dictionary and thesaurus. They offer a free and kid-friendly version of this dictionary called **Kids.Wordsmyth (kids.wordsmyth.net/we). Wordsmyth (wordsmyth.net)** is another good third-grade option. **Little Explorers (tinyurl.com/2swjc)** from Enchanted Learning is a limited picture dictionary that requires a subscription. This is a good tool to use with students who struggle with vocabulary. While digital dictionaries and thesauruses are not updated as often as encyclopedias, they are convenient. Bookmark these sites or add them to your website for easy access. The more students use them, the more comfortable they will become. Offer lessons and activities to learn and practice the necessary skills with an online dictionary, just as you would when using hard-copy dictionaries, glossaries, and thesauruses.

One lesson idea is to have students locate difficult vocabulary words in a piece of informational text and then use an electronic dictionary to define them. You could give students a website to read (preferably on a standards topic from literacy or science) and ask them to write down all of the words they don't know. After using an electronic dictionary to find the definitions to these words, have students reread the text. With luck, they will come away with a better understanding of the content they read.

The **Trading Cards (tinyurl.com/8lqftek)** app or website is a great way to document vocabulary words by adding definitions, a picture, and recordings of pronunciations. You can also use Trading Cards by doing an activity with an online thesaurus. Simply give students a word on a trading card and ask them to make as many trading cards as they can of synonyms and antonyms of that word. They can print these out and trade them with others or make them into a digital book.

# Math Resources

There are two main sets of standards for the Common Core math standards: processes and practices. First, you have the math targets, written similarly to ELA (Counting and Cardinality; Operations and Algebraic Thinking; Number and Operation in Base Ten; Numbers and Operations; Fractions in Base Ten; Measurement and Data; and Geometry). While you work with third-grade students on mathematical processes, such as operations and algebraic thinking, you need to teach them how to apply the SMP (which include problem solving and precision) to those processes. One practice, the only one that includes technology, is mathematical practice 5: "Use appropriate tools strategically."

## MP5 • MATH

Use appropriate **tools** strategically.

Following is the explanation CCSS provides for **MP5**. As this is the standard explanation for Grades K–12, it does include references to higher grades.

> Mathematically proficient students consider the available tools when solving a mathematical problem. These tools might include pencil and paper, concrete models, a ruler, a protractor, **a calculator, a spreadsheet, a computer algebra system, a statistical package, or dynamic geometry software**. Proficient students are sufficiently familiar with tools appropriate for their grade or course to make sound decisions about when each of

these tools might be helpful, recognizing both the insight to be gained and their limitations. For example, mathematically proficient high school students analyze graphs of functions and solutions generated using a **graphing calculator**. They detect possible errors by strategically using estimation and other mathematical knowledge. When making mathematical models, they know that technology can enable them to visualize the results of varying assumptions, explore consequences, and compare predictions with data. Mathematically proficient students at various grade levels are able to identify relevant external mathematical resources, such as **digital content located on a website**, and use them to pose or solve problems. They are able to use **technological tools** to explore and deepen their understanding of concepts.

Because this description does not give examples for all grades, we have provided a list of appropriate apps, websites, software, and lessons that will help translate this standard for third grade.

Your students will be using technology as a tool to help them become better at math. That is essentially what this math standard—the only one that explicitly includes technology—states. Many math programs, websites, and apps allow students to explore and deepen their understanding of math concepts. The best of them have students learning in creative ways and are not merely electronic worksheets. They automatically adapt to the students' skill levels and tell you where the students are in their learning and what they need to advance. Of course, these usually do not come free. We list many good math resources here. Some are free; some are not. The free resources (many with ads) are often less interesting and not as well organized. They don't give you the feedback you need. It is up to you to decide what is best for your circumstances and budget.

There are many sites that allow you to use mathematical tools, such as a graphing calculator (see **Table 11.8**). Another option is to use software that comes with your whiteboard, which typically has all sorts of built-in math tools, such as protractors, rulers, and grids. **Table 11.7** contains some resources we recommend for teaching to the third-grade math standards.

**Table 11.7: Math Resources**

 **ScootPad**
scootpad.com

This web-based math site is totally customizable for individual students. It adapts to the student and keeps the teacher in the loop with multiple reports. It is completely aligned to the CCSS. Pricing is available on the website.

 **DreamBox Learning**
dreambox.com

Individualized, adaptive game-based math resource that keeps kids coming back for more. Available online or through an app. Check out the website for pricing information. Educational pricing is available if purchasing for a class or school.

 **Explain Everything**
explaineverything.com

This app uses text, video, pictures, and voice to help students present a variety of possible creations. The company offers educational pricing.

 **IXL Math**
ixl.com/math

This site features adaptive individualized math through gameplay, including data and graphing problems. It gives students immediate feedback and covers many skills, despite its emphasis on drills. Levels range from prekindergarten to Grade 8. Educational pricing is available.

 **PrimaryGames**
tinyurl.com/72ojhan

These sites offer free math games covering all math topics at each grade level. However, these sites have ads, are not able to track a student's success rate, and are not generally self-adaptive to the student's skill level.

 **Coolmath Games**
coolmathgames.com

 **SoftSchools**
softschools.com

**Sheppard Software**
tinyurl.com/ccrxoa

 **Starfall**
starfall.com

This free website has a few clever activities for early literacy and math exploration, but you can purchase a membership for a full range of activities.

**Table 11.8: Math Resources**

| | | |
|---|---|---|
|  | **XtraMath**<br>xtramath.org | A free site that lets you practice math facts. It tracks student progress, it's easy to pick what you want your students to work on, and it's easy for kids to use it independently. |
|  | **Math Blaster HyperBlast**<br>mathblaster.com | The classic game many teachers used when they were students, now updated. Pricing available on the website. |
|  | **Pet Bingo**<br>tiny.cc/gv5g3y | This app is adaptable to each individual's level and will have students practicing math facts, measurement, and geometry while enjoying it with their very own pets. There is progress monitoring. See the website for pricing. |
|  | **Geoboard**<br>tinyurl.com/kzyxjv7 | This free app is the digital recreation of a geoboard. It is simple to use, and the geometry activities are open ended and endless. |
|  | **Pattern Shapes**<br>tinyurl.com/nbl5osu | This free website is all about exploring geometry. Students can drag shapes to learn area, symmetry, fractions, and much more. Write equations and line of symmetry right on the screen. There is also a free app. |
|  | **Swipea Tangram Puzzles for Kids**<br>tinyurl.com/nsnoazj | This is a digital version of tangrams where students can manipulate, flip, and rotate shapes to create different pictures. App is free. Full upgrade is available for a fee. |
|  | **Math Playground, Thinking Blocks**<br>tinyurl.com/3c6eoa | This free website has manipulatives with blocks so you can model, solve word problems, and practice with fractions. Thinking Blocks is also available as a free app. |
| | **A Maths Dictionary for Kids**<br>tiny.cc/hfhl3y | A free animated, interactive, online math dictionary for students that explains over 630 common mathematical terms and math words in simple language with definitions, examples, activities, practice, and calculators. |

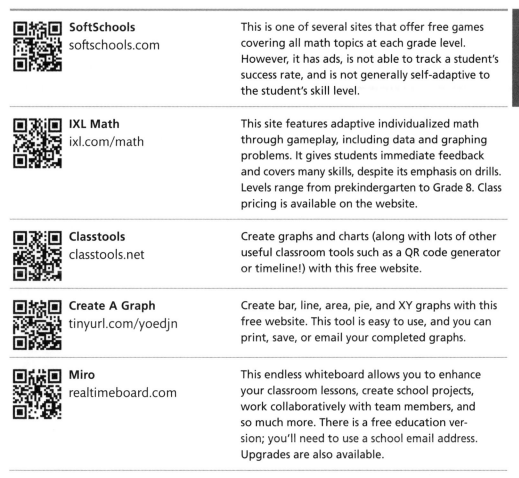

| | **SoftSchools** softschools.com | This is one of several sites that offer free games covering all math topics at each grade level. However, it has ads, is not able to track a student's success rate, and is not generally self-adaptive to the student's skill level. |
|---|---|---|
| | **IXL Math** ixl.com/math | This site features adaptive individualized math through gameplay, including data and graphing problems. It gives students immediate feedback and covers many skills, despite its emphasis on drills. Levels range from prekindergarten to Grade 8. Class pricing is available on the website. |
| | **Classtools** classtools.net | Create graphs and charts (along with lots of other useful classroom tools such as a QR code generator or timeline!) with this free website. |
| | **Create A Graph** tinyurl.com/yoedjn | Create bar, line, area, pie, and XY graphs with this free website. This tool is easy to use, and you can print, save, or email your completed graphs. |
| | **Miro** realtimeboard.com | This endless whiteboard allows you to enhance your classroom lessons, create school projects, work collaboratively with team members, and so much more. There is a free education version; you'll need to use a school email address. Upgrades are also available. |

Many studies in recent years have shown how math games can increase student learning. In addition, a survey **(tinyurl.com/pqms3nj)** from the Games and Learning Publishing Council indicates that the use of digital games in the classroom is becoming more popular with teachers. According to the survey, 55% of teachers who responded have students play digital games in their classroom weekly (2014).

With this in mind, pick a math unit of study. You may wish to first research this math topic and find videos to show as an introduction. Videos from **BrainPOP (brainpop.com)**, **Khan Academy (khanacademy.org)**, and **SchoolTube (schooltube. com)** are only a few good sources. Please be advised that you should preview any video before showing it to the class. These videos are also a great resource for guided math stations or learning centers in your classroom. See our website **(tinyurl.com/ybk4exvr)**.

# Literacy Lessons

Cross-curriculum planning is encouraged with CCSS by using ELA standards in history, science, and technical subjects. Getting through all of the standards you need in third grade is very difficult in the time given. The key to planning with CCSS is to teach multiple standards in one lesson, when you can. We hope the following sample lessons for third grade will inspire you to become an effective technology lesson planner.

## QR Code Activity

Scan and/or take pictures from nonfiction books that focus on a subject you are studying in social studies or science. Pictures can be mounted on large pieces of construction paper. Link the poster through a QR code reader like **i-nigma Reader (tiny.cc/vxdf3y)** or **QR Code Generator (qr-code-generator.com)** to a web-based document that contains facts about the concepts that go with each picture. This primarily satisfies **W.3.6,** "with guidance and support from adults, use technology to produce and publish writing." This also satisfies **SL.3.2**, which determines the main ideas and supporting details in writing using diverse media formats. In addition, if you have students use these posters to review new information, it satisfies **W.3.8**, to "gather information from print and digital sources."

### ISTE STUDENT STANDARDS

Students will use this ISTE Standard in this lesson:

- **Empowered Learner** by understanding fundamental concepts of technology operations, demonstrating the ability to choose, use, and troubleshoot current technologies.

## iMovie Trailer

Coaches in our former building worked with third-grade teachers to help with this lesson because a little prep is needed before you begin. Start with an internet search for student iMovie Trailer examples. There are some good examples on YouTube. Of course, you will want to preview these iMovie Trailers before showing them to your students. Begin the lesson with a discussion on the last movie trailers students have seen. Ask them to identify what makes a good trailer: one that captures the interest of the audience, does not reveal the ending, has music that reflects the mood of the movie, and so on. After viewing several examples, lead students through a discussion about what made those trailers interesting.

Next, have a discussion about these important elements and how they can be included in a movie trailer:

- Readable text

- Clear recordings

- Interesting, clear images

- Timing of images

- Concise language

- Music that reflects the mood of the book

- Narration that is louder than the background music

- Enough details to be interesting but not enough to give away the ending

- Ends with a question or scene that makes the audience want to read the book[/

Third-grade teachers we worked with chose to do this project with a book they were reading in class. However, you can also have students use a self-selected book they are reading independently because movie trailers make an excellent alternative to book reports. Let the students know your expectations for the completed project. Short and sweet is best. For example, have students:

- Introduce the book: Include the title, the author's name, and the genre.

- Tell about the book: Introduce the main characters and action. Don't try to tell every detail.

- Tell about a favorite part of the book or make a connection: Persuade the audience to read the book and leave them wanting to know more. For example, explain what the main character has to overcome, but don't tell if he or she is successful.

- Give a recommendation: Provide closure for the book trailer. This helps match the perfect reader and the book.

If students work together collaboratively, **W.3.6** will be satisfied, using technology, including the internet, to produce and publish writing. In the beginning, you may find your students need to plan and organize for their trailers. Apple's iMovie for Mac website has more than twenty-nine free templates to help students work through their trailers. Students may need adult supervision and assistance when the time comes to scan, upload, or download pictures for their trailer. Certainly, students can provide their own illustrations and graphics, either by hand or digitally by using any graphic art program (such as Microsoft Draw or Google Draw). If their book has pictures, students can scan and use them for trailers. Or, students can also search the internet for pictures to use. Once all trailers are complete, students can share their iMovie Trailers with the class.

Finished projects can be saved to the class ebook shelf for students to explore throughout the year. In addition to **W.3.6**, other standards satisfied include **SL.3.5**, as students are using technology to clarify information in their presentations. **SL.3.2** is also satisfied, because students are interpreting information using a diverse media format all to develop a coherent understanding of a topic (their novels or books). **W.3.8** is also satisfied, as students will need help, support, and guidance with finding and downloading images for their trailers.

ISTE STUDENT STANDARDS

Students will use these ISTE Standards in this lesson:

- **Knowledge Constructor** by employing research, evaluating and building knowledge using digital resources.

- **Creative Communicator** with their presentations choosing the appropriate platform and publishing and presenting customized content.

- **Global Collaborator** by using digital tools to enrich their learning and by collaborating with others.

## Getting to Know You

The beginning of the year is the perfect time to get to know each other. If you introduce yourself with this activity using Prezi (or any other presentation tool), you can use it for any activities throughout the year, especially book reports. As you go through your introduction, instruct the students on how to use Prezi. You may want to have a paper template handy, so students can get their ideas on paper first.

Or, if you have 1:1 tablets for your students, have them use Kidspiration, Bubbl.us, or Evernote to get their ideas down digitally. Students can draw or bring in pictures to go with each section. At the beginning of the year, it may be a good idea to have extra sets of hands to help with the uploading and attaching to the Prezis. If you do not have help, consider having students draw directly on Prezi. Other ideas are to have parents take pictures digitally at home and then email them to you, or let students check out a digital camera to take pictures at home.

Things to include:

- **Name**

- **Future Career**: What career would you like to pursue when you are older? Why? How will you go about pursuing this career?

- **All About Me**: Write words that describe you. Draw or bring in a picture. What are your different interests? What do you like to do in your spare time? List four or five of your favorite interests. Include a picture or drawing.

- **My Family**: Write about your immediate family, including pets. Give details about their occupations and interests. Include a picture or drawing.

- **My Goals**: Write three learning goals you have for this school year. What is it you would like to achieve? How will you go about achieving these goals?

- **Past Education**: What teachers have you had in the past? What have been your favorite subjects? Why?

- **My Favorites**: Write about your favorite things. What are your favorite foods, books, movies, sports, people, and so on?

You may have more ideas to add, or students can add more if they like. Using your whiteboard or Miro, encourage students to share. Audience members should be encouraged to ask clarifying questions. This project is a great way for new students joining your class during the year to introduce themselves and learn about their new classmates.

Continue using Prezi for various assignments throughout the year. You can introduce other presentation tools to your students, such as **Seesaw (web.seesaw.me), Powtoon (powtoon.com/home), Toontastic (tiny.cc/lv9e3y), Haiku Deck (haikudeck.com), Animoto (animoto.com),** or **Tellagami (tellagami.com).** Save these projects in student's digital portfolios. By the end of the year, your students will have a nice collection of technology skills and projects.

**W.3.8** (recall information from experiences; sort into categories) is one of the primary focuses of this lesson. **RI.3.5** could also be satisfied throughout the year when students use text features and search tools to locate information about a topic and then include it in their presentations. **W.3.6** is also satisfied when students utilize adult support to help them make their Prezi presentations, as well as upload their drawings and pictures. When students present their information to the class, they are interacting and collaborating with others. **SL.3.2** and **SL.3.5** are also satisfied with this lesson, as students learn to present their information, read at an understandable pace, and enhance their information with visual displays. In future lessons, encouraging students to include a digital glossary in their Prezi presentations will satisfy **L.3.4d.**

### ISTE STUDENT STANDARDS

Students will use this ISTE Standard in this lesson.

- **Creative Communicator** by choosing the appropriate platform for their presentations and publishing and presenting customized content.

# Social Studies and Science Lessons

The following sample lessons address standards and teach lessons based on national standards in social studies and science:

## Ecosystem Relationships

Third-grade classrooms across the country study interdependent relationships in ecosystems. For this activity, students create a set of weather and climate trading cards using Wixie. They make at least one trading card for each season, which must include a typical weather condition for that season (monsoon–summer, blizzard–winter, tornado–spring, and hurricane–fall). Each card must include the definition of the weather event and describe conditions that cause the event. Students must make one trading card for climate and one trading card for weather; they must include the definitions of *weather* and *climate* and information on how the terms differ. One trading card should be be made for the water cycle, including the names of each part in the order it occurs. When students have finished, they should have seven trading cards. They might make additional cards for other weather vocabulary they have been using. Students can record themselves on the Wixie app, narrating their trading cards. Or, if you prefer to use something a little more authentic, ReadWriteThink's **Trading Card** app **(tinyurl.com/8lqftek)** is a great alternative. Students follow the same procedure, but this app allows trading cards to be printed and cut out for trading with students within the classroom or perhaps another classroom.

With students getting to know and use various text features to locate key facts or information in a text efficiently, specifically with their research, this lesson satisfies **RI.3.5**. This activity also satisfies **RL.3.8**. Working on their trading cards, whether on Wixie or the trading card app, satisfies **W.3.6**. Interaction and collaborating with others will come later as students trade and discuss their trading cards. **SL.3.2** is also satisfied with this activity. Though students are not creating stories or poems, they are creating facts for their trading cards, specifically if they narrate their Wixie trading cards. Therefore, this activity also satisfies **SL.3.5**.

### ISTE STUDENT STANDARDS

Students will use these ISTE Standards in this lesson:

- **Empowered Learner** by choosing terms to define and explain in their trading cards and researching and designing the finished product.

- **Knowledge Constructor** by employing research, evaluating and building knowledge using digital resources.

- **Creative Communicator** by choosing the appropriate platform for their presentations and publishing and presenting customized content.

> Technology helps me learn because I have learned with online typing classes to type with two fingers, which helps me explore new internet sites, especially Google. Technology also helps me understand things, and that helps me accelerate my learning. —**Abigail Rhodes, student**

## Important Leaders

Another lesson that third-grade classrooms across the country study focuses on important people (past and present) who helped shape our nation, state, and community. With your class, brainstorm a list of leaders. Stay away from obvious choices (George Washington, Abraham Lincoln, etc.). Instead, steer students toward choices such as important Native Americans from your area, local community leaders, or national leaders, as students may not know much about supreme court justices, Secretary of State, and so on.

Break your students into groups of four (if you have a group of three, that is fine). Name each table. For example, you may want to do something fun and name each table after a type of candy or popular destination. This is an important component so students can keep track of the tables they have visited. For each group, pick a table host. The table host is the leader and does not move when the groups switch. The table host is in charge of writing down the words, descriptions, and brief phrases the group brainstorms. Arrange desks/tables to accommodate the number of groups you have.

In the center of the area is an iPad. Using any of the mind-mapping sources we mentioned earlier, place a name in the center of the mind-map (make sure each group has a different name). Using the **World Café Method (bit.ly/1WN4w0Y),** students will have five to twenty minutes to brainstorm anything they know about the person in the center of their map. The timing and duration of this activity is up to you, keeping in mind that students need to rotate through all groups.

At the end of the allotted time, the table host thanks the group and holds up the table picture as the teacher announces the groups switch. Students are reminded that they must go to every table and cannot repeat a table. The new group gets the allotted time to go over what the previous group wrote and brainstorm new ideas about the person, as the table host records their thoughts. This process is repeated until all groups have gone to all tables. Make sure the mind-map for each table is saved, as students will need to refer to these. Repeat this process another day, if you wish, with more names.

Next, students will select a leader from the original list (which you have modified if necessary) whom they would like to research and report on. You may want to review the techniques we outlined earlier for having students search the internet and using search engines.

Before students begin their note-taking, you may wish to guide them with some essential questions to include in their research. For example: Who is this person? How have they contributed to our community? What qualities make this person an important member of our community?

Using tools such as Safe Search Kids **(safesearchkids.com)**, students can search for information they need to complete the assignment. Make sure they consult reference materials for definitions or pronunciations of words they do not know. This lesson easily satisfies **RI.3.5** and **W.3.8;** instructing students on how to take notes and having them take notes on information gathered  is helpful in writing their rough drafts and eventually their projects.

There are so many wonderful ways students can present their writing using technology. It is also important to mention that this project can definitely be differentiated for your classroom. Consider using **Trading Cards**, where students can write short text on cards and add pictures. Options requiring a little more text are **Evernote**, **PowerPoint**, **Google Docs**, or **WikiSpaces**. Students present key ideas from their research and import pictures to illustrate their points. More in-depth ways for students to present what they have learned include **iMovie**, **iMovie Trailer**, **Prezi**, **Wixie**, and **Pixie**. Backgrounds and music can be added. Pictures can be scanned or imported to enhance their writing.

Students may need some guidance and support from adults to produce, publish, and share their writing projects; thus this activity also satisfies **W.3.6**. Depending on which tool the students choose to use for producing their work, both **SL.3.2** and **SL.3.5** may also be satisfied, as well as **L3.4d**.

### ISTE STUDENT STANDARDS

Students will use these ISTE Standards in this lesson:

- **Empowered Learner** Students leverage technology to take an active role in choosing, achieving and demonstrating competency in their learning goals, informed by the learning sciences.

- **Knowledge Constructor** by employing research, evaluating and building knowledge using digital resources.

- **Creative Communicator** with their presentations choosing the appropriate platform and publishing and presenting customized content.

- **Global Collaborator** Students use digital tools to broaden their perspectives and enrich their learning by collaborating with others and working effectively in teams locally and globally.

# Math Lessons

The following lesson ideas satisfy the math standard **MP5.**

## Area and Perimeter Activity

The third-grade team at our former school had students involved in a unique math investigation for area and perimeter. Marilyn Burns, founder of **Math Solutions (mathsolutions.com)** and one of today's most highly respected mathematics educators, originally designed this math activity, but we updated it to include technology. Students read the book *Spaghetti and Meatballs for All!* by Marilyn Burns. You can find a link for the story online. The third-grade teachers sent everyone a Google Doc with the task, directions, and story link. Students then used their tablets and earbuds to listen to the story. Afterward, students received the following task:

> There are thirty-two people coming to dinner. Other than the arrangement that the host (insert any name here) designed, please arrange the seating in as many different ways as you can to seat thirty-two people. In other words, arrange the seating in ways that will have a perimeter of thirty-two. You can use apps such as Pattern Shapes to drag tiles to form arrangements, or you can use grid paper or online grid paper **(incompetech.com/ graphpaper).** You can change the area as much as you want. You can use more than eight tiles as long as each of your arrangements has a perimeter of thirty-two. You can put as many tables together or keep as many separate, as you want, as long as the perimeter is thirty-two.

Student directions are then to record each new way on the centimeter square grid paper. There are also links for interactive grid paper websites, where students can do their work. See the appendix or our website **(tinyurl.com/ybk4exvr).**

First, students should highlight the key words and important information in the task. Next, they solve the problem on the centimeter grid paper. Students need to make sure they label their thinking, so that another person can follow along easily. Once students have come up with as many arrangements as possible, have them choose one arrangement and explain (using Explain Everything) how they know the arrangement will work, using good math vocabulary (perimeter, area, square centimeters, etc.). This lesson addresses the **MP5** by using digital tools to enhance math learning. Though students are not creating stories or poems, they are creating explanations for their seating arrangements and must be able to explain using the appropriate math vocabulary for this lesson. Therefore, this activity also satisfies **SL.3.5**. **W.3.6** is satisfied because students are using the app Explain Everything to produce and publish their mathematical thinking, reasoning, and problem solving for this task.

### ISTE STUDENT STANDARDS

Students will use these ISTE Standards in this lesson:

- **Computational Thinker** Students develop and employ strategies for understanding and solving problems in ways that leverage the power of technological methods to develop and test solutions.

- **Global Collaborator** Students use digital tools to broaden their perspectives and enrich their learning by collaborating with others and working effectively in teams locally and globally.

## Multiplication Strategies

The following lesson appeared in first grade and was also adapted for third grade, after a former colleague of ours heard about it. As third-grade teachers begin to teach multiplication strategies, each student will make a page for the class multiplication ebook. Using your favorite media-publishing tool (Wixie, eBook, iBook Author, etc.), students can pair up to write and illustrate their favorite multiplication strategy. There will be duplicates—that is OK because every illustration and explanation is different. Students are encouraged to make their own drawings to go along with their strategies. However, they may need adult help to locate and download a picture (such as arrays or grids) from the internet.

Some suggestions for students:

- Show the problem in an array, a set that shows equal groups in rows and columns.

- Show the problem in a grid.

- Write the problem and use skip counting.

- Write the problem and use repeated addition.

Each page should include a heading for the strategy. As a class, making a table of contents as well as a glossary will help students learn and apply text features to math and thus satisfy **RI.3.5**. Finished books should be shared with the class, placed on a class ebook shelf, or shared with each student in an electronic math folder. Using this ebook at the beginning of the year as you introduce and work through the multiplication tables is a great way to help your students with their strategies (especially the more difficult ones). Making a similar book with division strategies is an awesome way to ensure that your students are learning multiplication and division strategies throughout the year. Students should also be encouraged, as they learn and/or find new strategies, to add them to the electronic multiplication and division books. This activity satisfies **W.3.6**, to produce and publish writing, including collaboration with peers. Furthermore, **SL.3.5** is addressed, as students are adding their digital photos (visual displays) to descriptions of their addition or subtraction strategies. This addresses the MP5 by using digital tools to enhance mathematical learning. Projecting the book as well as having a class discussion where students are answering questions about the material presented in the strategy book satisfies **SL.3.2**.

### ISTE STUDENT STANDARDS

Students will use these ISTE Standards in this lesson.

- **Computational Thinker** Students develop and employ strategies for understanding and solving problems in ways that leverage the power of technological methods to develop and test solutions.

- **Creative Communicator**  Students communicate clearly and express themselves creatively for a variety of purposes using the platforms, tools, styles, formats and digital media appropriate to their goals.

- **Global Collaborator** Students use digital tools to broaden their perspectives and enrich their learning by collaborating with others and working effectively in teams locally and globally.

## Happy Birthday

This is an adaptation of an activity we used with second-grade classes. It can also be used with fourth- or fifth-graders. Begin by using your Smart Board or **Miro (real-timeboard.com)** to display **A Maths Dictionary for Kids (tinyurl.com/38vkvrs).** Look up and discuss words such as *spreadsheet, budget, requirement,* and so on. Discuss how these words are important to what the students will be doing. By using the online dictionary, and encouraging your students to use this practice whenever they are unsure of the meaning of a word, standard **L.3.4d** is satisfied.

The first step is to present this task to your students using **LiveBinders (livebinders.com), Webquest (tiny.cc/xvgk3y),** or **Explain Everything (explaineverything.com).**

### TASK

Your birthday will be here soon! You are excited and want to have a party for you and a group of your friends. Your parents have agreed and said you can invite thirty of your friends and family, but only if you take care of all the arrangements. You will be the party planner and organize the best possible party within the budget set by your parents. They have given you a budget of $350, which has to cover all aspects of your party, from food and drinks to cake and games.

Your job is to shop online at different stores to find the best deals and best prices on all of the items you will need, in order to get the most for your money. You will be given a list of required items that are necessary to have a successful birthday party. The goal is to stay on or under budget, fulfilling enough of the requirements to accommodate thirty guests.

### REQUIREMENTS

When planning your party, you must include the following:

- Invitations (30 total)
- At least 3 types of decorations
- One main meal (enough to feed thirty guests)
- Two snack food options (chips, popcorn, etc.) (enough for thirty guests)
- Drinks (enough for two drinks per guest)

- Birthday cake (big enough to feed thirty guests, with plenty for seconds and leftovers)

- Ice cream (enough to feed thirty guests)

- Birthday candles

- At least three games (with everything you need) for entertainment

You will be provided with links to different stores that provide all of the items you will need. Each store varies in price for the same items. It is up to you to make the best possible choices to get the best and most items within your budget while fulfilling all of the requirements.

Remember, your goal is to convince your parents that you can throw this party within the budget. To help convince them, create a presentation that shows each section of the requirements with detailed information about the items you chose, complete with the prices. At the end of your presentation, you will need to include a grand total to show your parents you stayed within your $350 budget!

Search the following websites to choose items for your party. Use **Simplenote (simplenote.com)**, **Evernote (evernote.com)**, or **Penzu (penzu.com)** to keep track of what you find and would like to buy. These are not your final choices.

Invitations:

- **Walmart (tinyurl.com/ycuta53z)**

- **Party City (tiny.cc/s6hk3y)**

- **Zazzle (zazzle.com/invitations)**

- **Vista Print (tinyurl.com/yay8dvnl)**

Food, snacks, and drinks:

- **Walmart (walmart.com)**

- **Target (target.com)**

- **Amazon (tinyurl.com/yaz5matd)**

- **Pizza Hut (pizzahut.com)** eight pieces per large pizza

- **Domino's (dominos.com)** eight pieces per large pizza

- **Papa John's (papajohns.com)** eight pieces per large pizza
- **Subway Catering (subway.com/en-US/Catering)**
- **Quiznos Catering (quiznos.com/catering.aspx)**

Games and Decorations:

- **Oriental Trading (orientaltrading.com)**
- **Walmart (walmart.com)**
- **Target (target.com)**
- **Amazon (tinyurl.com/yaz5matd)**
- **Party City (partycity.com)**

Birthday Cake and Ice Cream (Don't forget the candles!):

- **Walmart (walmart.com)**
- **Target (target.com)**
- **Bake Me A Wish (tinyurl.com/ycpsg3z5)**
- **I Am Baker (tiny.cc/6dik3y)**
- **Cold Stone Creamery (coldstonecreamery.com)**
- **Baskin Robbins (baskinrobbins.com)**

From the lists you have made, now choose exactly the items you want to buy. Pick your favorite spreadsheet to track your purchases: **Google Spreadsheets (spreadsheets.google.com); Microsoft Office Excel (onedrive.live.com).** Don't forget, you aren't actually purchasing now! Calculate the total cost for each item, as well as a grand total for your party. If you are over budget, go back and see what you can replace or eliminate to lower your total cost while still fulfilling the minimum requirements for your party. If you are under budget, see what other items you can add or replace to make your party even better while still staying within your budget. Once you have finalized your choices and are close to your budget (without going over), create a presentation to show your parents, describing the items you want to purchase.

There are many presentation tools your students can choose: **Google Slides (tiny. cc/zjik3y)** or **Microsoft PowerPoint (tiny.cc/tlik3y)** are some of the more popular choices. Encourage your students to try some of the new presentation tools available: **Powtoon (powtoon.com), Moovly (moovly.com), and Adobe Spark (spark. adobe.com).** There are many presentation tools available. Some are free, some are not. Your students should be encouraged to present their findings to the class, as well as their parents.

For each section of your presentation, include a picture of the item, price, and store where you will purchase it. You must include these sections in your presentation:

- Invitations
- Food (main meal)
- Snacks
- Drinks
- Games
- Decorations
- Birthday cake, ice cream, and candles
- A breakdown of all items with a price and a grand total

Good luck and happy birthday!

As mentioned above, **L.3.4d** is satisfied (when using online dictionaries) as well as **MP.5**. Other standards satisfied include **RI.3.5** when using text features and search tools to locate information; **W.3.8**, which recalls information from digital sources, taking notes in the process; **W.3.6** when using technology to produce and publish writing;  and **SL.3.2** by having students present and explain their presentations aloud to their parents (and the class) and answering questions about key details. Students should also request clarification if something in their presentation is not understood. Have students rework their presentations if there are parts that need clarification. Also satisfied is **SL.3.5**, as students explain the data they gathered researching their items for their party.

ISTE STUDENT STANDARDS

Students will use these ISTE Standards in this lesson:

- **Empowered Learner** by understanding fundamental concepts of technology operations, demonstrating the ability to choose, use, and troubleshoot current technologies.

- **Digital Citizen** Students recognize the rights, responsibilities and opportunities of living, learning and working in an interconnected digital world, and they act and model in ways that are safe, legal and ethical.

- **Computational Thinker** Students develop and employ strategies for understanding and solving problems in ways that leverage the power of technological methods to develop and test solutions.

- **Creative Communicator** Students communicate clearly and express themselves creatively for a variety of purposes using the platforms, tools, styles, formats and digital media appropriate to their goals.

# A Final Note

As students progress through the elementary grades, they establish their baseline of proficiency in technology. This will definitely enhance their experiences with technology in the upper grades, as well as satisfy the CCSS performance standards at the K-5 levels. We hope that you find the resources and lesson ideas presented in this chapter useful and that they are easy to adapt to your class.

You will find more resources on our website **(tinyurl.com/y9dfltpr)**, which may be helpful as you look to differentiate your instruction. Visit our online site for updated information about this book. To learn more about meeting technology standards found within the CCSS in other grades, look for our additional title in this series.

# 12 Practical Ideas for Fourth Grade

We realize that you will want to focus on your particular grade or subject when you are planning your lessons and implementing CCSS, so we have organized the Practical Ideas chapters by grade level and subject. Each grade starts with an overview followed by ELA technology standards with accompanying apps, software, and websites that you can use to help your students succeed with that standard. We then continue with the math standard for the grade level and review appropriate resources. Finally, we have included sample lessons for each grade level in various subject areas. Although we have organized the book so you can find your specific grade and subject easily, please do not disregard other sections of this chapter. It is often helpful to see what the standards require before and after the grade you teach. To see grades other than K–5, look for our additional title in this series covering grades 6–12, as it provides information to help you differentiate for students at all levels of your class.

Fourth-graders are expected to use technology to enhance their literacy skills. The literacy standards place an emphasis on information gathering and publishing of student writing. Students should also use technology to practice math skills. This includes the use of digital math tools in the form of software programs, apps, or websites. We offer ideas and suggestions for which technologies to use and how to teach with them. At the fourth-grade level, students are expected to use technology with many of their literacy skills as well as possess an understanding of what technology tools are best used when solving math problems. In this chapter, we list all fourth-grade CCR standards that require teaching and learning with technology, and we have included our ideas on how to integrate technology into these standards using tablets, computers, software, apps, and websites.

# Reading Resources

There are many ways in which students can make visual and/or oral presentations of a story or drama. Using programs that help students to create the stories in a format that allows them to illustrate, as well as type, helps students with the visual presentation of the text. In many cases, these presentation programs allow students to pick backgrounds from templates and to import pictures. Most present in a slide-show format, but they can also be printed as a storybook. Some even allow you to save presentations as ebooks. Movie creation apps, websites, and software are not conducive to stories in paragraph form. However, you can use your voice to speak the text and use photos and video to illustrate in an animated format. We have also included apps and websites that allow students to create shorter versions of their stories in an animated way. Although not as inclusive, they can be a lot of fun!

# Reading Literature

## RL.4.7 • READING LITERATURE

Make connections between the text of a story or drama and a **visual or oral presentation** of the text, identifying where each version reflects specific descriptions and directions in the text.

The CCSS for reading are designed to help ensure that students gain adequate exposure to a range of texts and tasks. Rigor is infused through the requirement that students read increasingly complex texts through the grades and make connections between text and visual or oral presentations. **Table 12.1** lists student-friendly tools that allow them to transform text into slideshows, books, animations, and movies.

## Slideshow Software

Slideshows, which are easy to use, are a great way for students to demonstrate their understanding and share ideas with the class. The slideshow tools share in **Table 12.1** can get them started.

Table 12.1: Slideshow and Animation Tools

| | | |
|---|---|---|
| | **Kid Pix**<br>kidpix.com | This software is not free, but students can use it to publish collaborative writing that uses pictures and text. A new version called Kid Pix 3D features more animation. For an alternative, try Tux Paint (tuxpaint.org). It is a free online download that is also for primary students and has similar features. |
| | **Wixie**<br>wixie.com | This software for purchase uses multimedia, pictures, sound, video, and text to create presentations and stories stored in the cloud for mobile access. The apps are free, but there are online versions with more features available with educational pricing. |
| | **Pixie**<br>tech4learning.com/pixie | |
| | **Smilebox**<br>smilebox.com | A free program linked to the website to create slideshows, invitations, greetings, collages, scrapbooks, and photo albums right on your computer. Don't miss applying for the free Teacher's Toolbox! |

## Book Creation Websites

**Table 12.2** lists some free sites that also allow you to add pictures to your text and create ebooks or printed versions.

Table 12.2: Book Creation Tools

| | | |
|---|---|---|
| | **Storybird**<br>storybird.com | This free website uses art to inspire storytelling. Students can write, read, share, and print short books. |
| | **StoryJumper**<br>storyjumper.com | This free site gives your students a fun set of tools for writing and illustrating stories that can be shared online. (You must pay for a hardbound book.) |

| | | |
|---|---|---|
| | **Little Bird Tales**<br>littlebirdtales.com | This website is free. Students can draw original artwork or import pictures to create and write stories. You must pay to download as a digital movie, but you can print stories for free. |
| | **Canva**<br>canva.com | Create a free digital poster to display student work in a fun and unique way. There are many templates with photos, graphics, and fonts to use in this drag-and-drop, easy-to-use website. It is free to teachers and students. |

## Story Animation Apps

Some apps allow students to create shorter versions of their stories in an animated way. **Table 12.3** shares some of our recommendations.

**Table 12.3: Animation Tools**

| | | |
|---|---|---|
| | **Puppet Pals**<br>tinyurl.com/btxmr9b | This app allows students to create a puppet production using familiar characters to tell or retell a story. It is free, but see the website for add-on pricing. |
| | **iFunFace**<br>ifunface.com | Students can create a read-aloud to show how the main idea and details flow by using a photo and audio recording to create an animation. It helps students visualize how to support details that branch off from the main ideas and how they flow together. The app is free but can be upgraded for a price. |
| | **Blabberize**<br>blabberize.com | Students speak the text and use photos to illustrate in an animated format. Free. |
| | **Voki**<br>voki.com | Students speak the text and use photos to illustrate in an animated format. It is free, but there are ads. |
| | **Fotobabble**<br>fotobabble.com | Students speak the text and use photos to illustrate. Free. |

**ChatterPix Kids**
tinyurl.com/ptwhtxd

This free app is for creating and sharing videos. Make anything talk! Just take a picture, draw a line to make a mouth, and record your voice. Great for reading aloud and poetry sharing.

## Movie Creation Apps, Websites, and Software

Creating movies, although more time consuming, is a fun and interactive way to present information. **Table 12.4** shares some tools that can be used.

Table 12.4: Movie-Making Tools

 **iMovie and iMovie Trailer**
apple.com/ios/imovie

These are great programs to use when creating stories. Templates make the program faster and easier to use in iMovie Trailer, and iMovie has many great features. These programs come free with Apple computers, but you can also buy the app.

 **MovieMaker**
tiny.cc/6bmk3y

Microsoft's version of iMovie. It comes standard with any Windows computer.

 **Animoto**
animoto.com

This website allows you to create professional movies, and it is free to educators.

 **Wideo**
wideo.co

Wideo allows you to easily make animation videos. Education pricing is available.

 **Movavi**
movavi.com

Make movies using your photos and videos or create slideshows, video blogs, or screen-capture tutorials. It's easy to enhance, edit, and tell your story, and it's a lot of fun! Check the website for educational pricing.

# Reading Information

## RI.4.7 • READING INFORMATIONAL TEXT

Interpret information presented visually, orally, or quantitatively (e.g., in charts, graphs, diagrams, timelines, **animations, or interactive elements on web pages**) and explain how the information contributes to an understanding of the text in which it appears.

You can find many websites that show charts, graphs, diagrams, timelines, and interactive animations. Picking a topic from your science standards and finding websites on this information is a great way to integrate technology. You can then discuss all of the ways people depict information on websites.

## Software and Websites to Create Charts and Graphs

There are several software programs and websites (some must be purchased, others are free) that students can use to create their own charts and graphs. We have listed some of them in **Table 12.5**.

Table 12.5: Charting and Graphing Tools

| SOFTWARE & WEBSITES | | |
|---|---|---|
|  | **Microsoft Excel**<br>office.com | These programs offer a great approach to teaching students about charts and graphs as they learn how to interpret and present information. |
|  | **Apple Numbers**<br>apple.com/mac/numbers | |
|  | **Google Sheets**<br>google.com/sheets/about | |
|  | **Create A Graph**<br>tinyurl.com/yoedjn | Create bar, line, area, pie, and XY graphs with this free website. This tool is easy to use, and you can print, save, or email your completed graphs. |
| | **Classtools**<br>classtools.net | Create graphs and charts and use many helpful classroom tools, such as a QR code generator or timeline, with this free website. |

| | **FASTT Math**<br>bit.ly/1nmvNe6 | This program really helps students visualize how charts and graphs compare, and it's extremely easy to use. The program includes ready-made activities in all subject areas, including rubrics and sample graphs. District purchasing and volume CDs are available. Contact a representative through the website for specific prices. |
|---|---|---|
| | **Gliffy**<br>gliffy.com | Create professional-quality flowcharts, wireframes, diagrams, and more with this tool. It is free for limited use; upgrades are available for a fee. |
| | **ChartGizmo**<br>chartgizmo.com | With your free account from ChartGizmo, you can start creating dynamic charts from static or collected data and place them on your website in minutes. |

## Software and Websites to Create Timelines

Students can make the connections between time and events visually. This can be difficult because it requires abstract thinking. Use a topic from your literacy social studies standards to integrate this standard **(RL4.7)** into your curriculum using timelines and interactive elements, such as pictures and videos (See **Table 12.6**).

**Table 12.6: Timeline Tools**

| | **Timeline JS by KnightLab**<br>timeline.knightlab.com | TimelineJS is an open-source tool that enables anyone to build visually rich, interactive timelines. Beginners can create a timeline using nothing more than a Google spreadsheet. Experts can use their JSON skills to create custom installations, while keeping TimelineJS's core functionality. This is a free site. |
|---|---|---|
| | **SoftSchools**<br>softschools.com | Timeline Maker, which is an easy program to use and print, is included in SoftSchools' free site; however, there are ads. |
| | **Sutori**<br>sutori.com | This is a collaborative timeline. You can create and share privately or publicly. It is free; however, you do need to sign up on their website. |

 **ReadWriteThink**
readwritethink.org

A free site that has many good teacher resources, including great ways for students to make their own timelines. It is so easy to make and display them!

# Writing Resources

Presenting information digitally to aid comprehension is another standard fourth-graders will be expected to meet. Traditionally, **Microsoft PowerPoint (office. com)** has been the presentation tool of choice. Although this is still a great program to use, other presentation programs have emerged. Apple offers **Keynote (apple. com/mac/keynote)** as part of its software package. Its features are similar to Power-Point. **Google Slides (google.com/slides/about)** is geared toward business presentations, but it is free and web-based. It is easy to share a project that multiple users can work on at once, which makes this an especially useful program for interacting and collaborating remotely. You can add audio recordings to your slides, as well as visual displays such as pictures and short video clips. These can be used to enhance the development of main ideas or the themes of your presentations. **Evernote (ever-note.com)** is a free app that allows your students to share notes as well as audio and video recordings. It's easy to use and share with others. There are also places to save your writing. Digital portfolios can be saved to **Edmodo (edmodo.com), eBackpack (ebackpack.com),** or **LiveBinders (livebinders.com),** just to name a few.

# Writing

## W.4.2a • WRITING

Introduce a topic clearly and group-related information in paragraphs and sections; include formatting (e.g., headings), illustrations, and multimedia when useful to aiding comprehension.

## W.4.6 • WRITING

With some guidance and support from adults, use technology, including the internet, to produce and publish writing as well as to interact and collaborate with others; demonstrate sufficient command of keyboarding skills to type a minimum of one page in a single sitting.

Presenting digitally is not limited to slideshow presentations. There are many websites out there that allow you to publish student writing. Using blogging websites such as **Edmodo (edmodo.com)** and **Google Classroom (classroom.google.com)** is another way to share student writing in a safe, protected environment. It is also a great way for students to interact and collaborate with others. Both of these sites allow teachers to set themselves up as administrators and add students to different groups. All student writing is secure in these groups.

## Publishing Websites

You can give assignments asking for short answers where everyone can respond in a blog format or you can ask them to write longer assignments on their own that they work on as a document, then submit privately to you or post on a website to share. There are also websites that ask students to submit their work for possible publication. **Table 12.7** shares a few of our recommendations.

**Table 12.7: Publishing Resources**

| | | |
|---|---|---|
|  | **PBS Kids Writer's Contest** <br> wtvp.org/writers-contest | This free site asks for student writing and serves as a nice incentive to get students to do their best. |
|  | **Lulu** <br> lulu.com | These sites allow you to create real books and publish them online. Parents can purchase the books as keepsakes. The site is free to use, but a fee is required to publish. |
|  | **Lulu Junior** <br> lulujr.com | |

**WEBSITES**

**Table 12.7: Publishing Resources**

| | | |
|---|---|---|
| | **TikaTok**<br>tikatok.com | This is another site that allows students to write, create, and publish stories as ebooks or hardcover books. Classroom pricing is available on the website. TikaTok StorySpark, is the app version, also available for purchase. |
| | **CAST UDL Book Builder**<br>bookbuilder.cast.org | This free site lets you publish your ebook and see what others have published. |
| | **Poetry Idea Engine**<br>tinyurl.com/2cuowf | This Scholastic site allows students to use templates to make different forms of poetry—another great way technology gets kids writing. Better still, it is free! |
| | **eBackpack**<br>ebackpack.com | This learning management system features built-in assignments, note-taking, student portfolios, lesson planning, standard alignments, parent communication, and much more. An app is available. Look for education pricing. |
| | **LiveBinders**<br>livebinders.com | Opens up new possibilities for collaboration, organization, and sharing. All your lessons and content are in one place, including documents, links, presentations, student portfolios, and more. Educational pricing available. |

## Keyboarding Software

By fourth grade, students are expected to type a page in one sitting. There are lots of keyboarding programs that you can buy, or free sites that offer instruction and games. **Table 11.4** in the previous chapter shares keyboarding resources that are free as well as programs for purchase.

Some districts send students to computer labs to practice keyboarding at given times, others fit it in where they can in the classroom, and still others have students practice and learn at home. The best way is to combine all three approaches.

Students benefit from formal keyboarding instruction, but they need to practice both in the classroom and at home. When students are working at the computers in your classroom, remind them to practice good technique, such as sitting up straight, keeping hands in home row, holding wrists slightly curved, and moving fingers instead of hands.

# Writing Research

## W.4.8 • WRITING RESEARCH

Recall relevant information from experiences or gather relevant information from print and digital sources; take notes and categorize information, and provide a list of sources.

By the time students are in fourth grade, they should be able to search the internet to gather information on a given topic. Your class will need guidance, of course, so lessons on internet searching are critical, as well as lessons on media literacy. (Media literacy is especially crucial because students need to be able to critique a website before using it—anyone can put up a webpage.) As stated by the **W.4.8** standard, students will also need to be able to take notes off these sites and summarize or paraphrase information as well as provide a list of sources. We discuss these techniques in the following paragraphs.

Although students are sufficiently net-savvy these days, they still need assistance with the basics of searching. Different search engines work in different ways, and each will give you different information. Your students need to know how to use multiple engines.

Smart searching will help avoid a lot of wasted time. Teaching students to analyze search results will definitely help them find better information and to think more critically about any information they find on the internet. Following are a few rules of thumb.

- Choose your search terms carefully. Be precise about what you are looking for, but use phrases and not full sentences.

- Adding more words can narrow a search. Use Boolean searches to narrow your topic with quotation marks. There's a big difference between "gopher" and "habitats of gophers in North America."

- Use synonyms! If students can't find what they're looking for, have them try keywords that mean the same thing or are related.

- Type "site:". Typing the word *site:* (with the colon) after your keyword and before a URL will tell Google to search within a specific website.

- Add a minus sign. Adding a minus sign (a hyphen) immediately before any word, with no space in between, indicates that you don't want that word to appear in your search results. For example, "Saturn-cars" will give you information about the planet, not the automobile.

## Kid-Friendly Search Engines

Browsing safe content is the most important reason for using search engines made specifically for kids. Allowing your students to have the run of the web using a search engine for young students helps you because it is difficult to monitor many students at once if your class is using unfiltered search engines.

There is no guarantee that every search will be kid-safe. However, some search engines, such as **Cybersleuth Kids (cybersleuth-kids.com)** and S**afe Search Kids (safesearchkids.com)** are specifically for young children. See a list of recommended search engines that are recommended for children in Chapter 11.

## Note-Taking Apps and Websites

Tried-and-true methods for taking notes and categorizing information from books can still be used to gather information and take notes on websites. Teaching students to use data sheets, note cards, and Know, What, Learn (KWL) techniques still works. However, technology can make this easier. The **Kentucky Virtual Library (kyvl.org)** is an excellent resource for some of these techniques.

Modeling is essential when teaching students how to glean information from a website. An interactive whiteboard is a perfect tool for modeling lessons. Don't have an interactive whiteboard? Use **Miro (realtimeboard.com).** It's a free website that allows you to turn an ordinary whiteboard into an interactive, virtual one. All you need is a computer and a projector. Using the many tools an interactive whiteboard and software have to offer will really help teach your students how to navigate through information posted on the internet because they can follow along as you demonstrate.

**Table 12.8: Note-Taking Tools**

| | | |
|---|---|---|
| **Evernote**<br>evernote.com | This free app allows you to import a worksheet, document, or picture, including a snapshot of a webpage, and then annotate it using tools common to interactive whiteboard software. You can highlight words, cut and paste, and add sticky notes. It also allows you to use voice recognition. You can then send your annotated sheet to someone else. |
| **Simplenote**<br>simplenote.com | This note-taking app is simple to use and has the ability to share notes with others, search notes, track changes, and use it over multiple platforms. All notes are backed up online and synchronized. Best of all, it's free. |
| **Penzu**<br>penzu.com | This writing website can be accessed with their app, and it's free! Created for journaling and diaries, it is very customizable and secure. It even allows you to set up reminders. |

## Mind-Mapping Tools

Mind-mapping tools will help your students organize their research when gathering information. Several wonderful software programs have been used for mind-mapping for many years. However, there are also free sites out there. **Table 12.9** shares some digital tools you can use to teach note-taking and categorizing.

Fourth-graders will also need to provide a list of sources. Of course, making your own template for sources and having students fill it in using a word-processing program works. However, there are websites, such as **EasyBib (easybib.com),** that students can use to generate citations in MLA, APA, and Chicago formats easily. EasyBib is a free website and app for grades 4–12. Simply copy and paste or scan a book's barcode to create its citation. Students can also cite a list of sources on their own by including URL, publisher or author, topic/title, and date a website

**Table 12.9: Mind-Mapping Resources**

| | | |
|---|---|---|
| | **Kidspiration**<br>tinyurl.com/dg2cxa | A mind-mapping software program that helps students organize their writing. It can be especially helpful for students who are learning to create paragraphs and organize big ideas into smaller parts. See the website for pricing. The web-based version is called Webspiration Classroom (**tinyurl.com/bmop3nh**) and is available for purchase. |
| | **Webspiration Classroom**<br>tinyurl.com/bmop3nh | |
| | **Bubbl.us**<br>Bubbl.us | This is a free (with limited use) mind-mapping website for Grades K–12. It can be shared by multiple students at a time and comes with an app. See the website for more options and to purchase a package. |
| | **MindMeister**<br>tiny.cc/826i3y | This is a free, basic, mind-mapping website for Grades 2–12. Upgrades are available and have a free trial period. See the website for details. |
| | **FreeMind**<br>tinyurl.com/5qrd5 | This is a free mind-mapping tool using Java for Grades 2–12. Options for a basic or maximum install are available. |
| | **Classtools**<br>classtools.net | Create graphs and charts and use many helpful classroom tools, such as a QR code generator or timeline, with this free website. |

was published. If the publication date is not available, they should note the date retrieved from the internet.

## Media Literacy Resources

Your class also needs to be aware that links come up in searches that may have strings attached—not to the research topic, but to advertisers. This should be a part of your media literacy lesson. Students can waste a great deal of time if they aren't focused on specific research. Students need to know that anyone can put up a website, and they need to know how to tell whether a site is credible. Determining a website's domain register is the first step in evaluating credibility: .com (company), .gov (government site), or .org (nonprofit organization, such as a school). Then students need to identify the author of the site (this will usually be posted at the beginning or the end), who they are affiliated with, or what is the author's background or expertise on the topic. Advertisers abound, and students will need to be careful what they click. The class needs to be taught what to do if they go to an inappropriate site (e.g., clicking the back button immediately and letting a teacher know).

# Speaking and Listening

## SL.4.2 • SPEAKING AND LISTENING

Paraphrase portions of a text read aloud or information presented in **diverse media and formats**, including visually, quantitatively, and orally.

## SL.4.5 • SPEAKING AND LISTENING

Add **audio recordings** and **visual displays** to presentations when appropriate to enhance the development of main ideas or themes.

There are many diverse media formats that will read aloud to students. Audiobooks on CD or ebooks are good sources. Sites such as **Follett (tiny.cc/cb2q3y).** and **TumbleBooks (tumblebooks.com)** must be purchased but allow access to multiple ebook collections that include both fiction and nonfiction. You can also check out ebooks at your local library or purchase them from booksellers such as Amazon or Barnes & Noble (especially if you have e-readers). There are some free ebooks available. Of course, pay sites offer a much better selection.

Using ebooks or a website with your interactive whiteboard (or free whiteboard sites) allows interaction when modeling or for student engagement. Informational text works especially well with this standard, but fictional pieces can also be used.

## Paraphrasing Apps

After listening to text read aloud, students can use different media formats to paraphrase what they heard. Because students are paraphrasing and keeping it short, they can use these fun, interactive apps (see T**able 12.10**).

## Presentation Apps and Websites

Scanning finished book pages into Microsoft PowerPoint, Apple Keynote, or Google Slides allow you to make ebooks or presentations for your classroom by adding audio recordings and visual displays to enhance the development of main ideas or themes as stated in **SL.4.5.** These programs allow you to speak directly into the program, and then store the ebooks for all students. Options include controlling the speed of page advancement, recording narration, adding action buttons, adjusting mouse-over and mouse-click actions, incorporating preset animation, and setting page transition effects. **Table 12.10** shares just some of the available resources that students can use to share work and create presentations.

Table 12.10: Speaking and LIstening Resources

| | | |
|---|---|---|
| | **Prezi**<br>prezi.com | You can sign up for a free educational account, and your students can create and share presentations online. Prezi has mind-mapping, zoom, and motion, and it can import files. Presentations can be downloaded. A Prezi viewer app is available. |
| | **Adobe Spark**<br>tinyurl.com/yamq84lg | This free app from Adobe gives students and teachers a great way to make video presentations. Create a movie and narrate in your own voice. The app provides themes, photos, animations, and templates to organize the videos. |
| | **Comic Life**<br>tinyurl.com/oj5o2qd | Make a comic from your own images with fonts, templates, panels, balloons, captions, and lettering art. This tool is available for purchase as software or an app. |
| | **ToonDoo**<br>toondoo.com | Create your own comics to upload online, or create a comic storybook. The app is free, but you can also purchase printable images or ToonDooSpaces. |
| | **Puppet Pals**<br>tinyurl.com/btxmr9b | This app allows students to create a puppet production using familiar characters to tell or retell a story. It is free, but see the website for add-on pricing. |

**SOFTWARE & APPS**

 **iFunFace**
ifunface.com

Students can create a read-aloud to show how the main idea and details flow by using a photo and audio recording to create an animation. It helps students visualize how to support details that branch off from the main ideas and how they flow together. The app is free but can be upgraded for a price.

 **CAST UDL Book Builder**
bookbuilder.cast.org

This free site lets you publish your ebook and see what others have published.

 **WebQuests**
webquest.org

 **SiteBuilder**
sitebuilder.com

These are good tools to use for presentations. The WebQuest site allows students to follow an already-created, project-based lesson where information is found solely on the internet. Students can create their own WebQuest if a website-building program or a website such as SiteBuilder (**sitebuilder.com**) is available. **WebQuest.org** is the original and most popular site. However, if you search the internet, you will find more sites that you can use.

# Language

## L.4.4c • LANGUAGE

Consult reference materials (e.g., dictionaries, glossaries, thesauruses), both print and **digital**, to find the pronunciation and determine or clarify the precise meaning of key words and phrases.

One lesson idea is to have students locate difficult vocabulary words in a piece of informational text and then use an electronic dictionary to define them. You could give students a website to read (preferably on a standards topic from literacy or science) and ask them to write down all of the words they don't know. After using an electronic dictionary to find the definitions to these words, have students reread the text. With luck, they will come away with a better understanding of the content they read.

Table **12.11** shares online vocabulary and reference resources that students can use. Bookmark these sites or add them to your website for easy access. The more students use them, the more comfortable they will become. Offer lessons and activities to learn and practice the necessary skills with an online dictionary, just as you would when using hard-copy dictionaries, glossaries, and thesauruses.

**Table 12.11: Vocabulary and Reference Tools**

| | |
|---|---|
|  **Trading Cards**<br>tinyurl.com/8lqftek | The app or website is a great way to document vocabulary words by adding definitions, a picture, and recordings of pronunciation. You can also use Trading Cards by doing an activity with an online thesaurus. Simply give students a word on a trading card and ask them to make as many trading cards as they can of synonyms and antonyms of that word. They can print these out and trade them with others or make them into a digital book. The Explain Everything app is also easy to use to import a picture, record your voice, and make a digital presentation. |
|  **Merriam-Webster**<br>merriam-webster.com | is still the most commonly used digital dictionary and thesaurus. They also offer a kid-friendly version of this dictionary called Word Central (**wordcentral.com**). |
|  **Word Central**<br>wordcentral.com | This resource includes the pronunciation of the word as well as its definition. The original Merriam-Webster site has this as well, and it includes multiple definitions. |
|  **Kids.Wordsmyth**<br>kids.wordsmyth.net/we<br><br>**WordSmyth**<br>wordsmyth.net | These sites are both good fourth-grade options. The kids' version includes pronunciation (as does the adults' version) and shows how words are used as parts of speech with examples and pictures where applicable. |

| | | |
|---|---|---|
| **Little Explorers** <br> tinyurl.com/2swjc | This is another good option for a dictionary and thesaurus, and it includes a glossary maker. You can sign up for an ad-free version, which will not cost your school. |
| **Thesaurus.com** <br> thesaurus.com | This is a great thesaurus site. While digital dictionaries and thesauruses are not updated as often as encyclopedias, they are still very convenient. |

# Math Resources

There are two main sets of benchmarks for Common Core math standards: processes and practices. First, you have the math targets, written similarly to ELA (Counting and Cardinality; Operations and Algebraic Thinking; Number and Operation in Base Ten; Measurement and Data; and Geometry). While you work with fourth-grade students on mathematical processes, such as algebra and fractions, you need to teach them how to apply the SMP (which include problem solving and precision) to those processes. One practice, the only one that includes technology, is mathematical practice 5: "Use appropriate tools strategically."

## MP5 • MATH

Use appropriate **tools** strategically.

Following is the explanation CCSS provides for **MP5**. As this is the standard explanation for Grades K–12, it does include references to higher grades.

> Mathematically proficient students consider the available tools when solving a mathematical problem. These tools might include pencil and paper, concrete models, a ruler, a protractor, a **calculator, a spreadsheet, a computer algebra system, a statistical package, or dynamic geometry software**. Proficient students are sufficiently familiar with tools appropriate for their grade or course to make sound decisions about when each of these tools might be helpful, recognizing both the insight to be gained and their limitations. For example, mathematically proficient high school students analyze graphs of functions and solutions generated using a

**graphing calculator**. They detect possible errors by strategically using estimation and other mathematical knowledge. When making mathematical models, they know that **technology** can enable them to visualize the results of varying assumptions, explore consequences, and compare predictions with data. Mathematically proficient students at various grade levels are able to identify relevant external mathematical resources, such as **digital content located on a website**, and use them to pose or solve problems. They are able to use **technological tools** to explore and deepen their understanding of concepts.

Because this description does not give examples for all grades, we have provided a list of appropriate apps, websites, software, and lessons that will help translate this standard for fourth grade.

This is the only fourth-grade math standard that involves technology. Many math programs, websites, and apps allow students to explore and deepen their understanding of math concepts. The best of them have students learning in creative ways and are not merely electronic worksheets. They automatically adapt to the students' skill levels and tell you where the students are in their learning and what they need to advance. Of course, these usually do not come free. We list many good math resources here. The free resources (many with ads) are often less interesting and not as well organized. They don't give you the feedback you need. It is up to you to decide what is best for your circumstances and budget.

## Math Resources

As stated in the standard, "Mathematically proficient students consider the available tools when solving a mathematical problem."

The websites in **Table 12.12** allow you to use various mathematical tools, such as a graphing calculator. Another option is to use software that comes with a whiteboard. These have all sorts of mathematical tools, such as protractors, rulers, and grids, built in.

## Graphing Apps and Software

In fourth grade, students are also expected to use a protractor to measure angles. They can use the protractor feature of the Toolkit app **(skypaw.com),** which includes a converter that can measure pairs of units. **Softpedia (softpedia.com)** allows you to download a protractor to use online. The site is free, but it has ads.

Many studies in recent years have shown how math games can increase student learning. In addition, a survey **(tinyurl.com/pqms3nj)** from the Games and Learning Publishing Council indicates that the use of digital games in the classroom is becoming more popular with teachers. According to the survey, 55% of teachers who responded have students play digital games in their classroom weekly (2014).

With this in mind, pick a math unit of study. You may wish to first research this math topic and find videos to show as an introduction. Videos from **BrainPOP (brainpop.com), Khan Academy (khanacademy.org),** and **School Tube (schooltube. com)** are only a few good sources. Please be advised that you should preview any video before showing it to the class. These activities are also a great resource for guided math stations or learning centers in your classroom. See our website **(tinyurl.com/ybk4exvr)** for more.

**Table 12.12: Math Resources**

| | | |
|---|---|---|
|  | **ScootPad**<br>scootpad.com | This web-based math site is totally customizable for individual students. It adapts to the student and keeps the teacher in the loop with multiple reports. It is completely aligned to the CCSS. Pricing is available on the website. |
|  | **DreamBox Learning**<br>dreambox.com | Individualized, adaptive game-based math resource that keeps students coming back for more. Available online or through an app. Check the website for pricing information. |

WEBSITES

**Table 12.12: Math Resources**

| | | |
|---|---|---|
| | **Explain Everything**<br>explaineverything.com | This app uses text, video, pictures, and voice to help students present a variety of possible creations. The company offers educational pricing. |
| | **IXL Math**<br>ixl.com/math | This site features adaptive individualized math through gameplay, including data and graphing problems. It gives students immediate feedback and covers many skills, despite its emphasis on drills. Levels range from prekindergarten to Grade 8. Educational pricing is available. |
| | **Starfall**<br>starfall.com | This free website has a few clever activities for early literacy and math exploration, but you can purchase a membership for a full range of activities. |
| | **XtraMath**<br>xtramath.org | A free site for practicing math facts. It tracks student progress, it's easy to pick what you want your students to work on, and students can use it independently. |
| | **A Maths Dictionary for Kids**<br>tiny.cc/hfhl3y | A free animated, interactive, online math dictionary for students that explains over 630 common mathematical terms and math words in simple language with definitions, examples, activities, practice, and calculators. |
| | **Math Salamanders**<br>tinyurl.com/yau2yd7c | Here, you will find a range of printable multiplication problems to practice multiplication and times tables skills to solve real life fourth-grader problems. |
| | **Geoboard**<br>tinyurl.com/kzyxjv7 | This free app is the digital recreation of a geoboard. It is simple to use, and the geometry activities are open ended and endless. |

**Swipea Tangram Puzzles for Kids**
tinyurl.com/nsnoazj

This is a digital version of tangrams where students can manipulate, flip, and rotate shapes to create different pictures. App is free. Full upgrade is available for a fee.

**Math Playground, Thinking Blocks**
tinyurl.com/3c6eoa

This free website has manipulatives with blocks so you can model, solve word problems, and practice with fractions. Thinking Blocks is also available as a free app.

**SoftSchools**
softschools.com

This is one of several sites that offer free games covering all math topics at each grade level. However, it has ads, is not able to track a student's success rate, and is not generally self-adaptive to the students' skill levels.

**IXL Math**
ixl.com/math

This site features adaptive individualized math through gameplay, including data and graphing problems. It gives students immediate feedback and covers many skills, despite its emphasis on drills. Levels range from prekindergarten to Grade 8. Class pricing is available on the website.

**Create A Graph**
tinyurl.com/yoedjn

Create bar, line, area, pie, and XY graphs with this free website. This tool is easy to use, and you can print, save, or email your completed graphs.

**Miro**
realtimeboard.com/ education

With Miro for Education, teachers can invite students to collaborate with the whole class in real time. Create as many boards as you need. Teachers must sign in and invite students. Educational account is free. Upgrade is available for a price.

**FASTT Math**
bit.ly/1nmvNe6

This program really helps students visualize how charts and graphs compare, and it's extremely easy to use. The program includes ready-made activities in all subject areas, including rubrics and sample graphs. District purchasing and volume CDs are available. Contact a representative through the website for specific prices.

**Table 12.12: Math Resources**

| GAMES | | |
|---|---|---|
|  | **Math Blaster HyperBlast**<br>mathblaster.com | The classic game many teachers used when they were students, now updated. Pricing available on the website. |
|  | **PrimaryGames**<br>tinyurl.com/72ojhan | offer math games covering all math topics at each grade level. However, these sites have ads, are not able to track students success rates, and are not generally self-adaptive to the students skill level. |
|  | **Coolmath Games**<br>coolmathgames.com | |
| | **SoftSchools**<br>softschools.com | |
| | **Sheppard Software**<br>tinyurl.com/ccrxoa | |

| VIDEOS | | |
|---|---|---|
|  | **BrainPOP**<br>brainpop.com | This website has been around for a long time. It offers educational videos on multiple math topics, in a fun, cartoon format. Prices vary based on the subscription you choose. |
|  | **SchoolTube**<br>schooltube.com | This is educators' best free source for a video-sharing community where students can watch or post math videos. |

# Literacy Lessons

Cross-curriculum planning is encouraged with CCSS by using ELA standards in history, science, and technical subjects. Getting through all of the standards you need in fourth grade is very difficult in the time given. The key to planning with the standards is to teach multiple standards in one lesson, when you can. We hope the following sample lessons for fourth grade will inspire you to become an effective technology lesson planner.

## Immigration

As coaches, we teamed up with our former colleagues who taught fourth grade and designed a literacy unit on immigration. This is what they were covering in social studies, and the teachers wanted to integrate the social studies topic with literacy, writing, and technology, thus covering a myriad of standards. Using a variety of informational as well as fictional text, students read about immigration over the centuries: the hardships and obstacles immigrants faced, their contributions, and the impact they made. Students also compared and contrasted immigrants from the past with those of today. To show knowledge, students chose from several writing prompts. Sample prompts include the following.

> **Narrative:** After reading multiple informational pieces and some historical fiction, create an imaginative narrative that describes an immigrant's journey and experience in the United States.
>
> **Info/Explain:** Write a piece that informs and explains the different tests that immigrants underwent to enter the United States.
>
> **Info/Explain:** Write a piece that informs and explains the effects of immigrants on the United States. What contributions did immigrants make to the United States? How is your present-day life affected by the "things" immigrants brought with them?
>
> **Opinion:** Write an opinion piece that explains which island you would rather come through, Ellis Island or Angel Island, and why.

Using tools such as **Cybersleuth (cybersleuth-kids.com)** or Safe Search Kids **(safe-searchkids.com),** students can search for information they need to complete the assignment (making sure they stop to consult reference materials for definitions or pronunciations of words they do not know). This easily satisfies **W.4.8.** As we mentioned earlier, instructing students on how to take notes and then having them take notes on information gathered will be very beneficial in helping them to write their rough drafts and eventually their projects.

There are so many wonderful ways students can present their writing using technology. It is also important to mention that this project can definitely be differentiated for your classroom. Consider using Trading Cards, where students can write short text on cards and add pictures. Options requiring a little more text are Evernote, PowerPoint, Google Docs, or Classroom. Students present key ideas from their research and import pictures to illustrate their points. More in-depth ways for students to present what they have learned include iMovie, iMovie Trailer, Prezi, Wixie, and Pixie. Backgrounds and music can be added. Pictures can be scanned or imported to enhance their writing.

This interesting and in-depth activity satisfies many standards, including **RI.4.7, RL.4.7,** and **W.4.2a.** Students may need some guidance and support from adults to produce, publish, and share their writing projects; thus this activity also satisfies

**W.4.6.** Depending on which tool the students choose to use for producing their work, both **SL.4.2** and **SL.4.5** may also be satisfied, as well as **L4.4c.**

ISTE STUDENT STANDARDS

Students will use these ISTE Standards in this lesson:

- **Empowered Learner** by understanding fundamental concepts of technology operations, demonstrating the ability to choose, use, and troubleshoot current technologies.

- **Digital Citizen** by acting and modeling technology ways that are safe, legal, and ethical.

- **Knowledge Constructor** by employing research, evaluating and building knowledge using digital resources.

- **Creative Communicator** with their presentations choosing the appropriate platform and publishing and presenting customized content.

## Animal Adaptations

This next lesson about how animals adapt to their habitats, characteristics of animals, and animal survival nicely integrates literacy and science. We adapted it with our former fourth-grade teachers after learning about it from a coach at a neighboring school. This particular lesson can be differentiated very easily.

Once again, using a tool mentioned earlier, such as Cybersleuth or Kids Safe Search (or your own favorites), students search for information (making sure they stop to consult reference materials for definition or pronunciation of words they do not know). This easily satisfies **W.4.8.** As we mentioned earlier, instructing students on how to take notes and then having them take notes on information gathered is very beneficial.

Using Comic Life, students make a dictionary entry for an animal. Using a favorite presentation tool, such as Google Classroom, Keynote, iMovie, or PowerPoint, all dictionary entries can be combined and then shared through the classroom ebook shelf, Microsoft PowerPoint, Google Docs, CAST UDL Book Builder, and so on.

Alternatively, students can display their information by making presentations about their animal's habitat, characteristics, and survival. You may want to make a guide for your students, outlining what information must be included. For example: What kind of habitat, characteristics, and survival did you research? What animals or plants can be found in your habitat? What problems did the topic you researched have? Using your favorite presentation tool (i.e., Keynote, Evernote, PowerPoint, Google Slides or Classroom, iMovie, iMovie trailer, Wixie, or Pixie), students make a slideshow displaying the information they learned. Student drawings can be scanned and uploaded to their presentations. Pictures from the internet (with adult supervision, of course) can also be imported and placed in the presentation to illustrate the information presented. Students can also record facts, a narrative, or music to accompany their slideshow.

Students may also like to make a brochure to display the information they learned about their habitat, animal characteristics, and animal survival. Once again, you may want to make a guide for your students outlining what information must be included. The teachers we worked with created a template using any of the online brochure templates, which also included the headings listed for each section. Students also had the option to use word-processing software, such as Office or Pages. The brochure can be two sided and printed as such. Students found and uploaded pictures to go with each section. Use a reader like **i-nigma Reader (tiny.cc/vxdf3y)** or **QR Code Generator (qr-code-generator.com).** QR codes are also added to include more information in each section. Parents loved this display in the hallway! It kept them busy reading and using their QR readers.

Many standards are satisfied with this very engaging lesson, including **RI.4.7, RL.4.7,** and **W.4.2a.** Students may need some guidance and support from adults to produce, publish, and share their projects; thus, this activity also satisfies **W.4.6.** Depending on which tool the students choose to use for producing their work, both **SL.4.2** and **SL.4.5** may also be satisfied, as well as **L.4.4.**

### ISTE STUDENT STANDARDS

Students will use these ISTE Standards in this lesson:

- **Empowered Learner** by understanding fundamental concepts of technology operations, demonstrating the ability to choose, use, and troubleshoot current technologies.

- **Digital Citizen** by acting and modeling technology ways that are safe, legal, and ethical.

- **Knowledge Constructor** by employing research, evaluating and building knowledge using digital resources.

- **Creative Communicator** with their presentations choosing the appropriate platform and publishing and presenting customized content.

## Fun with Idioms

A fourth-grade standard is to "Demonstrate understanding of figurative language, word relationships, and nuances in word meanings **(L.4.5)**." In this project, students will be asked to illustrate and translate the meaning of phrases such as: "She took second period by storm," "Today's homework is going to be a piece of cake," or "Roll up your sleeves and put your noses to the grindstone. It's time to get cracking!"

Begin by reading and discussing with your class a variety of idiom storybooks. Some examples include:

- *Parts* (#1) by Tedd Arnold
- *More Parts* (#2) by Tedd Arnold
- *Even More Parts* (#3) by Tedd Arnold
- *A Chocolate Mousse for Dinner* by Fred Gwynne
- *The King Who Reigned* by Fred Gwynne
- *Fowl Play* by Travis Nichols

- *Butterflies in My Stomach and Other School Hazards* by Serge Bloch

- *Stink and the Super-Galactic Jawbreaker* by Megan McDonald

- *The World Is Your Oyster* by Tamara James

- *In A Pickle: And Other Funny Idioms* by Marvin Terban

- *Catch My Breath* by Paul Briggs

- *You're Pulling My Leg!: 400 Human-Body Sayings from Head to Toe* by Pat Street

- *There's A Frog in My Throat: 400 Animal Sayings a Little Bird Told Me* by Loren Leedy

There are also several resources you may find interesting and want to have on hand:

- *I'm Not Hanging Noodles on Your Ears and Other Intriguing Idioms from Around the World* by Jag Bhalla

- *101 American English Idioms: Understanding and Speaking English Like an American* by Harry Collis

- *Essential American Idioms* by Richard Spears

- *Scholastic Dictionary of Idioms* by Marvin Terban

- *Speak English Like an American* by Amy Gillett

- *Say It Better in English: Useful Phrases for Everyday Life* by Marianna Pascal

There are many more online idiom sites. As you read the idiom books to your class, ask students to describe what they hear. Next, share the illustrations and have another discussion. You can also video students making these idioms as a class. For example, record students cracking an egg for the idiom "It's time to get cracking." Then record them "Buckling down and getting to work," and so on. You may even wish to use **Puppet Pals (tinyurl.com/btxmr9b)** or **ChatterPix Kids (tinyurl. com/ycdwnpca)** to create idiom pages as a class, so students get a better idea of what idioms are as well as what you are looking for in a final project. This step satisfies **RI.4.7** interpreting information presented orally and visually, as well as explaining how the text and illustrations contribute to an understanding of the text in which they appear.

Introduce the word *idiom* to your students as well as its definition. Idioms are colorful and convey a lot of information in a small number of words. Idioms are more often used in speech than in writing, probably because you may need to be familiar with the background of a speaker to decode the meaning of the words. In fact, you can often recognize a word or phrase as an idiom because the literal meaning doesn't make sense.

You might want to explore the etymology of the Greek *idí ma,* which means *peculiarity.* The idea is that these phrases are "one of a kind" or have meanings different from the literal translations.

The English language includes over 15,000 idioms, but idioms are not unique to English; they are found in almost every language. For example, the English idiom "a bull in a china shop" is similar to the German *ein Elefant in einem Porzellangeschäft* (an elephant in a china shop). The English idiom "make a mountain out of a molehill" is similar to the French *la montagne accouche d'une souris* (the mountain gives birth to a mouse).

But similar combinations of words in different languages can also have very different meanings. For example, "to be long in the tooth" means to be old or out of date in English. But in French, *avoir les dent longues* (to have long teeth) means to be ambitious.

If your class or school includes students and teachers who speak languages other than English, ask them to share idioms they know in these languages! Students can continue this conversation at home and by asking parents or other relatives who speak a different language what idioms they know in their native languages. Share with the class!

Divide your class into pairs or small teams. Each group needs to agree on the final product. You may wish to brainstorm possible products as a class. Encourage students to come up with their own ideas. Some may include:

- Digital storybooks similar to the ones you read. You could use **PBS Kids Writer's Contest (wtvp.org/writers-contest), Tikatok (tikatok.com),** or **Lulu (lulu.com).**

- Digital posters (which will be printed out) to illustrate idioms. You could use **Canva (canva.com)** or **Adobe Spark (tiny.cc/qkpl3y)**

- A digitally illustrated idiom dictionary. Students could use **KidPix (kidpix.com), Wixie (wixie.com), Pixie (tech4learning.com/pixie),** or **Smilebox (smilebox.com).**

- Schoolhouse-Rock-style animated shorts. Students can try **iMovie (apple.com/los/imovie), Animoto (animoto.com),** or **Wideo (wideo.co).**

Have students explore the idiom resources listed above to understand how the guides are laid out. Encourage students to use online dictionaries and thesauruses to help them understand meanings of any words with which they are unfamiliar. Talk with students as they work to illustrate their idiomatic language. Encourage them to add more details and create more complete and specific illustrations.

Allow students to share their final projects. Having these projects available throughout the year for students to leisurely look through is very beneficial. Uploading and sharing with parents through your webpage or another sharing method is also something to consider.

In addition to **RI.4.7** and **W.4.2a, W.4.8,** and **W.4.6** are also satisfied with this lesson. Speaking and listening skills **SL.4.2** and **SL.4.5** are also addressed. When students consult the resource materials you have available for idioms (print or digitally), they are satisfying **L.4.4c.**

## ISTE STUDENT STANDARDS

Students will use these ISTE Standards in this lesson:

- **Empowered Learner** by understanding fundamental concepts of technology operations, demonstrating the ability to choose, use, and troubleshoot current technologies.

- **Digital Citizen** by acting and modeling technology ways that are safe, legal, and ethical.

- **Knowledge Constructor** by employing research, evaluating and building knowledge using digital resources.

- **Creative Communicator** with their presentations choosing the appropriate platform, and publishing and presenting customized content.

# Social Studies and Science Lessons

The following sample lessons address CCSS ELA standards based on national standards in social studies and science.

## Social Studies Review

Fourth-grade teachers we previously worked with decided to try something new. The teachers worked with the reading specialist and the technology coach to devise a plan for students to demonstrate their learning in social studies. After studying regions of the United States all year, students picked a region they wanted to visit and then researched that region. Teachers made a template with Google Docs, which students then made a copy of and renamed using their name and chosen region.

Next, students chose two separate resources on the same topic (region) and entered the title/author on the research page. Taking notes in a three-column format (provided for students on the Google Docs), students researched the following big ideas: geography, resources, tourism, climate, and any other interesting facts they found. At least two supporting details were required for each source. Next, students were asked to turn their research into an opinion piece designed to convince others that their region was a great place to visit. Once this work was done, students created an advertisement showing others why they should visit the region. Students were provided with several examples of advertisements and reflected on things they noticed in them. Next, students were given four choices, using four different tools, from which they could choose to make their advertisement.

Following are the options.

**Choice 1:** Sometimes you might see advertisements in magazines, on city buses, or flyers hanging around town. Comic Life is an excellent app that allows you to use headings, text, speech bubbles, and insert fascinating photos.

**Choice 2:** Wixie is a tool you've probably used before and are most comfortable with. This allows you to take images, drawings, or clipart and narrate with a voice recording to make a slideshow. You cannot use video with this tool.

**Choice 3:** Many advertisements these days come in the form of websites. Google Sites allows you to create your very own website where you can add as many pages as you want to promote your region. This gives you more flexibility with adding more information, pictures, videos, and links to other websites.

**Choice 4:** iMovie Trailers are a great way to include real images and a short amount of text. They are captivating and allow you to keep the advertisement short and sweet. On the other hand, you may want to create a new project as an iMovie so you can also narrate with your own voice. The choice is yours!

This intriguing activity satisfies many standards, including **RI.4.7** and **W.4.2a.** Students will need some guidance and support from adults to produce, publish, and share their advertisements; thus, this activity also satisfies **W.4.6.** Also, standard **W.4.8** will be met. Depending on which tool the students select, both **SL.4.2** and **SL.4.5** may also be satisfied.

### ISTE STUDENT STANDARDS

Students will use these ISTE Standards in this lesson:

- **Empowered Learner** by understanding fundamental concepts of technology operations, demonstrating the ability to choose, use, and troubleshoot current technologies.

- **Digital Citizen** by acting and modeling technology ways that are safe, legal, and ethical.

- **Knowledge Constructor** by employing research, evaluating and building knowledge using digital resources.

- **Creative Communicator** with their presentations choosing the appropriate platform and publishing and presenting customized content.

## Mapping Activities

Another engaging lesson teaches students about mapping. Using latitude and longitude as the learning targets, students use a research outline to find the latitude and longitude for an assigned continent. Students need to find information such as where a continent is located (hemisphere, coordinates, etc.). Then, as a group, students choose three or four different landforms that can be found on their continent. Next, they find the coordinates of each landform and provide information about it. Finally, students choose one of the landforms they want to visit as a group.

They explain why they would like to visit their location and what they would do while there. After finding their information, students make slides using Wixie, outlining and illustrating all of their information. One of the slides is a coordinate graph grid where students place their continent, coordinating latitude and longitude. Students take turns narrating their pages. Finally, presentations are turned into ebooks to be shared with the class through ebook shelf. This lesson plan addresses standards **RL.4.7** and **SL.4.5.** When students orally narrate their Wixie projects, **W.4.2a** is also satisfied with this lesson.

### ISTE STUDENT STANDARDS

Students will use these ISTE Standards in this lesson:

- **Empowered Learner** by understanding fundamental concepts of technology operations, demonstrating the ability to choose, use, and troubleshoot current technologies.

- **Digital Citizen** by acting and modeling technology ways that are safe, legal, and ethical.

- **Knowledge Constructor** by employing research, evaluating and building knowledge using digital resources.

- **Creative Communicator** with their presentations choosing the appropriate platform and publishing and presenting customized content.

# Math Lessons

The following two lesson ideas satisfy the **MP5** standard as well as several other ELA standards.

## Explain Your Work

Our colleagues who taught fourth grade were concerned about how their students might show and explain math standard **4.OA.A**: "use the four operations with whole numbers to solve problems." Teachers needed an innovative way for students to clearly analyze, synthesize, and explain what steps they took to solve a problem and identify which strategies they used to find their answers, including math vocabulary, in their explanations. Using a screen-casting app, such as **Show Me**

**(tiny.cc/w8ql3y)** or **Explain Everything (explaineverything.com)**, students can work on a problem, create a video (recording of their explanation) for solving the problem, and point to or write on their tablets as they present to the class. This lesson addresses the **MP5** standard. Even though students are not creating stories or poems, they are creating explanations, and they must be able to explain using the appropriate math vocabulary for this lesson. Therefore, this activity also satisfies **SL.4.5.** Also satisfied is **W.4.6,** as students are using the Explain Everything app to produce and publish their mathematical thinking, reasoning, and problem solving for this task.

## ISTE STUDENT STANDARDS

Students will use these ISTE Standards in this lesson:

- **Empowered Learner** by understanding fundamental concepts of technology operations, demonstrating the ability to choose, use, and troubleshoot current technologies.

- **Digital Citizen** by acting and modeling technology ways that are safe, legal, and ethical.

- **Knowledge Constructor** by employing research, evaluating and building knowledge using digital resources.

- **Innovative Designer** students use a variety of technologies within a process to identify and solve problems by creating new, useful, or imaginative solutions.

- **Computational Thinker** students develop and use strategies for understanding and solving problems in ways that use technology to develop and test solutions.

- **Creative Communicator** students use their presentations choosing the appropriate platform and publishing and presenting customized content.

## California Trip

This next lesson is very popular with fourth-grade students and teachers across the country. There are many versions on the internet, as well as ways to differentiate and extend this lesson. Search the web with the phrase "California Here We Come" to see alternative versions and extensions to this lesson.

This lesson is perfect after teaching graphing and map reading, and when you begin the fourth-grade social studies unit on states and capitals. Students work in teams to travel across the United States. Each team of students will decide which East Coast capital in which they will begin the race, discuss which way they think will be the fastest, and analyze why they have made that decision. They should make sure to keep track of their decisions and rationale using any of your favorite programs, such as Wixie, Keynote, or Microsoft Word.

First, the team designs a chart or table to record the mileage from capital to capital. This can be done in a table or spreadsheet. Using MapQuest, they begin the trip.

Teams travel west and must stop at the capital for each state they drive through. The route they choose is up to them, but they must record all miles traveled, as well as plot their routes onto a blank U.S. map that has been uploaded and shared with each team. Students need to be able to draw on the map, so importing it into your favorite drawing program (Wixie, Microsoft Draw, etc.) is beneficial. The team reaching Sacramento, California, with the fewest number of miles traveled wins!

Upon reaching Sacramento, each team totals the number of miles traveled. The students' next task is to determine how much money would be needed to buy gas for the trip (using the average of 23 miles per gallon of gas at the current price found online). Students will resolve the problem using 60 miles-per-hour average speed and nine traveling hours per day. This will give them the number of days it would have taken to make the trip. Then students can calculate the number of days needed if they traveled only 7 hours a day averaging 60 miles per hour.

Teams also decide how much money was spent on food if breakfast cost $4.50 each, lunch cost $5.25, and supper cost $7.35. Then teams need to determine how much money was spent for each night in a hotel. Students present their findings to the class and discuss what they discovered along the way.

Teams should be sure to cite all resources. Some potentially helpful resources include the following.

- **Blank map of U.S. (tinyurl.com/obcmptm):** There are many free sites available to choose the kind of blank United States map you would like to use. This map has the capitals marked.

- **MapQuest (mapquest.com):** This free site will help students find the shortest route from one point to another. They type in the addresses of their starting and ending points. They also have the capability of finding alternate routes by moving the route marker. This site does have ads.

- **Hotels (hotels.com):** This free site will help students find the cheapest hotel for any city they decide to stop in for the night. Students type in the city and state or point of interest location. Students can choose the type of hotel they want. This site does have ads.

- **Gas Prices (gasbuddy.com):** This free site will help students find the price of gas for any state in the United States. Simply enter the starting and ending points to generate a list of gas stations and prices. This site does have ads.

This lesson addresses the **MP5** standard. Even though students are not creating stories or poems, they are taking notes, gathering relevant information from digital sources, citing sources, categorizing information, and creating explanations and justifications for travel across the country. They must also explain using the appropriate math vocabulary for this lesson. Therefore, this activity satisfies **SL.4.5** and **W.4.8.** Also satisfied is **W.4.6,** as students must find a way to produce and publish their mathematical thinking, reasoning, and problem solving for this task. When students present to the class, **W.4.7** and **SL.4.2** are satisfied, as they need to interpret and paraphrase the information they are presenting orally and explain how the information being presented contributes to the understanding and justification that their team should finish first (especially so all other teams agree with their thinking and rationalizations).

## ISTE STUDENT STANDARDS

Students will use these ISTE Standards in this lesson:

- **Empowered Learner** by understanding fundamental concepts of technology operations, demonstrating the ability to choose, use, and troubleshoot current technologies.

- **Digital Citizen**  by acting and modeling technology ways that are safe, legal, and ethical.

- **Knowledge Constructor** by employing research, evaluating and building knowledge using digital resources.

- **Innovative Designer** students use a variety of technologies within a process to identify and solve problems by creating new, useful, or imaginative solutions.

- **Computational Thinker** students develop and use strategies for understanding and solving problems in ways that use technology to develop and test solutions.

- **Creative Communicator** students use their presentations choosing the appropriate platform and publishing and presenting customized content.

- **Global Collaborator** students use collaborative technologies to work with peers to examine solutions to a problem from multiple viewpoints.

## Multiplication Problem-Solving Flip Books

Students in elementary school learn multiplication. This is a lesson and activity that can be adapted for any grade learning and/or practicing multiplication. Students will make a multiplication flipbook of strategies to use throughout the year to strengthen their multiplication fluency and problem-solving skills.

Using your Smart Board or **Miro (realtimeboard.com),** display A Maths Dictionary for Kids **(tinyurl.com/38vkvrs).** Start by looking up and discussing *multiplication*. Next, do the same with other multiplication words: *multiplicand, multiplier,* and *product.* Discuss how these words are important to what the students will be learning. Standard L.4.4c is satisfied by using the online dictionary and encouraging your students to use this practice whenever they are unsure of a word's meaning.

Remind your students that, although they have already learned multiplication, it is important to continue strengthening their fluency, and to remember and recall multiplication strategies, so they can apply them to multiplication problem-solving skills.

**BrainPOP (brainpop.com/math)** has several multiplication videos and warm-up activities. Start this lesson by watching these videos and working through some of the activities. Afterward, discuss with your students the strategies they use for multiplication.

In small groups, have students use **Simplenote (simplenote.com), Evernote (evernote.com),** or **Penzu (penzu.com)** to generate a list of strategies they use when doing multiplication. Have them include examples of each strategy. Groups can share their strategies, keeping a list on your Smart Board. Some strategies may include:

- Show the problem in an array (a set that shows equal groups in rows and columns)

- Show the problem in a grid

- Write the problem and use skip counting

- Write the problem and use repeated addition

- Estimation and mental math

- Using factors

- Breaking up the numbers

After each team has shared, ask them to discuss which method is easiest for them to use. Can students think of a situation when they might use each method?

Using ReadWriteThink's **Interactive Flipbook (tinyurl.com/yd7y6r7),** give each student five-to-ten problems they must use to illustrate, solve, and explain all of the multiplication strategies you earlier listed. This activity can be differentiated to make sure all students understand the multiplication strategies. There are many sites where you can locate multiplication story problems. Try **Math Salamanders (tinyurl.com/yau2yd7c), ScootPad (scootpad.com), IXL Math (ixl.com/math),** or **Math-Aids.com (tinyurl.com/y92o9ozl).**

Throughout my elementary school adventures in extended math, we utilized technology to help our learning. However, I specifically remember utilizing the internet for the entirety of a project. The goal of the project was to travel across the United States as cheaply as possible. We had to evaluate food costs, hotel accommodations, and the route we took to minimize the expenses. We utilized MapQuest, along with hotel booking sites, to collect information on costs. I remember having fun researching and planning, along with maximizing every dollar. These projects first introduced me to resources that would later become even more popular as the internet grew in size. **—Joshua Christensen, student**

When students finish their flipbooks, have them present their strategies and problem-lem solving to the class or in small groups. Finished flipbooks should be saved to students' digital portfolios: **Edmodo (edmodo.com), eBackpack (ebackpack.com), Evernote (evernote.com), or LiveBinders (livebinders.com),** to name a few. Throughout the year, use the sites listed above, or your favorites, to have students practice their multiplication problem-solving skills. Encourage students to work toward solving more difficult problems, or write their own.

As mentioned above **L.4.4c** is satisfied (when using online dictionaries) as well as **MP5.** Other standards satisfied include **RI.4.7** when interpreting information and explaining how what they learned contributes to their understanding. **W.4.8** and **W.4.2a,** when students take notes and use their notes to introduce a topic clearly and group related information in sections to aid comprehension. Also satisfied is **W.4.6** when using technology to produce and publish writing, **SL.4.2** by having students present and explain their flipbooks aloud to the class and answering questions about key details. Students should also request clarification if something in their presentation is not understood. Have students rework their presentations if there are parts that need clarification. Also satisfied is **SL.4.5,** as students explain their problems, strategies, and illustrations from their flipbooks.

ISTE STUDENT STANDARDS

Students will use these ISTE Standards in this lesson:

- **Empowered Learner** by understanding fundamental concepts of technology operations, demonstrating the ability to choose, use, and troubleshoot current technologies.

- **Digital Citizen** by acting and modeling technology ways that are safe, legal, and ethical.

- **Knowledge Constructor** by employing research, evaluating and building knowledge using digital resources.

- **Innovative Designer** students use a variety of technologies within a process to identify and solve problems by creating new, useful, or imaginative solutions.

- **Computational Thinker** students develop and use strategies for understanding and solving problems in ways that use technology to develop and test solutions.

- **Creative Communicator** students use their presentations choosing the appropriate platform and publishing and presenting customized content.

# A Final Note

As students progress through the grades, they establish their baseline of proficiency in technology. This will definitely enhance their experiences with technology in the upper grades, as well as satisfy the CCSS performance standards at the K–5 levels. We hope that you find the resources and lesson ideas presented in this chapter useful and that they are easy to adapt to your class.

You will find more resources on our website **(tinyurl.com/y9dfltpr),** which may be helpful as you look to differentiate your instruction. Visit our online site for updated information about this book. To learn more about meeting technology standards found within the CCSS in other grades, look for our additional title in this series.

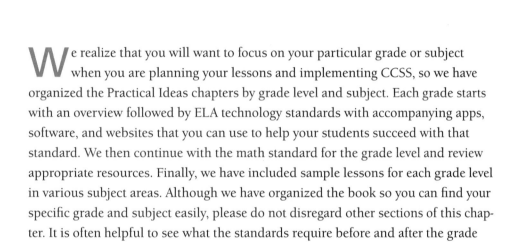

# CHAPTER

# 13 Practical Ideas for Fifth Grade

We realize that you will want to focus on your particular grade or subject when you are planning your lessons and implementing CCSS, so we have organized the Practical Ideas chapters by grade level and subject. Each grade starts with an overview followed by ELA technology standards with accompanying apps, software, and websites that you can use to help your students succeed with that standard. We then continue with the math standard for the grade level and review appropriate resources. Finally, we have included sample lessons for each grade level in various subject areas. Although we have organized the book so you can find your specific grade and subject easily, please do not disregard other sections of this chapter. It is often helpful to see what the standards require before and after the grade you teach. To see grades other than K–5, look for our additional title in this series covering 6–12, as it provides information to help you differentiate for students at all levels of your class.

Fifth-graders are expected to use technology to enhance their literacy skills. The emphasis here is to find information that is needed quickly and to efficiently take notes and document sources. They will need to take this information and publish their writing in a variety of ways, using tools such as digital dictionaries and thesauruses. Reading texts is also emphasized. Finally, students must be quite proficient keyboardists by fifth grade. Technology should also be used to practice math skills, because students will need to use digital math tools available through software programs, apps, or websites. In this chapter, we list all fifth-grade CCR standards that require teaching and learning with technology. We also offer ideas and suggestions on which technologies to use and how to teach with them.

# Reading Resources

**Microsoft PowerPoint (office.com)** is often the presentation tool of choice—even with students—when using technology to produce and publish writing in a collaborative way. While this is a great program, other presentation tools are just as useful. Apple offers **Keynote (apple.com/mac/keynote)** as part of its software package; its features are similar to PowerPoint's. Another program that has emerged is **Google Slides (google.com/slides/about)**. It is aimed toward business presentations, but it is free and web-based. Google Slides makes it easy to share a project that multiple users can work on at once, which makes it an especially good program to use when interacting and collaborating remotely. Students can also add audio recordings to their slides as well as visual displays such as pictures and short video clips. Having students create and present multimedia presentations allows the class to analyze how visual and multimedia elements of the presentation contribute to the meaning, tone, or beauty of a text.

# Reading Information

## RL.5.7 • READING LITERATURE

> Analyze how visual and **multimedia** elements contribute to the meaning, tone, or beauty of a text (e.g., graphic novel, **multimedia presentation** of fiction, folktale, myth, poem).

The CCSS for reading are designed to ensure that students gain adequate exposure to a range of texts and tasks. Rigor is also infused through the requirement that students read increasingly complex texts through the grades and make connections between text and visual or oral presentations.

### Slideshow Software and Websites

There are many ways that students can make visual and/or oral presentations from a piece of fiction, a folktale, myth, or poem. Using programs that allow students to illustrate as well as type improves the visual presentation of the text. **Table 13.1** shares examples of these programs.

All of these programs allow students to type in text and create their own illustrations. Students can pick backgrounds from templates or import pictures; presentations are put in a slideshow format or they can be printed as storybooks. Some programs even allow you to save presentations as ebooks. Smilebox and Movavi allow you to make decorative slideshows.

**Table 13.1: Slideshow Software and Websites**

**Kid Pix**
kidpix.com

This software is not free, but students can use it to publish collaborative writing that uses pictures and text. A new version called Kid Pix 3D features more animation. For an alternative, try Tux Paint (**tuxpaint.org**). It is a free online download that is also for primary students and has similar features.

**Wixie**
wixie.com

This software for purchase uses multimedia, pictures, sound, video, and text to create presentations and stories stored in the cloud for mobile access. The apps are free, but there are online versions with more features available with educational pricing.

**Pixie**
tech4learning.com/pixie

**Smilebox**
smilebox.com

A free program linked to the website to create slideshows, invitations, greetings, collages, scrapbooks and photo albums right on your computer. Don't miss applying for the free Teacher's Toolbox!

**Movavi**
movavi.com

Make movies using your photos and videos or create slideshows, video blogs, or screen-capture tutorials. It's easy to enhance, edit, and tell your story, and it's a lot of fun! Check the website for educational pricing.

## Animation Apps

The resources in **Table 13.2** are not easy to use with stories in paragraph form. However, you can use your voice to speak the text, and photos can be used to illustrate in an animated format. These apps allow students to create shorter, animated versions of their stories.

**Table 13.2: Animation Resources**

| APPS | | |
|---|---|---|
| | **Puppet Pals**<br>tinyurl.com/btxmr9b | This app allows students to create a puppet production using familiar characters to tell or retell a story. It is free, but see the website for add-on pricing. |
| | **iFunFace**<br>ifunface.com | Students can create a read-aloud to show how the main idea and details flow by using a photo and audio recording to create an animation. It helps students visualize how to support details that branch off from the main ideas and how they flow together. The app is free but can be upgraded for a price. |
| | **Blabberize**<br>blabberize.com | Students can speak the text and use photos to illustrate in an animated format. Free. |
| | **Voki**<br>voki.com | Students speak the text and use photos to illustrate in an animated format. It is free, but there are ads. |
| | **Fotobabble**<br>fotobabble.com | Students speak the text and use photos to illustrate. Free. |

## RI.5.7 • READING INFORMATION

Draw on information from multiple print or **digital sources**, demonstrating the ability to locate an answer to a question quickly or to solve a problem efficiently.

Fifth-grade students need to understand that, although they can find information on any topic on the internet, finding the information that they need in a timely manner is not always easy. Learning which tool to use is important, as is understanding which sources are credible. Students can post a question on the search engine and sift through all of the sites, first reading the title of the link and, if it is appropriate, the short summary. If, after glancing through the webpage, they find it is not a site they are looking for (not the right information, or not a credible source), they can click the back button and try again. Sometimes knowing exactly which site to use is helpful. For example, if they are looking for a definition, they should use an online dictionary such as **Merriam-Webster (merriam-webster.com).** A news site such as **Time for Kids (timeforkids.com)** can be used to find an answer

**Table 13.3: Reading Information Resources**

| | | |
|---|---|---|
| | **WatchKnowLearn** watchknowlearn.org | The site has free educational videos that allow you access to everything from frog dissection simulations to earthquake destruction. It organizes content by age range and provides reviews. |
| | **NeoK12** neok12.com | There are many science experiments, simulations, and videos on all sorts of topics on this website, and they are guaranteed to be kid safe. As an added bonus, it is free. |
| | **EarthCam** earthcam.com | This interesting site allows you to view live video from many different places around the world (e.g., Times Square or Wrigley Field). |
| | **iTunesU** tinyurl.com/lbjbarh | As stated on their website, "Choose from more than 750,000 free lectures, videos, books, and other resources on thousands of subjects from Algebra to Zoology." Access it free through iTunes. A free app is also available. |
| | **BrainPOP** brainpop.com | This website has been around for a long time. It offers educational videos on multiple educational topics in a fun, cartoon format. Price varies based on the subscription you choose. |
| | **Open Culture** tinyurl.com/d8ww8ez | This free website is a one-stop shop for audiobooks, ebooks, and movies. There are even courses for teachers! They do not create the media. They just compile it so we can find it more easily. |

WEBSITES

to a current event, as could a local newspaper site like **Newsela (newsela.com)**. **Weather.com** is a good place to see the weather forecast for different areas. Bookmarking sites that are popular for fifth grade can help students find answers to their questions quickly.

Doing an activity, such as giving the class a sample question/problem and researching the answer together, is a good way to get students started. They can be given additional sample questions with answers to be found with a partner. Those answers can be reviewed with the class as a group to discuss how everyone found them.

# Writing Resources

Producing and publishing writing is not limited to slideshow presentations, although **Google Docs (google.com/docs/about)** is great because it makes collaboration easy, especially from home. There are many websites out there that allow you to publish student writing. Blogging websites such as **Edmodo (edmodo.com)**, **Kidblog (kidblog.org)**, and **Google Classroom (tiny.cc/6kxm3y)** are other places to share student writing in a safe, protected environment where they can interact and collaborate with others. These sites (see **Table 13.4**) allow teachers to set themselves up as administrators and add students to different groups. All student writing is kept secure in these groups.

# Writing

The CCR standards for K-5 writing offer a focus for instruction each year to ensure that students gain adequate mastery of a range of skills and applications. Each year in their writing, students should demonstrate increasing sophistication in all aspects of language use, from vocabulary and syntax to the development and organization of ideas, and they should address increasingly demanding content and sources. Students advancing through the grades are expected to meet each year's grade-specific standards and retain or further develop skills and understandings mastered in preceding grades.

## W.5.2. • WRITING

Introduce a topic clearly, provide a general observation and focus, and group related information logically; include formatting (e.g., headings), illustrations, and **multimedia** when useful to aiding comprehension.

## W.5.6 • WRITING

With some guidance and support from adults, **use technology, including the internet**, to produce and publish writing as well as to interact and collaborate with others; demonstrate sufficient command of **keyboarding skills** to type a minimum of two pages in a single sitting.

### Publishing Websites

You can give assignments asking for short answers where everyone can respond in a blog format, or you can ask students to write longer assignments on their own that they work on as a document, then submit privately to you or post on a website to share. Using blogging programs, as well as other publishing tools, aids in comprehension, which satisfies standards **W.5.2** and **W.5.6**.

There are also websites that ask students to submit their work for possible publication. **Table 13.4** contains publishing websites to explore.

Table 13.4: Publishing Resources

 **Scholastic Publishing**
tinyurl.com/plwnn6f

This free website allows teachers to submit student writing for publication.

 **PBS Kids Writer's Contest**
wtvp.org/writers-contest

 **Lulu**
lulu.com

 **Lulu Junior**
lulujr.com

This free site asks for student writing and serves as a nice incentive to get students to do their best. Lulu (**lulu.com**) and Lulu Junior (**lulujr.com**) These sites allow you to create real books and publish them online. Parents can purchase the books as keepsakes. The site is free to use, but a fee is required to publish.

WEBSITES

| | | |
|---|---|---|
| | **TikaTok**<br>tikatok.com | This is another site that allows students to write, create, and publish stories as ebooks or hardcover books. Classroom pricing is available on the website. TikaTok StorySpark is the app version, also available for purchase. |
| | **CAST UDL Book Builder**<br>bookbuilder.cast.org | This free site lets you publish your ebook and see what others have published. |
| | **Poetry Idea Engine**<br>tinyurl.com/2cuowf | The Scholastic site allows students to use templates to make different forms of poetry—another great way technology gets kids writing. Better still, it is free! |
| | **Storyboard That**<br>storyboardthat.com | Create your own free storyboards and animate them! You can create two storyboards per week for free, or upgrade anytime for more advanced features. |
| | **Storyboarder**<br>tiny.cc/ufzm3y | This website makes it easy to visualize a story as fast you can draw stick figures. Quickly draw to test if a story idea works. Create and show animatics to others. Express your story idea without making a movie. |
| | **eBackpack**<br>ebackpack.com | This learning management system features built-in assignments, note-taking, student portfolios, lesson planning, standard alignments, parent communication, and much more. An app is available. Look for education pricing. |
| | **LiveBinders**<br>livebinders.com | Opens up new possibilities for collaboration, organization, and sharing. All your lessons and content are in one place, including documents, links, presentations, student portfolios, and more. Educational pricing available. |
| | **PosterMyWall**<br>tinyurl.com/yd76ko2j | Create an online scrapbook using this scrapbook template. |

**Canva**
canva.com

Create a free digital poster to display student work in a fun and unique way. There are many templates with photos, graphics, and fonts to use in this drag-and-drop, easy-to-use website. It is free to teachers and students.

**Mixbook Photo Company**
tinyurl.com/y7wxucqg

Scrapbook template site where you can also purchase the books you make.

## Keyboarding

By fifth grade, students are expected to be able to type two pages in one sitting. Paying for a good typing program is worth the expense. Quality programs track student progress and levels of proficiency, teach necessary skills, and allow students access from home. If you can't buy a program, there are many free sites that offer instruction and games. **Table 11.4** in Chapter 11 shares keyboarding resources that are free as well as programs for purchase:

Some districts send students to computer labs to practice keyboarding. Other schools fit it in where they can in the classroom, and still others have students practice and learn at home. The best way is to combine all three approaches. Students benefit from formal keyboarding instruction, but they need to practice both in the classroom and at home. When students work at the computers in your classroom, remind them to practice good technique, such as sitting up straight, keeping hands in home row, holding wrists slightly curved, and moving the fingers instead of the hands.

# Writing Research

## W.5.8 • WRITING RESEARCH

Recall relevant information from experiences or gather relevant information from print and **digital sources**; summarize or paraphrase information in notes and finished work, and provide a list of sources.

By the time students are in fifth grade, they should be able to search the internet independently to gather information on a given topic. Your class will need guidance, of course, so lessons on internet searching are critical, as well as lessons on media literacy. Media literacy is especially crucial because students need to be able to critique a website before using it—anyone can put up a webpage. As stated by the **W.5.8** standard, students will also need to be able to take notes from these sites and summarize or paraphrase information as well as provide a list of bibliographic sources. We discuss these techniques in the following paragraphs.

Although students are sufficiently net-savvy these days, even fifth-graders still need assistance with the basics of searching. Various search engines work differently, and each will give you different information. Your students need to know how to use multiple engines.

Smart searching will help avoid a lot of wasted time. Teaching students to analyze search results will definitely help them find better information and to think more critically about any information they find on the internet. Following are some basic guidelines for students.

- Choose your search terms carefully. Be precise about what you are looking for, but use phrases and not full sentences.

- Adding more words can narrow a search. Use Boolean searches to narrow your topic with quotation marks. There's a big difference between "gopher" and "habitats of gophers in North America."

- Use synonyms! If students can't find what they're looking for, have them try keywords that mean the same thing or are related.

- Type "site:". Typing the word *site:* (with the colon) after your keyword and before a URL will tell many search engines to search within a specific website.

- Add a minus sign. Adding a minus sign (a hyphen) immediately before any word, with no space in between, indicates that you don't want that word to appear in your search results. For example, "Saturn-cars" will give you information about the planet, not the automobile.

## Kid-Friendly Search Engines

Browsing safe content is the most important reason for using search engines made specifically for kids. You may need to allow students to begin using adult search engines (e.g., Google, Firefox, or Ask) in fifth grade to find more information than what is available in search engines for kids. However, it is always best for students to use kid-safe search engines when possible.

There is no guarantee that every search will be kid-safe. However, the search engines listed in **Table 13.5**, as well as those found in previous chapters, are your best bet.

Table 13.5: Search Engines

| | | |
|---|---|---|
| | **Kidtopia**<br>kidtopia.info | A web search site designed for kids by librarians with kid-friendly results. This site is free and intended for Grades 2–5. |
| | **Ask Kids**<br>ask.com | This is a free, filtered search engine for Grades K–6. |

## Mind-Mapping Apps and Websites

Modeling is essential when teaching students how to glean information from a website. An interactive whiteboard is a perfect tool for modeling lessons. Don't have an interactive whiteboard? Use Miro (**realtimeboard.com**). It's a free website that allows you to turn an ordinary whiteboard into an interactive, virtual one. All you need is a computer and a projector! Using the many tools an interactive whiteboard and its software have to offer will really help teach your students how to navigate through information posted on the internet. Using note-taking tools when gathering information will help your students organize their research.

Mind-mapping tools will help your students organize their research when gathering information. **Inspiration (inspiration.com)** is a wonderful software program that has been used for mind-mapping for many years. There are also free sites out there that you can use, such as those listed in **Table 13.6**.

**Table 13.6: Mind-Mapping Tools**

| | | |
|---|---|---|
| | **Bubbl.us**<br>bubbl.us | This is a free (with limited use) mind-mapping website for Grades K–12. It can be shared by multiple students at a time and comes with an app. See the website for more options and to purchase a package. |
| | **MindMeister**<br>tiny.cc/826i3y | This is a free, basic, mind-mapping website for Grades 2–12. Upgrades are available and have a free trial period. See the website for details. |
| | **FreeMind**<br>tinyurl.com/5qrd5 | This is a free mind-mapping tool using Java for Grades 2–12. Options for a basic or maximum install are available. |
| | **Classtools**<br>classtools.net | Create graphs and charts, and use many other helpful classroom tools, such as a QR code generator or timeline, with this free website. |
| | **Character Attribute Map**<br>tinyurl.com/yal8okq6 | Print out character maps to help students organize their characters. |

## Note-Taking Apps and Websites

Tried-and-true methods for taking notes, paraphrasing, and summarizing information from books can still be used to gather information and take notes on websites. Teaching students to use data sheets, note cards, and Know, What, Learn (KWL) techniques still works. However, technology can make this easier. The **Kentucky Virtual Library (kyvl.org)** is an excellent resource for some of these techniques. Apps such as **Evernote (evernote.com)** are a great way to take notes, as well as using a word-processing program. Evernote allows you to import a worksheet, document, or picture, including a snapshot of a webpage. Students can then annotate their information using tools common to interactive whiteboard software. Whiteboards let them highlight words, cut and paste, and add sticky notes. The sticky notes are especially useful to summarize or paraphrase students' notes. This website also allows students to use voice recognition. They can then send their annotated sheet to someone else (including the teacher).

Of course, students can also use word-processing programs such as **Microsoft Office (office.com), Pages (apple.com/mac/pages),** or **Google Docs (google.com/docs/about)**. Some teachers make digital templates with spaces to summarize or paraphrase to help students find specific information and organize their notes.

**Table 13.9: Note-Taking Tools**

| | | |
|---|---|---|
| QR | **Evernote** evernote.com | This free app allows you to import a worksheet, document, or picture, including a snapshot of a webpage, and then annotate it using tools common to interactive whiteboard software. You can highlight words, cut and paste, and add sticky notes. It also allows you to use voice recognition. You can then send your annotated sheet to someone else. |
| QR | **Simplenote** simplenote.com | This note-taking app is simple to use and has the ability to share notes with others, search notes, track changes, and use it over multiple platforms. All notes are backed up online and synchronized. Best of all, it's free. |
| QR | **Penzu** penzu.com | This writing website can be accessed with their app, and it's free! Created for journaling and diaries, it is very customizable and secure. It even allows you to set up reminders. |
| QR | **Double Entry Journals** tiny.cc/tf1m3y | Students can digitally record their responses to what they have read and work collaboratively in this journal website. |
| QR | **Storyboard Graphic Organizer** tinyurl.com/y8gm4o3e | Printable storyboard graphic organizer to help students stay organized when writing. |

Fifth-graders will also need to provide a list of sources. Of course, making your own template for sources and having students fill it in using a word-processing program works. However, there are websites, such as **EasyBib (easybib.com),** that students can use to generate citations in MLA, APA, and Chicago formats easily. EasyBib is a free website and app for grades 5–12. Simply copy and paste or scan a book's barcode to generate its citation. Students can also cite a list of sources on their own by including URL, publisher or author, topic/title, and date a website was published. If the publication date is not available, they should note the date retrieved from the internet.

## Media Literacy Resources

Your class also needs to be aware that links come up in searches that may have strings attached—not to the research topic, but to advertisers. This should be a part of your media literacy lesson. Students can waste a lot of time if they aren't focused on specific research. Students need to know that anyone can put up a website, and they need to know how to tell whether a website is credible. Determining a website's domain register is the first step in evaluating credibility: a .com (company), .gov (government site), or .org (nonprofit organization, such as a school). Then students need to identify the author of the site (this will usually be posted at the beginning or the end), who they are affiliated with, or what is the author's background or expertise on the topic. Advertisers abound, and students will need to be careful what they click.

The class needs to be taught what to do if they go to an inappropriate site (e.g., clicking the back button immediately and letting a teacher know) The website Media Smarts **(mediasmarts.ca)** is a good site to use. Teachers must register first. Then permission is granted to use the licensed material. It provides online media literacy lessons complete with quizzes.

# Speaking and Listening

## SL.5.2. • SPEAKING AND LISTENING

Summarize a written text read aloud or information presented in **diverse media and formats**, including visually, quantitatively, and orally.

## SL.5.5 • SPEAKING AND LISTENING

Include **multimedia** components (e.g., graphics, sound) and **visual displays** in presentations when appropriate to enhance the development of main ideas or themes.

There are many diverse media formats that read aloud to students. Audiobooks on CD or ebooks are good sources. Sites such as **Follett (tiny.cc/cb2q3y)** and **Tumble-Books (tumblebooks.com)** must be purchased, but allow access to multiple ebook collections that include both fiction and nonfiction. You can also check out ebooks at your local library or purchase them from booksellers such as Amazon or Barnes & Noble (especially if you have e-readers). There are some free ebooks available. **Project Gutenberg (gutenberg.org), FreeReadFeed (freereadfeed.com),** and **Free-BookSifter (freebooksifter.com)** are possibilities. There are adult titles on these sites, too, so choose carefully. Of course, pay sites offer a much better selection. Using ebooks or a website with your interactive whiteboard (or free whiteboard site) allows interaction when modeling or for student engagement. Informational text works especially well with this standard, but fictional pieces can also be used.

### Interactive Apps and Websites

After listening to text read aloud, students can use different media formats to summarize what they heard. Because students are summarizing and keeping it short, they can use fun, interactive apps like **iFunFace (ifunface.com)** or **PuppetPals (tinyurl.com/btxmr9b)** to create fun, interactive projects. **Table 12.3** in Chapter 12 lists some of the tools available.

## Mind-Mapping Software, Websites, and Apps

Working with the teacher or on their own, students need to understand the development of the main idea or themes of a text. Mind-mapping programs are a good place to organize text with main ideas. Students can visually see how the supporting details branch off from the main idea and how they flow together. Tools like SimpleMind (tinyurl.com/y7ualejm) allow you to create custom mind maps with photos and videos. For more examples of these programs, see **Table 12.12** in Chapter 12.

## Animation Apps and Websites

Students can include multimedia components and visual displays when presenting their main ideas or themes by taking their mind maps and creating a read-aloud using an app that allows them to have a character recite their presentation. Of course, PowerPoint, Google Slides, or Keynote also work well when presenting and including multimedia components and visual displays. **Table 13.10** shares some apps and websites that use visuals as well as sound.

**Table 13.10: Note-Taking Tools**

| | | |
|---|---|---|
| **APPS & WEBSITES** | **Blabberize** blabberize.com | Students can speak the text and use photos to illustrate in an animated format. Free. |
| | **Voki** voki.com | Students speak the text and use photos to illustrate in an animated format. It is free, but there are ads. |
| | **Fotobabble** fotobabble.com | Students speak the text and use photos to illustrate. Free. |
| | **ChatterPix Kids** tinyurl.com/ptwhtxd | This free app is for creating and sharing videos. Make anything talk! Just take a picture, draw a line to make a mouth, and record your voice. Great for reading aloud and poetry sharing. |

**Prezi**
prezi.com

You can sign up for a free educational account, and your students can create and share presentations online. Prezi has mind-mapping, zoom, and motion, and it can import files. Presentations can be downloaded. A Prezi viewer app is available.

 **Wixie**
wixie.com

This software for purchase uses multimedia, pictures, sound video, and text to create presentations and stories stored in the cloud for mobile access. The apps are free, but there are online versions with more features available with educational pricing.

 **Pixie**
tech4learning.com/pixie

# Language Resources

**Merriam-Webster (merriam-webster.com)** is still the most commonly used digital dictionary and thesaurus. They also offer a kid-friendly version of this dictionary called **Word Central (wordcentral.com).** This resource includes the pronunciation of the word as well as its definition. The original Merriam-Webster site has this as well, and includes multiple definitions. **Kids.Wordsmyth (kids.wordsmyth.net/we)** and **Wordsmyth (wordsmyth.net)** are good fifth-grade options. The kids' version includes pronunciation (as does the adults' version) and shows how words are used as parts of speech with examples and pictures where applicable. **Little Explorers (tinyurl.com/2swjc)** is another good option for a dictionary and thesauruses, and it includes a glossary maker. You can sign up for an ad-free version, which will not cost your school. **Thesaurus.com (thesaurus.com)** is a great thesaurus site. While digital dictionaries and thesauruses are not updated as often as encyclopedias, they are still very convenient to use and are kept current. Bookmark these sites or add them to your website for easy access. The more students use them, the more comfortable they will become. Offer lessons and activities to learn and practice the necessary skills with an online dictionary, just as you would when using hard-copy dictionaries, glossaries, and thesauruses.

# Language

## L.5.4c • LANGUAGE

Consult reference materials (e.g., dictionaries, glossaries, thesauruses), both print and **digital**, to find the pronunciation and determine or clarify the precise meaning of key words and phrases.

A lesson plan idea when using electronic dictionaries is to look up difficult vocabulary words in a piece of informational text. You could give students a website (preferably on a standards topic from literacy or science) and ask them to write down all of the words they don't know. After using an electronic dictionary to find the definitions to these words, have students reread the text. With luck, they will come away with a better understanding of the content they read.

The **Trading Cards (tinyurl.com/8lqftek)** app or website is a great way to document vocabulary words by adding definitions, a picture, and recordings of pronunciations. You can also use Trading Cards by doing an activity with an online thesaurus. Simply give students a word on a trading card and ask them to make as many trading cards as they can of synonyms and antonyms of that word. They can print these out and trade them with others or make them into a digital book. The Explain Everything app is also easy to use to import a picture, record your voice, and make a digital presentation.

# Math Resources

There are two main sets of benchmarks for Common Core math standards: processes and practices. First, you have the math targets, written similarly to ELA (Counting and Cardinality; Operations and Algebraic Thinking; Number and Operation in Base Ten; Measurement and Data; and Geometry). While you work with fifth-grade students on mathematical processes such as base ten and fractions, you need to teach them how to apply the SMP (which include problem solving and precision) to those processes. One practice, the only one that includes technology, is mathematical practice 5: "Use appropriate tools strategically."

## MP5 • MATH

Use appropriate **tools** strategically.

Following is the explanation CCSS provides for **MP5**. As this is the standard explanation for Grades K–12, it does include references to higher grades.

> Mathematically proficient students consider the available tools when solving a mathematical problem. These tools might include pencil and paper, concrete models, a ruler, a protractor, **a calculator, a spreadsheet, a computer algebra system, a statistical package, or dynamic geometry software.** Proficient students are sufficiently familiar with tools appropriate for their grade or course to make sound decisions about when each of these tools might be helpful, recognizing both the insight to be gained and their limitations. For example, mathematically proficient high school students analyze graphs of functions and solutions generated using a graphing calculator. They detect possible errors by strategically using estimation and other mathematical knowledge. When making mathematical models, they know that technology can enable them to visualize the results of varying assumptions, explore consequences, and compare predictions with data. Mathematically proficient students at various grade levels are able to identify relevant external mathematical resources, such as **digital content located on a website,** and use them to pose or solve problems. They are able to use **technological tools** to explore and deepen their understanding of concepts.

Because this description does not give examples for all grades, we have provided a list of appropriate apps, websites, software, and lessons that will help translate this standard for fifth grade.

Currently, this is the only fifth-grade math standard that involves technology. Because using any kind of technology to have students practice math can grab their attention, help long-term learning, and make math fun, technology is a math tool that students should use as much as possible. Many math programs, websites, and apps allow students to explore and deepen their understanding of math concepts. The best of them have students learning in creative ways and are not merely electronic worksheets. They automatically adapt to the students' skill levels and tell

**Table 13.11: Math Resources**

APPS

| | | |
|---|---|---|
|  | **ScootPad**<br>scootpad.com | This web-based math site is totally customizable for individual students. It adapts to the student and keeps the teacher in the loop with multiple reports. It is completely aligned to the CCSS. Pricing is available on the website. |
|  | **DreamBox Learning**<br>dreambox.com | Individualized, adaptive game-based math resource that keeps students coming back for more. Available online or as an app. Check the website for pricing information. |
|  | **IXL Math**<br>ixl.com/math | This site features adaptive, individualized math through gameplay, including data and graphing problems. It gives students immediate feedback and covers many skills, despite its emphasis on drills. Levels range from prekindergarten to Grade 8. Educational pricing is available. |
|  | **Starfall**<br>starfall.com | This free website has a few clever activities for early literacy and math exploration, but you can purchase a membership for a full range of activities. |
|  | **XtraMath**<br>xtramath.org | A free site for practicing math facts. It tracks student progress, it's easy to pick what you want students to work on, and it's easy for students to use independently. |
|  | **AdaptedMind**<br>tinyurl.com/997geeg | This free website provides good practice for all sorts of fifth-grade mathematical problems. |
|  | **Fun Brain, Shape Surveyor**<br>tinyurl.com/yczb2vh4 | Play math games and calculate the area and perimeter of shapes to receive pieces of a puzzle. Complete the puzzle and win. |

**Education.com**
tinyurl.com/y8bvf3ng

Alfalfa the turtle is always up for an adventure—especially when it involves math! In this sweet story, kids help Alfalfa find the area and perimeter of new, unfamiliar spaces she finds herself in by answering questions along the way. With the help of a grumpy chameleon named Harold, Alfalfa uses her number smarts to find her way back into the wild after she's caught.

 **TurtleDiary**
tinyurl.com/ybk79uka

Play a variety of math games, specifically involving area and perimeter, to help fifth-grade students with this standard.

 **Explain Everything**
explaineverything.com

This app uses text, video, pictures, and voice to help students present a variety of possible creations. The company offers educational pricing.

 **Swipea Tangram Puzzles for Kids**
tinyurl.com/nsnoazj

This is a digital version of tangrams where students can manipulate, flip, and rotate shapes to create different pictures. The app is free; a full upgrade is available for a fee.

 **The Geometer's Sketchpad**
keycurriculum.com

Students can manipulate dynamic models of fractions, number lines, and geometric patterns. Middle school students can build their readiness for algebra by exploring ratio and proportion, rate of change, and functional relationships through multiple representations. More advanced students can use Sketchpad Explorer to construct and transform geometric shapes and functions, from linear to trigonometric. Pricing for the software version is determined by number of computers used.

 **SoftSchools**
softschools.com

This is one of several sites that offer free games that cover all math topics at each grade level. However, it has ads, is not able to track a student's success rate, and is not generally self-adaptive to students' skill levels.

**Table 13.11: Math Resources**

| | | |
|---|---|---|
| | **IXL Math**<br>ixl.com/math | This site features adaptive individualized math through gameplay, including data and graphing problems. It gives students immediate feedback and covers many skills, despite its emphasis on drills. Levels range from prekindergarten to Grade 8. Educational pricing is available. |
| | **Create A Graph**<br>tinyurl.com/yoedjn | Create bar, line, area, pie, and XY graphs with this free website. It is easy to use, and you can print, save, or email your completed graphs. |
| | **Classtools**<br>classtools.net | Create graphs and charts and use many helpful classroom tools, such as a QR code generator or timeline, with this free website. |

you where students are in their learning and what they need to advance. Of course, these usually do not come free. We list many good math resources here. The free resources (many with ads) are often less interesting and not as well organized. They don't give you the feedback you need. It is up to you to decide what is best for your circumstances and budget.

## Graphing Software and Websites

As stated in the standard, "Mathematically proficient students consider the available tools when solving a mathematical problem. These tools might include a calculator, a spreadsheet, a computer algebra system, a statistical package, or dynamic geometry software. Proficient students are sufficiently familiar with tools appropriate for their grade or course to make sound decisions about when each of these tools might be helpful, recognizing both the insight to be gained and their limitations."

There are many sites that allow you to use math tools such as a graphing calculator. Another option is to use software that comes with your whiteboard. These have all sorts of built-in mathematical tools such as protractors, rulers, and grids. You can use your interactive whiteboard for many of these functions. Don't have an interactive whiteboard? Use **Miro (realtimeboard.com)**! It's a free website that allows you to turn an ordinary whiteboard into an interactive, virtual one. All you need is a computer and a projector! Following are some good programs and sites to use when graphing.

In fifth grade, students are also expected to use a protractor to measure angles. They can use the app protractor feature of the Toolkit app **(skypaw.com/apps)**, which includes a converter that can measure pairs of units. **Softpedia (softpedia. com)** allows you to download a protractor to use online. The site is free, but it has ads. Using your interactive whiteboard protractor tool also works well.

Many studies in recent years have shown how math games can increase student learning. In addition, a survey **(tinyurl.com/pqms3nj)** from the Games and Learning Publishing Council indicates that the use of digital games in the classroom is becoming more popular with teachers. According to the survey, 55% of teachers who responded have students play digital games in their classroom weekly (2014).

With this in mind, pick a math unit of study. You may wish to first research this math topic and find videos to show as an introduction. Videos from **BrainPOP (brainpop.com)**, **Khan Academy (khanacademy.org)**, and **School Tube (schooltube. com)** are only a few good sources. Please be advised that you should preview any video before showing it to the class. These activities are also a great resource for guided math stations or learning centers.

Problem-solving activities are also an effective way to differentiate if you happen to have some students who are moving through lessons faster than the rest of the class.

## Literacy Lessons

Cross-curriculum planning is encouraged with the CCSS by using ELA standards in history, science, and technical subjects. Getting through all of the standards you need in fifth grade is very difficult in the time given. The key to planning with the CCR standards is to teach multiple standards in one lesson, when you can. We hope the following list of sample lessons for fifth grade will inspire you to become an effective technology lesson planner.

## Summary Writing

Several fifth-grade colleagues have used the following activity when they want their students to show what they know for summary writing. Choose a nonfiction or current-event text for students to read. Our teachers like **Newsela (newsela.com).** You may also switch things around and have your students choose their own article for this activity. When students finish reading, they begin brainstorming for their summaries. You can use any form of brainstorming writing technique that suits you.

Using the iMovie Trailer app, students make a movie trailer for their nonfiction summaries, using pictures they find on the internet. Students must include titles, subtitles, and keywords to describe their article summaries. Students also select music to fit the summaries and import them into iMovie Trailer. As students read, they should be encouraged to look up and determine the meaning of unfamiliar words. When they do this, standard **L.5.4c** will be satisfied. Using iMovie Trailer, picking pictures to illustrate their summaries, and selecting the music will satisfy standard **RL.5.7,** as students are taking responsibility for establishing the meaning and tone of their iMovie Trailer summaries. Also satisfied with this activity are **W.5.2, W.5.6,** and **W.5.8.** Furthermore, **SL.5.2** and **SL.5.5** are satisfied, as students are using iMovie Trailer as their multimedia presentation.

### ISTE STUDENT STANDARDS

Students will use these ISTE Standards in this lesson:

- **Empowered Learner** by understanding fundamental concepts of technology operations, demonstrating the ability to choose, use, and troubleshoot current technologies.

- **Digital Citizen** by acting and modeling technology ways that are safe, legal, and ethical.

- **Knowledge Constructor** by employing research, evaluating and building knowledge using digital resources.

- **Creative Communicator** with their presentations choosing the appropriate platform and publishing and presenting customized content.

## Culminating Raps

Even though this next lesson focused on literacy, it works with any subject or topic. This fifth-grade class was studying metaphors and similes. As a culminating project, students wrote raps and performed them for the class.

- First, the class brainstormed fifteen to twenty key words for metaphors and similes, with the teacher writing and displaying the words on the whiteboard.

- Working in pairs or groups of no more than four, students discussed and picked eight to ten of the keywords they felt were interesting and would work in their raps.

- Next, students took each keyword and found eight to ten rhymes.

- Then, using the keywords and rhymes, students wrote sentences. These sentences all related to the topic of metaphors and similes. Each keyword had at least four sentences, and students could choose their rhyming pattern (for example, AA BB or AB AB).

- Once students completed their writing, they found the beat for their rap. Using **GarageBand (tiny.cc/dx8n3y )** or any other app or software that promotes music creation, students rehearsed their raps (slowing the beat down or speeding it up if need be).

- Students could perform their raps "live" in front of the class. But most chose to record themselves with their tablets (one tablet videoing the performance and the other playing their rap on GarageBand). Students then streamed the audio or video to show the class.

This engaging project satisfies a myriad of fifth-grade standards, specifically **L.5.4c,** as students should be encouraged to be creative to find words that rhyme with their keywords and therefore should consult reference materials, such as dictionaries and thesauruses. **SL.5.2** and **SL.5.5** are also satisfied, as students are summarizing what they learned about metaphors and similes and presenting using diverse media, including sound. All of the fifth-grade writing standards are also satisfied with this lesson—**W.5.2, W.5.8,** and especially **W.5.6,** as students will need guidance and support from adults as they work with others to produce their rap.

ISTE STUDENT STANDARDS

Students will use these ISTE Standards in this lesson:

- **Empowered Learner** by understanding fundamental concepts of technology operations, demonstrating the ability to choose, use, and troubleshoot current technologies.

- **Digital Citizen** by acting and modeling technology ways that are safe, legal, and ethical.

- **Knowledge Constructor** by employing research, evaluating and building knowledge using digital resources.

- **Creative Communicator** with their presentations choosing the appropriate platform and publishing and presenting customized content.

- **Global Collaborator** students use collaborative technologies to work with peers to examine solutions to a problem from multiple viewpoints.

## Digital Character Scrapbook

When we read novels, authors provide details about the main character through descriptive sentences, events that directly involve the character, and what other characters think and say about the main character. To show what they know about the main character in a novel they are reading, students will create a digital scrapbook for the main character.

Scrapbooking has been a popular pastime for quite some time. Students demonstrate their knowledge in this format, which provides them with an opportunity to express individuality and creativity in an authentic, popular format. You might want to assess their knowledge of scrapbooking prior to introducing the activity. Invite community members who scrapbook to share their projects and techniques. Perhaps parents or other teachers who scrapbook can come and speak to the class.

Share examples of traditional and digital scrapbooks with students. Here are a few resources you might consult on the subject:

BOOKS

- *Picture Yourself Creating Digital Scrapbooks* by Lori J. Davis

- *Characters, Emotion and Viewpoint: Techniques and Exercises for Crafting Dynamic Characters and Effective Viewpoints* by Nancy Kress

WEBSITES

- **Heritage Scrapbooks (tiny.cc/6rjn3y)**

- **Lewis Carroll Scrapbook Collection (tinyurl.com/4n27k)**

As a class, discuss differences between traditional and digital scrapbooks. Ask students to consider how images are composed as well as how text, narration, and sound effects are used. Discuss how multimedia elements change the impact of a scrapbook.

Next, students should choose a novel for their projects, or you may want to assign novels. Students should focus their attention on the main character of the story. Have students reread their story, taking notes in the form of a **double-entry journal (tiny.cc/tf1m3y),** or use **Simplenote (simplenote.com), Evernote (evernote.com),** or **Penzu (penzu.com)** for online note-taking. Students should pay particular attention to passages that describe the main character, events that the main character is directly involved in, and what other characters in the story say about the main character. To help students get an even deeper understanding of the character, you may wish to have them complete a **character attribute map (tinyurl.com/yal8okq6)** or other character graphic organizer. Any mind-mapping apps or websites will work as well, such as **Bubbl.us (bubbl.us), MindMeister (mindmeister.com), SimpleMind (tinyurl.com/y7ualejm),** or **Freemind (tinyurl.com/5qrd5).** Consider having students share their preliminary ideas for the scrapbook on a **storyboard graphic organizer (tinyurl.com/y8gm4o3e), Storyboard That (storyboardthat.com)** or **Storyboarder (tiny.cc/ufzm3y).**

This is a great time to check for understanding. The more students understand the actions, behavior, and events involving the main character, the easier it will be for them to create a scrapbook from the main character's point of view. Now is also a good time to share your expectations for their scrapbooks. Decide what students must include, allowing for a page or two for students to add what they think is important. Remind students to decorate each page with background, text, and pictures. Some ideas are:

- Page 1, Cover: This should include the character's name, the book title, author's name, and student's name.

- Page 2, Journal Entry #1: This is a summary from the main character's perspective.

- Page 3, Pictures and Photographs: Include images that reflect events important to the main character. Include a caption for each that explains why it was included.

- Page 4, Letters: One letter from the main character to a secondary character about a problem in the story. Also include a second letter from the secondary character with their likely response.

- Page 5, Souvenirs and Mementos: Include at least three objects that reflect events in the story or important aspects of the main character. Please include captions, explaining each object.

- Page 6, Journal Entry #2: This should be an entry from the main character's diary that reflects how the character has grown over time.

- Page 7, Glossary of Terms: Include any vocabulary your audience may need help understanding.

Once students have submitted their storyboards and you have approved their ideas, have them gather resources. They may wish to search the internet for how to age paper (for their letters or diary entries). Once students age their letters, they can take pictures and/or scan their entries into their presentations. Students will also need to decide what presentation tool to use for their scrapbooks. Some online scrapbook templates are listed below, or students can use **Wixie (wixie.com).**

- **Canva (tinyurl.com/mxvbw7y)**

- **PosterMyWall (tinyurl.com/yd76ko2j)**

- **Mixbook Photo Company (tinyurl.com/y7wxucqg)**

- **Smilebox (tinyurl.com/y7cej4ob)**

Encourage students to share their online scrapbooks. Audience members should be encouraged to ask clarifying questions. Students presenting must be able to answer questions quickly and efficiently. Post projects in students' digital portfolios as well as on your website for colleagues, parents, and other students to see.

This lesson satisfies a myriad of standards. **RL.5.7** is satisfied when students study examples of original and digital scrapbooks and discuss the differences. **W.5.2** and **W.5.6** are also satisfied. **W.5.8** is satisfied as students are gathering information from their text and digital resources, and **SL.5.2** and **SL.5.5** are satisfied when students summarize and present their projects to the class. Also, **L.5.4c** is addressed when students consult dictionaries and include glossaries in their projects.

## ISTE STUDENT STANDARDS

Students will use these ISTE Standards in this lesson:

- **Empowered Learner** by understanding fundamental concepts of technology operations, demonstrating the ability to choose, use, and troubleshoot current technologies.

- **Digital Citizen** by acting and modeling technology ways that are safe, legal, and ethical.

- **Knowledge Constructor** by employing research, evaluating and building knowledge using digital resources.

- **Creative Communicator** with their presentations choosing the appropriate platform and publishing and presenting customized content.

- **Global Collaborator** students use collaborative technologies to work with peers, parents, and members of the community to examine solutions to a problem from multiple viewpoints.

# Social Studies and Science Lessons

The following sample lessons address CCSS and ELA standards and teach content based on national standards in social studies and science.

## History of Slavery Activity

During social studies, fifth-grade students learn about the Civil War. As part of this unit, former fifth-grade colleagues of ours brought in a study of slavery and did an integrated lesson with literacy and art. The first step is to find interactive text, websites, videos, art, music, and so on, to share on your whiteboard. (BrainPOP has a multitude of movies, ideas, and activities on this topic.) After watching, listening, and discussing this period in our history, students work in pairs to find examples of songs, ballads, poems, and art in which they are interested. YouTube is a great source for songs, ballads, and spoken poems. As students search, they should be encouraged to look up and determine the meaning of unfamiliar words or phrases they encounter. When they do this, standard **L.5.4c** is satisfied. Next, students choose their favorite song, ballad, or poem to write alternate lyrics or verses that including any new vocabulary they learned. Teams may wish to write their rough draft using any document or presentation tool (PowerPoint, Keynote, etc.). Students will also make artwork (quilts, signs, drawings, etc.) to illustrate their song, ballad, or poem. This can be done using Google Draw, Microsoft Draw, or something similar. For students' final presentations, keeping in mind that they will be sharing with their classmates, students select which technology they will use to present their song/ballad/poem and artwork (iMovie Trailer, iMovie, Wixie, Explain Everything, GarageBand, etc.). Students present to the class by projecting their tablet onto the interactive whiteboard, or Miro. Students listen carefully to each presentation (taking notes using Evernote) and ask questions at the end. Students giving the presentation must be able to answer questions quickly and efficiently. Students research and understand the meaning, tone, and beauty of the songs, ballads, and poems of that time. This satisfies standards **RI.5.7, W.5.2, W.5.6,** and **W.5.8.** In addition, the presentation part of this activity satisfies **SL.5.2** and **SL.5.5.**

ISTE STUDENT STANDARDS

Students will use these ISTE Standards in this lesson:

- **Empowered Learner** by understanding fundamental concepts of technology operations, demonstrating the ability to choose, use, and troubleshoot current technologies.

- **Digital Citizen** by acting and modeling technology ways that are safe, legal, and ethical.

- **Knowledge Constructor** by employing research, evaluating and building knowledge using digital resources.

- **Creative Communicator** with their presentations choosing the appropriate platform and publishing and presenting customized content.

## Mystery Planets

Because fifth-graders across the country study the solar system, this activity coincides with a science lesson on astronomy or space. Create a planet riddle using the **Puppet Pals 2** app **(tiny.cc/aqln3y)** on a tablet. First, gather clues using BrainPOP and A Solar System Journey apps. Each student group provides clues for its "mystery" planet. Next, the group writes a "script" that includes the clues researched. For example: "My planet is the fifth planet from the Sun," or "This planet is the largest in the solar system. Who am I?" Next, students head to Puppet Pals 2 and create their riddles. When finished, students save their videos as "Mystery Planet" (with the appropriate group number). Upload the mystery planet videos to YouTube, and another fifth-grade class will try to solve the riddles. The "guest" teacher will have the answers, so your students shouldn't reveal the name of the planet in their videos! This engaging lesson satisfies **RI.5.5,** as students will get to know and use various text features to locate key facts or information in a text efficiently, specifically with their research. **RL.5.8** is also addressed by this activity. Working with and collaborating on their Puppet Pals 2 slideshows satisfies **W.5.6** and **SL.5.2.** Though students are not creating a story or poem, they are creating clues for riddles. Therefore, this activity also satisfies **SL.5.5.**

ISTE STUDENT STANDARDS

Students will use these ISTE Standards in this lesson:

- **Empowered Learner** by understanding fundamental concepts of technology operations, demonstrating the ability to choose, use, and troubleshoot current technologies.

- **Digital Citizen** by acting and modeling technology ways that are safe, legal, and ethical.

- **Knowledge Constructor** by employing research, evaluating and building knowledge using digital resources.

- **Creative Communicator** with their presentations choosing the appropriate platform and publishing and presenting customized content.

# Math Lessons

The following lesson samples satisfy standard **MP5** in addition to several ELA standards.

## Shape Geometry

Teacher friends of ours use this math activity for a unit on geometry, which involves students creating and comparing two-dimensional and three-dimensional shapes. They also list specific attributes of each shape in their comparison. Students can be paired or work in small groups while using the computer program Geometer's Sketchpad to create shapes from a teacher-made list. Students jot down attributes of each of the three-dimensional shapes, making sure they give proper number of sides, angles, and so on. Next, using the app Explain Everything, students create their two-dimensional shapes. Finally, students present their findings to the class by projecting their Geometer's Sketchpad and Explain Everything drawings. Students follow up with questions to the presenter, making sure they can distinguish between the two-dimensional and three-dimensional shapes presented. This intriguing and popular lesson addresses **MP5** by using digital tools to enhance mathematical learning. Though students are not creating stories or poems, they are creating explanations for their geometric shapes and must be able to explain them using the appropriate math attributes and other math vocabulary for this lesson. Therefore, this activity also satisfies **SL.5.5; W.5.6** is satisfied as well because students are using the app Explain Everything to produce and publish their mathematical thinking, reasoning, and problem solving for this task.

ISTE STUDENT STANDARDS

Students will use these ISTE Standards in this lesson:

- **Empowered Learner** by understanding fundamental concepts of technology operations, demonstrating the ability to choose, use, and troubleshoot current technologies.

- **Digital Citizen** by acting and modeling technology ways that are safe, legal, and ethical.

- **Knowledge Constructor** by employing research, evaluating and building knowledge using digital resources.

- **Innovative Designer** students use a variety of technologies within a process to identify and solve problems by creating new, useful, or imaginative solutions.

- **Computational Thinker** students develop and use strategies for understanding and solving problems in ways that use technology to develop and test solutions.

- **Creative Communicator** students use their presentations choosing the appropriate platform and publishing and presenting customized content.

## 3D Planets

The fifth-grade students in our state study the planets (addressing the NSTA Standards). This lesson combines our very successful science lesson with the applied math fifth-graders need to know, as well as a dose of reading, writing, and speaking. Students break into eight or nine small groups (one for each planet) to create a 3D model of the planets (we used a Styrofoam circle and added modeling clay to get the precise size) and a scale model of the solar system (lots of measurement and conversion). The groups create a scale model of their planet and where it fits into the solar system using the math standards **MP5**. Students also use their notes from videos they view, their internet research, trade books, and textbooks to create a presentation of their planet findings. Using iMovie Trailer, Prezi, Explain Everything, or any presentation app or program, students summarize their research, satisfying standard **RI.5.7**. Students draw on information from multiple print and digital sources, demonstrating the ability to locate an answer to a question quickly or to solve a problem efficiently. Also satisfied with this activity are **W.5.2**, **W.5.6**, and **W.5.8**. Furthermore, **SL.5.2** and **SL.5.5** are satisfied, as students are using digital media, such as iMovie, for their presentations.

## ISTE STUDENT STANDARDS

Students will use these ISTE Standards in this lesson:

- **Empowered Learner** by understanding fundamental concepts of technology operations, demonstrating the ability to choose, use, and troubleshoot current technologies.

- **Digital Citizen** by acting and modeling technology ways that are safe, legal, and ethical.

- **Knowledge Constructor** by employing research, evaluating and building knowledge using digital resources.

- **Innovative Designer** students use a variety of technologies within a process to identify and solve problems by creating new, useful, or imaginative solutions.

- **Computational Thinker** students develop and use strategies for understanding and solving problems in ways that use technology to develop and test solutions.

- **Creative Communicator** students use their presentations choosing the appropriate platform and publishing and presenting customized content.

- **Global Collaborator** students use collaborative technologies to work with peers to examine solutions to a problem from multiple viewpoints.

## Design Your Own Bedroom

This is a lesson we used in our classrooms. It can be adapted for use in Grades 2–4. In this lesson, students design their own bedroom. They will need to have a layout of their design, and then calculate how much paint they will need for the walls and ceiling. They will also have to decide how many floor tiles they will need. Lastly, they will need to take all of the information they gathered and put it together in a presentation.

Using your Smart Board or **Miro (realtimeboard.com),** display the task for the students. Consider making this task a **WebQuest (tiny.cc/j4mn3y),** so the students have all of the information in front of them. Also, display **A Maths Dictionary for Kids (tinyurl.com/38vkvrs).** Start by looking up and discussing *square footage.* Do the same with other words for which your students may need a refresher: *blueprints, width, length,* etc. Discuss how these words are important to what the students will be doing. Standard **L.5.4c** is satisfied by using the online dictionary and encouraging your students to use this practice whenever they are unsure of a word's meaning.

You may want to spend some time reviewing area and perimeter, having students practice finding each for a given shape. Some suggestions are:

- **Math Playground (mathplayground.com)**

- **Area and Perimeter (tinyurl.com/lrvmw64)**

- **Area Blocks (tinyurl.com/hg4hl5n)**

- **Fun Brain (tinyurl.com/yczb2vh4)**

- **Education.com (tinyurl.com/y8bvf3ng)**

- **TurtleDiary (tinyurl.com/ybk79uka)**

Students will also need to do some research online. It will be important for them to have a tablet or smartphone. If you decide to do a WebQuest, these links can be imbedded throughout. Also, have students use **Simplenote (simplenote.com), Evernote (evernote.com),** or **Penzu (penzu.com)** to take online notes and track data they find and want to use.

### OVERALL TASK

Your parents are building a new house and are in the blueprint stages. They have decided to let you design your own bedroom. You get to decide how big it will be, what color to paint the walls, and what type of tiles you want to cover the floor. You have three tasks to complete:

1. Design the size of your room. Your parents say it cannot be larger than 200 square feet.

2. Pick a paint color and figure out how much paint you will need to cover the walls and ceiling. Your parents say the ceiling must be a different color than the walls: white.

3. Decide what type of tiles you want for the floor. Calculate how many tiles you will need to cover the entire floor.

## TASK #1

Figure out the size of your new bedroom. Remember it cannot be larger than 200 square feet. Before you decide, you need to do some reading and research.

- **National Association of Home Builders (nahb.org)**

- **Houzz (tinyurl.com/y9zmjmvz)**

- **Credit Donkey (tinyurl.com/y9xxagqe)**

- **Answers.com (tinyurl.com/y7uvqf4q)**

Draw the design for your room using **Classroom Architect (classroom.4teachers. org)** or **RoomSketcher (roomsketcher.com)**. Remember, your floors have width and length. Your walls have width and height. Figure out your length and width and calculate the perimeter and area.

## TASK #2

Once the floor plan for your room has been calculated, pick a paint color. You will need to calculate how many cans of paint will be needed. Don't forget to keep track of your calculations using your note-taking apps Simplenote, Evernote, or Penzu. You can also use a spreadsheet such as **Microsoft Excel (tiny.cc/yknn3y)** or **Google Sheets (google.com/slides/about)** to keep track of your calculations. You will also need to let your parents know not only the color but the brand of paint you will be using. To do this you will need several resources:

- **Sherwin Williams Color Snap Visualizer (tinyurl.com/yajzlgbc)**

- **Home Depot Color Selector (paintcolor.homedepot.com)**

- **Valspar Paint Virtual Painter (tinyurl.com/yb4g5msl)**

To calculate the amount of paint you need, use these resources:

- **Benjamin Moore Paint Calculator (tinyurl.com/y8offvth)**

- **Glidden Paint Calculator (tinyurl.com/ycbot6be)**

- **Home Depot Paint Calculator (tinyurl.com/yakcrntz)**

**TASK #3**

Next, pick the tiles you wish to use. Make sure you check your tile size and calculate how many tiles you will need to cover your floor. You will need to convert inches to feet. There are several resources you will need for this task:

- You Tube Video, **Converting Inches to Feet (tinyurl.com/ybr5dnry)**

- **UnitConverters (tinyurl.com/yd5murtd)**

- **RapidTables (tinyurl.com/y89r934f)**

- **Lowe's Flooring (tinyurl.com/z2fbauh)**

- **Armstrong Flooring (tinyurl.com/ybl4uvkm)**

- **Flooring America (flooringamerica.com)**

Once you have finished your work, double-check it. Make sure you have all necessary components:

- Drawing of your room

- Length, width, and height of your room

- Area of floor and walls

- Amount and price of paint needed (store, color, and number of cans)

- Amount and price of tiles needed (store, style, and number of tiles needed)

When all work is completed, students will need to create a digital presentation to "show their parents" (the class). They can choose the application to present from PowerPoint, Keynote, Google Slides, or Prezi.

Or students can try **Powtoon (powtoon.com), Moovly (moovly.com), or Adobe Spark (tinyurl.com/yamq84lg).** All presentations or digital reports should include their room drawing, paint and tile data, and citations for any resources they used.

During presentations, allow time for the audience to look more deeply at the plans, including checking math data for accuracy.

All finished work should be saved to students' digital portfolios: **Edmodo (edmodo.com), eBackpack (ebackpack.com), Evernote (evernote.com),** or **LiveBinders (livebinders.com)** to name a few.

As mentioned earlier, **L.5.4c** is satisfied by this activity. Along with **MP5, SL.5.2** and **SL.5.5** are satisfied as students are sharing their work using technology. Also, standards **W.5.2a, W.5.6,** and **W.5.8** are covered because word processing and note-taking are used throughout this lesson. **RI.5.7** is also covered when they draw information from multiple digital sources to solve a problem efficiently.

## ISTE STUDENT STANDARDS

Students will use these ISTE Standards in this lesson:

- **Empowered Learner** by understanding fundamental concepts of technology operations, demonstrating the ability to choose, use, and troubleshoot current technologies.

- **Digital Citizen** by acting and modeling technology ways that are safe, legal, and ethical.

- **Knowledge Constructor** by employing research, evaluating and building knowledge using digital resources.

- **Innovative Designer** students use a variety of technologies within a process to identify and solve problems by creating new, useful, or imaginative solutions.

- **Computational Thinker** students develop and use strategies for understanding and solving problems in ways that use technology to develop and test solutions.

- **Creative Communicator** students use their presentations choosing the appropriate platform and publishing and presenting customized content.

M y daughter's math and reading skills have improved dramatically with the use of websites on the computer and apps on the iPad. Using technology not only allows her to learn how to type on the computer, use a mouse, and navigate an iPad—all skills she needs in this day and age – it has allowed her to get better at reading and math in a fun and creative way.
**—Gail Fischer Rhodes, parent**

# A Final Note

As students progress through the primary grades, they establish their baseline of proficiency in technology. This will definitely enhance their experiences with technology in the upper grades, as well as satisfy the CCSS performance standards at the K–5 levels. We hope that you find the resources and lesson ideas presented in this chapter useful and that they are easy to adapt to your class.

You will find more resources on our website **(tinyurl.com/y9dfltpr),** which may be helpful as you look to differentiate your instruction. Visit our site for updated information about this book. To learn more about meeting technology standards found within the CCSS in other grades, look for our additional title in this series.

# References

Bray, B. (1999, May 1). *Ten steps to effective technology staff development: Getting teachers on board.* Retrieved from edutopia.org/ten-steps-effective-technology-staff-development

Darling-Hammond, L., Hyler, M. E., & Gardner, M. (2017, June). Effective Teacher Professional Development. Palo Alto, CA: Learning Policy Institute. Page 12-13. Retrieved from https://www.teacherscholars.org/wp-content/uploads/2017/09/Effective_Teacher_Professional_Development_REPORT.pdf

DeWitt, P. (2013, July 7). Take a risk . . . Flip your parent communication! [Blog post]. Retrieved from blogs.edweek.org/edweek/finding_common_ground/2013/07/take_a_risk_flip_your_parent_communication.html

Devaney, L. (2016, May 6). Survey: Teachers now use twice as much gaming and video in the classroom. *eSchoolNews.* Retrieved from eschoolnews.com/2016/05/06/survey-teachers-now-use-twice-as-much-gaming-and-video-in-the-classroom/

Edutopia. (2007, November 5). What is successful technology integration? *Technology Integration Professional Development Guide.* Retrieved from edutopia.org/technology-integration-guide-description

Education Weekly. (Updated 2017.). Map: Tracking the Common Core State Standards. Retrieved from https://www.edweek.org/ew/section/multimedia/map-states-academic-standards-common-core-or.html?cmp=cpc-goog-ew-dynamic+ads&ccid=dynamic+ads&ccag=common+core+dynamic&cckw=&ccv=dynamic+ad&gclid=Cj0KCQjw1pblBRDSARIsACfUG13KQYIBOw-

HWbddp65eUNT2qvZczhTcn0Njb1ORuMM1G0AArW8CCsh0aApQTEALw_wcB

Games and Learning Publishing Council. (2014). Teachers surveyed on using digital games in class: A games and learning research report. Retrieved from http://www.gamesandlearning.org/2014/06/09/teachers-on-using-games-in-class

Gazzaley, A, & Rosen, L. (2016, September 16). The Distracted Mind: Ancient Brains in a High-Tech World. MIT Press.

Gerwitz, C. (2019, March 5). What Does Each State Require? *Education Week*. Retrieved from https://www.edweek.org/ew/section/multimedia/what-tests-does-each-state-require.html

Henderson. A., & Mapp, K. (2002). *A new wave of evidence: The impact of school, family, and community connections on student achievement*. Retrieved from sedl.org/connections/resources/evidence.pdf

LEAD Commission. (2012). Parents' and teachers' attitudes and opinions on technology in education [PDF]. Retrieved from leadcommission.org/sites/default/files/ LEAD Poll Deck.pdf

Meeuwse, K. (2013, April 11). Using iPads to transform teaching and learning [Blog post]. Retrieved from iteachwithipads.net/2013/04/11/using-iPads-to-transform-teaching-and-learning

National Governors Association Center for Best Practices, Council of Chief State School Officers. (2010). *Common core state standards*. Washington, DC.

New York University. (2007). *National symposium on the millennial student*. Retrieved from nyu.edu/frn/publications/millennial.student/Millennial.index.html

Partnership for 21st Century Skills. (2004). The partnership for 21st century skills— Framework for 21st century learning. Retrieved from p21.org/about-us/p21-framework

Sammons, L. (2009). *Guided math: a framework for mathematics instruction*. Huntington Beach: Shell Education.

Sammons, L. (2011, September 21). *Guided math: a framework for math instruction* [PowerPoint slides]. Retrieved from slideshare.net/ggierhart/guided-math-powerpointbytheauthorofguidedmath

Sparks, S. D. (2017, January 24). Common core revisions: What are states really changing? *Education Week (36)*. Retrieved October 5, 2018 from edweek.org/ew/articles/2017/01/25/clarifying-common-core.html

Strategic Learning Programs. (n.d.). Retrieved from iste.org/lead/professional-services/strategic-learning-programs

Sun, L. & Siklander, P. (2018). How to trigger students' interest in digital learning environments: A systematic literature review. Retrieved from https://www.researchgate.net/publication/326682783_How_to_trigger_students'_interest_in_digital_learning_environments_A_systematic_literature_review

Swanson, K. (2013, October 1). Five tips for explaining common core to parents. *THE Journal*. Retrieved from thejournal.com/2013/10/01/how-to-explain-common-core-to-parents.aspx

Szybinski, D. (2016). -Teaching a new generation of students. *NETWORK: A Journal of Faculty Development*. Retrieved from facultyresourcenetwork.org/publications/teaching-a-new-generation-of-students

United States Congress. (2010). Section 1015c. Chapter 28: Higher education resources and student assistance. *Title 20–Education*. Retrieved from gpo.gov/fdsys/pkg/USCODE-2010-title20/html/USCODE-2010-title20-chap28.htm

U.S. Department of Education, National Center for Education Statistics. (2018). Student Access to Digital Learning Resources Outside of the Classroom (NCES 2017-098) Retrieved from https://nces.ed.gov/pubs2017/2017098/index.asp

# Appendix A
# ISTE Standards

## ISTE Standards for Students

The ISTE Standards for Students emphasize the skills and qualities we want for students, enabling them to engage and thrive in a connected, digital world. The standards are designed for use by educators across the curriculum, with every age student, with a goal of cultivating these skills throughout a student's academic career. Both students and teachers will be responsible for achieving foundational technology skills to fully apply the standards. The reward, however, will be educators who skillfully mentor and inspire students to amplify learning with technology and challenge them to be agents of their own learning.

### 1. Empowered Learner

Students leverage technology to take an active role in choosing, achieving and demonstrating competency in their learning goals, informed by the learning sciences. Students:

    a.   articulate and set personal learning goals, develop strategies leveraging technology to achieve them and reflect on the learning process itself to improve learning outcomes.

    b.   build networks and customize their learning environments in ways that support the learning process.

    c.   use technology to seek feedback that informs and improves their practice and to demonstrate their learning in a variety of ways.

d.  understand the fundamental concepts of technology operations, demonstrate the ability to choose, use and troubleshoot current technologies and are able to transfer their knowledge to explore emerging technologies.

## 2. Digital Citizen

Students recognize the rights, responsibilities and opportunities of living, learning and working in an interconnected digital world, and they act and model in ways that are safe, legal and ethical. Students:

a.  cultivate and manage their digital identity and reputation and are aware of the permanence of their actions in the digital world.

b.  engage in positive, safe, legal and ethical behavior when using technology, including social interactions online or when using networked devices.

c.  demonstrate an understanding of and respect for the rights and obligations of using and sharing intellectual property.

d.  manage their personal data to maintain digital privacy and security and are aware of data-collection technology used to track their navigation online.

## 3. Knowledge Constructor

Students critically curate a variety of resources using digital tools to construct knowledge, produce creative artifacts and make meaningful learning experiences for themselves and others. Students:

a.  plan and employ effective research strategies to locate information and other resources for their intellectual or creative pursuits.

b.  evaluate the accuracy, perspective, credibility and relevance of information, media, data or other resources.

c.  curate information from digital resources using a variety of tools and methods to create collections of artifacts that demonstrate meaningful connections or conclusions.

d.  build knowledge by actively exploring real-world issues and problems, developing ideas and theories and pursuing answers and solutions.

## 4. Innovative Designer

Students use a variety of technologies within a design process to identify and solve problems by creating new, useful or imaginative solutions. Students:

    a.   know and use a deliberate design process for generating ideas, testing theories, creating innovative artifacts or solving authentic problems.

    b.   select and use digital tools to plan and manage a design process that considers design constraints and calculated risks.

    c.   develop, test and refine prototypes as part of a cyclical

design process.

    d.   exhibit a tolerance for ambiguity, perseverance and the capacity to work with open-ended problems.

## 5. Computational Thinker

Students develop and employ strategies for understanding and solving problems in ways that leverage the power of technological methods to develop and test solutions. Students:

    a.   formulate problem definitions suited for technology-assisted methods such as data analysis, abstract models and algorithmic thinking in exploring and finding solutions.

    b.   collect data or identify relevant data sets, use digital tools to analyze them, and represent data in various ways to facilitate problem-solving and decision-making.

    c.   break problems into component parts, extract key information, and develop descriptive models to understand complex systems or facilitate problem-solving.

    d.   understand how automation works and use algorithmic thinking to develop a sequence of steps to create and test automated solutions.

## 6. Creative Communicator

Students communicate clearly and express themselves creatively for a variety of purposes using the platforms, tools, styles, formats and digital media appropriate to their goals. Students:

    a.   choose the appropriate platforms and tools for meeting the desired objectives of their creation or communication.

    b.   create original works or responsibly repurpose or remix digital resources into new creations.

    c.   communicate complex ideas clearly and effectively by creating or using a variety of digital objects such as visualizations, models or simulations.

    d.   publish or present content that customizes the message and medium for their intended audiences.

## 7. Global Collaborator

Students use digital tools to broaden their perspectives and enrich their learning by collaborating with others and working effectively in teams locally and globally. Students:

    a.   use digital tools to connect with learners from a variety of backgrounds and cultures, engaging with them in ways that broaden mutual understanding and learning.

    b.   use collaborative technologies to work with others, including peers, experts or community members, to examine issues and problems from multiple viewpoints.

    c.   contribute constructively to project teams, assuming various roles and responsibilities to work effectively toward a common goal.

    d.   explore local and global issues and use collaborative technologies to work with others to investigate solutions.

# Index

**#**

21st Century Community Learning
Centers, 21
21st century learning, framework for, 47,
61
4C's, 61

**A**

accessibility, roadblocks to, 18
adoption (of CCSS), 2
animation apps and websites, 235
attention span, 8
audience of book, 4
audiobooks, 67, 91, 106, 136, 190, 221,
232

**B**

Baer, Edith, 77
Barrett, Judi, 78
books, creating, 177
Bureau of Education & Research (BER),
32–33
Burns, Marilyn, 166

**C**

Carle, Eric, 77
CCSS, criticism, 2
CCSS, misunderstandings, 14
standards vs. curriculum, 14
decreased test scores, 15
data collection and privacy, 15
CCSS, organization of, 36-44
CCSS standards by subject and grade, 40
CCSS standards assessment, 49-50
CCSS standards with technology, 45-57
Math, 56-57
ELA, 52-56
Writing, 51
Speaking and Listening, 51
Reading, 50
classroom technology
document cameras, 19
interactive whiteboards, 19
color printer, 19
scanner, 19
clusters, in standard organization, 43–44
College and Career Readiness Standards
(CCRS), 3

Common Core State Standards (CCSS)
    initiative, 2
computer lab, limitations of, 19
Council of Chief State School Officers
    (CCSSO), 2
Cronin, Doreen, 77

**D**
digital math games, 74
digital text, features, 87–88
domains, in standard organization,
    43–44

**E**
ebooks, 67, 83, 91, 93, 111, 114, 117, 149,
    150, 151, 176
Edmodo, 59, 61,
ELA standards, digital resources for
    teaching (table), 61
ELA Standards, organization, 36-39

**F**
Faculty Resource Network (NYU), 6
Fleming, Denise, 77
flipped classroom, 14, 60
fluency, sites to support, 151-152
Framework for 21st Century Learning,
    47, 61
funding, sources of, 21
funding, government, 21
funding, foundations, 22
funding, companies, 22
funding, other resources, 23

**G**
Global Family Research Project, 13
Google Earth, 78, 84, 89, 129

graphing calculators
        software and websites, 242-243
graphing lesson, 136

**I**
icons, for finding information easily, 87,
    99, 112
idioms, 204–207
interactive apps and websites, 233
internet access, lack of home access, 13,
    16-17
ISTE Standards
        Educators, 30-31
        Students, 129, 130, 132, 133–134,
            135, 138, 159, 161–162, 164,
            166, 167, 169, 173, 202, 203,
            207, 208–209, 210, 213, 215,
            246, 258–259

**K**
keyboarding, when to teach, 147
keyboarding, programs to teach, 148,
    184-185,
keyboarding practice, 149
kid-friendly search engines, 228

**L**
Laptops, classroom recommendations, 18
Leading Education by Advancing Digital
    (LEAD) commission, 16
lessons, fifth grade
        literacy, 244-250
        math, 252-259
        social studies/science, 250-252
lessons, first grade
        literacy, 99-102
        math, 104-107

social studies/science, 102-103
lessons, fourth grade
    literacy, 200-207
    math, 210-216
    social studies/science, 207-210
lessons, kindergarten
    literacy, 75-78
    math, 80-85
    social studies/science, 78-80
lessons, second grade
    literacy, 129-132
    math, 134-139
    social studies/science, 132-134
lessons, third grade
    literacy, 158
    math, 166-174
    social studies/science, 163-166

**M**

maker movement, 9
Marzollo, Jean, 77
math standards, organization, 41-44
media literacy resources, 231–232
Messner, Kate, 77
mind-mapping tools, 189, 229

**N**

narrative writing, lesson, 99
National Assessment of Educational
    Progress, 15
National Governors Association Center
    for Best Practices (NGA Center), 2
note-taking tools, 84, 143, 230, 248, 257,
    258

**P**

paraphrasing apps, 191
PARCC, 15–16, 20, 49–50

technical requirements, 20
parent teacher organization (PTO) See
    also Parent teacher association (PTA),
    21, 25, 66
parent teacher association (PTA) See also
    Parent teacher organization (PTO), 21,
    25, 66
parents, concerns with CCSS, 12-13
parents, and test preparation, 16
parents, and technology at home, 16
parents, as volunteers in the classroom,
    26
parent communication, 14
Partnership for 21st Century Learning
    (P21), 47, 61
Partnership for Assessment of Readiness
    for College and Careers (PARCC), see
    also State assessments
passwords, 27
patterns of technology use, 47
Peek, Merle, 77
professional development, 29
publishing student work, 223

**R**

reading informational text (standard),
    141, 180, 220
reading literature (standard), 41, 46, 52,
    176,
reading resources, 87, 218
Rhodes, Gail Fischer, 255
roadblocks
    to accessibility, 18
    software and hardware, 20
    policies, 24

**S**

Sammons, Laney, 60
scrapbooking, resources for, 247

screen time, 8

sentence writing, lesson, 75

shape geometry, fifth-grade lesson, 252-253

slideshows, 177, 179, 183, 203, 208, 218-219, 222, 258

Smarter Balanced Assessment Consortium, see also State assessments, 15-16, 20, 49-50

    technical requirements, 20

smart search, 227

social media, student use of, 8

speaking and listening (standard), 52-56, 149,

    resources, 117-121

staff development, 28-35

staff development, ideas for 32-33

staff development, learning about, 33-34

standards for Mathematical Practice (SMP), 42, 56

state assessments, technical requirements, 20

states adopting CCSS, 2-3

students, current generation, 6-7

summary writing, fifth-grade activity, 224-225

Sweeney, Joan, 83

Szybinski, Debra, 6

## T

technology, embedded in math standards, 46

technology, harmful effects, 9

technology, ideas for integrating, 58-62

    for Kindergarten, 63-85

    for first grade, 86-108

    for second grade, 109-139

    for third grade, 140-174

    for fourth grade, 175-216

    for fifth grade, 217-259

technology, in the common core, 44

technology, roadblocks to classroom, 18

technology committee, forming a, 29

technology grants, 33

technology plan, creation of, 29

## W

website for book, 5

Wise Brown, Margaret, 77

writing (standards)

    resources, 64-66

# Your opinion matters
# Tell us how we're doing!

Your feedback helps ISTE create the best possible resources for teaching and learning in the digital age.

Share your thoughts with the community or tell us how we're doing!

You can:

- Write a review at amazon.com or barnesandnoble.com.

- Mention this book on social media and follow ISTE on Twitter @iste, Facebook @ISTEconnects or Instagram @isteconnects.

- Email us at books@iste.org with your questions or comments.